In the Image of Her

Julius Gari Melchers, *Mother and Child*, 1906

In the Image of Her

Recovering Motherhood in the Christian Tradition

Amy E. Marga

BAYLOR UNIVERSITY PRESS

Waco, Texas 76798

Cover and book design by Kasey McBeath
Cover art: Julius Gari Melchers, *Mother and Child*, c.1906 (oil on canvas), The Art Institute of Chicago, IL, USA. Gift of James Deering / Bridgeman Images.

The Library of Congress has cataloged this book under ISBN 978-1-4813-1738-2.
Library of Congress Control Number: 2022940715

To Ben and Leo, who are the air that I breathe.
And to Origen's mother, who hid his clothes to save his life.

Contents

Acknowledgments

Every project is a team effort, just like mothering. Many people around me supported me and helped me in numerous ways as this book came together.

First, I would like to thank Luther Seminary in Saint Paul, Minnesota, especially Robin Steinke, the Luther Board, and Academic Deans Dirk Lange and Joy Moore, for giving me a sabbatical to complete this book. I cherish their confidence in me. Their encouragement of faculty scholarship in the turbulent landscape of theological education today is a gift. Included in this is the Luther Seminary librarian, Peter Watters, who tirelessly obtained books and resources for me. My long-standing theological conversation partner, Andy Root, helped me clarify my ideas and gave me confidence in the project. My colleagues Mark Granquist and Jennifer Wojciechowski read early drafts of my chapters and gave me insightful feedback.

I would like to heartily thank my editor at Baylor University Press, Cade Jarrell, who provided helpful feedback along the way. He has been a consistent source of encouragement, information, and help through the writing and publishing process.

Finally, I am deeply grateful to the friends who were my children's othermothers and who mothered me throughout this process. Carla

Dahl listened to it all. Nicole Bechtold and Theresa Okstad-Gardella reminded me that my goal was reachable, and Kamaria Skinner surrounded me and my boys with constant love and support. Most of all, my sister Beth Goobic and her two sons Crosby and Gustavo have provided daily doses of reality and unconditional love.

List of Figures

Introduction

The Institution of Motherhood in Western Civilization

The institution of motherhood has served the Western European world very well for centuries. Throughout history, maternity has been most often used for the purposes of male-dominated and male-defined social and economic goals, with female reproduction as a "currency"[1] within the power structures of male domination.[2] Male success has depended not only on the work of female bodies but especially on the work of maternal bodies.[3] Women who are mothers have

1 Uli Linke, "Manhood, Femaleness, and Power: A Cultural Analysis of Prehistoric Images of Reproduction," *Comparative Studies in Society and History* 34, no. 4 (1992): 579–620, here 580. Historical evidence suggests that women found ways to critique and show their opinions about the ways male culture dominated their bodies and reproductive lives. The festival of the Thesmorphia included a two-day festival in which only women of childbearing age could take place, as the "polis" of women. As it is described in Aristophanes' play, the *Thesmophoriazusae*, this festival allowed women to ritually rebel against the male norms of early (child) marriage and childbearing; it did not, however, actually give women any real power in Greek politics. See Nancy Demand, *Birth, Death, and Motherhood in Classical Greece* (Baltimore: Johns Hopkins University Press, 1994), 114–20.

2 See Nancy Polikoff, "Lesbians Choosing Children: The Personal Is Political Revisited," in *Maternal Theory: Essential Readings*, ed. Andrea O'Reilly (Bradford, Ont.: Demeter Press, 2007), 199.

3 In fact, in the classical Greek era, men were quite concerned about women's and midwives' control over the maternal body and female reproductive matters. They worried that women might abort their heirs or introduce other men's infants into their households. Hence, with medical works like that of Hippocrates, male decision-makers introduced *men* into the work of caring for

been expected to care for children: to feed them, nurture them, and educate them. The "good" mother raises children to be contributing members of society. This was especially true of mothers in the ancient world, such as Roman mothers, who were mainly recognized for the successes of their children. Motherhood was so valued in the Roman imagination that it emphasized two main categories for female human beings: a young virginal girl and a reproductive woman.[4]

Such ideas and expectations of women have continued through European history. In most European cultures, women have been given status and worth *because* they are mothers.[5] Motherhood retained its high value during the centuries of the colonizing and settling of North America, as Europeans imported their cultures and religions into the so-called New World. Motherhood played a role in the American imagination of "Republican Mothers" during the Revolutionary War,[6] and white supremacy has always depended upon white motherhood to maintain itself.[7] Today, American motherhood and domestic spaces mostly managed by women, with some exceptions, are still seen as the institutions responsible for raising children to be successful workers and citizens in an unforgiving Western capitalistic culture.[8]

---

pregnant and birthing women—in order to keep an eye on things, especially the midwives. See Demand, *Birth, Death, and Motherhood in Classical Greece*, 132.

4 Natalie Boymel Kampen, "Material Girl: Feminist Confrontations with Roman Art," *Arethusa* 27, no. 1 (1994): 111–37; Suzanne Dixon, *The Roman Mother*, Routledge Revivals (Hoboken, N.J.: Taylor and Francis, 2014).

5 This has been true throughout European history, from the early medieval Frankish and Carolingian dynasties through the Nazi regime in twentieth-century Germany. See Suzanne Fonay Wemple, *Women in Frankish Society: Marriage and the Cloister, 500 to 900*, Middle Ages (Philadelphia: University of Pennsylvania Press, 1981); Claudia Koonz, *Mothers in the Fatherland: Women, the Family and Nazi Politics* (New York: St. Martin's Press, 1987).

6 See for instance Sarah Robbins, "'The Future Good and Great of Our Land': Republican Mothers, Female Authors, and Domesticated Literacy in Antebellum New England," *New England Quarterly* 75, no. 4 (2002): 562–91. For some images of "republican mothers" during this time period, see the Smithsonian collection at https://learninglab.si.edu/collections/republican-motherhood/08wrTuRPgmUpUsXa#r/82071.

7 See for instance Elizabeth Gillespie McRae, *Mothers of Massive Resistance: White Women and the Politics of White Supremacy* (New York: Oxford University Press, 2020).

8 For just one examination of this contemporary, twenty-first century phenomenon, see Valerie Rose Brinton, "Capitalism and Performance Parenting,"

Historically, cultural norms have put pressure on women to be faithful to their husbands and to only bear legitimate children so that wealth and land stay within families. Mothers who bore sons often improved their own status in the family and society. However, there was another important reason to have legitimate children: women were not allowed to be part of the productive labor force. Their only economic security was bearing children, sons preferably, who could work and create wealth and take care of their mothers in the event of divorce or the death of their father. Having children ensured the continuation of a family bloodline and the traditions and commitments of a culture. Young women and girls were often married off to powerful cousins and households in order for wealthy families to maintain land and power. Up until the twentieth century, Western Europe was ruled by families such as the Hapsburgs who kept maternity and power within extended family networks.[9]

Cultural, social, and political expectations have also told women how to *feel*. Many of the expectations about the emotional lives of mothers—such as self-sacrificial practices, patience, gentleness, empathy, and long-suffering—are general human attributes that have been gendered and assigned to women throughout history. This has led to an ongoing and almost universal perception that such personality traits come "naturally" to women, or that all women "naturally" possess such personality traits. They have become seen as naturally "maternal" traits. Because women and girls have been expected to remain in or close to the home and to manage the details of home life, constructs such as domesticity, peacefulness, and other-centeredness have also been gendered and inscribed onto women who are mothers. These gendered constructs of behavior and emotion and their service to cultural-political power structures have become entrenched expectations of the institution of motherhood.

Motherhood, Mothering, and Women

But motherhood is not a natural desire for all women. Women are not born with the drive to procreate. Not all women want to

---

Journal of Psychohistory 42, no. 2 (2014): 161–69. But there are many more investigations of this available today.

[9] The Hapsburg Empire was notorious for marrying cousins in order to consolidate power. See for example Margaret MacMillan, *The Road to 1914: The War That Ended Peace* (New York: Random House, 2013), 212–44.

become mothers. Not all women are able to become mothers. The lively conversation about mothers and motherhood today cannot and must not determine how public discourse on *women* will go in America. It must remain separate from the important discussions of equality between men and women when it comes to pay disparities, workplace treatment, sexual assault, and all the other political and social issues for which women continue to fight in Western societies. Male-dominated goals of dominating lands, peoples, and natural resources have certainly upheld the grand narrative that the best and most "natural" destiny for women is motherhood. Christianity, Judaism, and Islam all have given religious weight to such a grand narrative. Despite the liveliness of contemporary debates about motherhood, motherhood must not be seen as a grand narrative for all women. Historically, women who did not pursue the scripts of motherhood were seen as unnatural *women*. After all, women were supposed to have one ambition and one ambition only—to have and raise children. Even within Euro-American feminism, a debate rages as to whether contemporary ideas about women and mothers still allow society to prioritize the mother over the woman, thus undermining the rights and status of women in society in general.[10]

In 1976, in a work that has widely been seen as the foundation of contemporary motherhood studies, author Adrienne Rich carved out a space between the experiences of motherhood and the institution of motherhood. It was a space that had resided in the shadow realms of the Western imagination for centuries. Rich's account of what it was like to be a mother in her memoir *Of Woman Born* put forth a brutally honest account of her own struggles with both anger and tenderness towards her young children as she tried to start a career as a writer. She gave a poignant and jarring description of being a mother of three boys. Her narrative was unlike any other up until then, for her entire analysis was based on motherhood as it was lived by her. She described in detail the joy, the pain, the interruption, and the complicated, mixed emotions that caring for a child brings, non-stop, to a mother every day.[11] She described

[10] See Elizabeth Badinter, *The Conflict: How Modern Motherhood Undermines the Status of Women* (New York: Metropolitan Books, 2012).

[11] See Lisa Baraitser, *Maternal Encounters: The Ethics of Interruption* (Hove, East Sussex: Routledge, 2009).

the profound inner struggles of mothering small children; it is the tension between self-care and the care of another who cannot take care of themselves. It is a tension that runs deep into a mother's psyche. It resides in her very body.[12]

Rich pulled the curtain back on the ideals of white Protestant mothering, which, up until then, had dominated the American imagination of what women should be. The ideal mother was white, feminine, heterosexual, gentle, and Christian. But behind the curtain, like the little man in the wizard of Oz, there stood regular women, everyday women, cut down to size and facing the daunting and monumental task of managing lives that had been profoundly transformed by bearing children. Becoming a mother involves a transformation of body, mind, spirit, career, finances, and every other aspect of life by the presence of another human being who is immature, vulnerable, adorable, and needy. Real wizardry would be nice for mothers. Caring for children—feeding them, nurturing them, responding to their emotional needs, and training them to be citizens of society—is often more than one woman can bear. This drastic transformation to a woman's life is so overwhelming that sometimes mental illness ensues—illness that can lead to maternal violence or the destruction of one's own children.

The public's reaction to *Of Woman Born* ranged from support to rage.[13] But despite the reactions it provoked, Rich's reflections gave mothers permission to combine their own mothering experiences with the values of second-wave white feminism that were sweeping the Western world in the mid-twentieth century. Her work offered a way into a new conversation about what it means to be a feminist and a mother. The quest for empowered, feminist mothering upon which Rich's book embarked paved the way for women *themselves* to talk about the chasm between their subjective experiences of mothering and the institutions of motherhood that shape so many women's lives.

12 Adrienne Rich, *Of Woman Born: Motherhood as Experience and Institution* (New York: W. W. Norton, 1976).

13 See Jane McCabe, review of *Of Woman Born: Motherhood as Experience and Institution,* by Adrienne Rich, *Frontiers: A Journal of Women's Studies* (1977): 77–78; Susan Sheridan, "Adrienne Rich and the Women's Liberation Movement: A Politics of Reception," *Women's Studies* 35 (2006): 17–45; D. Lynn O'Brien Hallstein, "The Intriguing History and Silences of *Of Woman Born*: Rereading Adrienne Rich Rhetorically to Better Understand the Contemporary Context," *Feminist Formations* 22, no. 2 (2010): 18–41.

That conversation is still going on today, and it is becoming broader and richer as more and more women join the conversation.

It is a conversation that also resists a single narrative. A mother can be biologically determined through pregnancy and birth or determined through the adoption of a child. A mother can be a mother without a man by her side. They can be lesbian or transgender. A mother can even be a man.[14] A mother can mother in a home or without a home. Mothers can be high-powered career women or incarcerated. They mother as migrants and as addicts.[15] Women mother as Christian,[16] Jewish,[17] or Muslim.[18] They mothered as Nazis[19] in twentieth century Germany and as slaves[20] and as slave holders in the American South.[21] As Sara Ruddick has shown, what makes a mother are the *practices* of "mothering," such as protecting, nurturing, training, and caring for young people.[22] Theorizing today what defines a mother is no longer

14 Izzy Lyons and Charles Hymas, "Mother Is No Longer Gender-Specific Term, Government Lawyers Say," *The Telegraph*, February 14, 2019, https://www.telegraph.co.uk/news/2019/02/14/mother-no-longer-gender-specific-term-government-lawyers-say/.

15 Susan C. Boyd, *Mothers and Illicit Drugs: Transcending the Myths* (Toronto: University of Toronto Press, 1999).

16 There is an entire cottage industry on mothering advice for American Christian women. One example is Gloria Furman, *Missional Motherhood: The Everyday Ministry of Motherhood in the Grand Plan of God* (Wheaton, Ill.: Crossway, 2016). See also Tina Schermer Sellers and Kris Thomas, "Women Called: A Qualitative Study of Christian Women Dually Called to Motherhood and Career," *Journal of Psychology and Theology* 33, no. 3 (2005): 198–209.

17 See for example Mara H. Benjamin, *The Obligated Self: Maternal Subjectivity and Jewish Thought*, New Jewish Philosophy and Thought (Bloomington: Indiana University Press, 2018). A powerful theology of mothering can be found in Melissa Raphael, *The Female Face of God in Auschwitz* (London: Routledge, 2003).

18 M. Aziza Pappano and Dana M. Olwan, eds., *Muslim Mothering: Global Histories, Theories, and Practices* (Bradford, Ont.: Demeter Press, 2016); Saktanber Ayşe, *Living Islam: Women, Religion and the Politicization of Culture in Turkey* (London: I.B. Tauris, 2002).

19 See for example Koonz, *Mothers in the Fatherland*; Johanna Haarer, *Die Deutsche Mutter und Ihr Erstes Kind* [The German Mother and Her First Child] (Munich: F.J. Lehmanns, 1934).

20 Basil Davidson, *Black Mother: The Years of the African Slave Trade* (Boston: Little, Brown, and Company, 1961).

21 Drew Gilpin Faust, *Mothers of Invention: Women of the Slaveholding South in the American Civil War*, Fred W. Morrison Series in Southern Studies (Chapel Hill: University of North Carolina Press, 1996).

22 See Sara Ruddick, *Maternal Thinking: Towards a Politics of Peace* (Boston: Beacon, 1995).

limited to ideologies about gender, women, "the family," or the (still very powerful) social imagination about the institution of "motherhood." Rather, contemporary understandings of motherhood seek to let mothers themselves say what it is like to be a mother.[23] No two experiences of oneself as a mother are alike.[24]

Motherhood's resistance to single narratives and grand theories has allowed mothers to have conversations about mothering in every corner of discourse today. These conversations can be found in self-help literature, memoirs, blogs, magazines, and even national newspapers.[25] They happen in the fields of economics,[26] globalization studies,[27] philosophy,[28] history, and politics.[29]

[23] A simple Google search brings up hundreds of memoirs about mothering. Famous authors such as Joan Didion (*Blue Nights*), Anne Lamott (*Operating Instructions*), Rachel Cusk (*A Life's Work*), and others share visceral and real stories about their subjective experiences as mothers. Tillie Olson is credited with beginning the twentieth-century form of reflecting on herself as a mother; see Tillie Olson, "I Stand Here Ironing," in *Tell Me a Riddle: A Collection* (Philadelphia: J.B. Lippincott, 1960). I daresay that there are almost as many different memoirs of motherhood and mothering as there are authors.

[24] One of the best publishing houses creating work on mothering and motherhood today is Demeter Press, based in Bradford, Ontario. It sees itself as the place to publish feminist perspectives on mothering, families, reproduction, and sexuality. See http://demeterpress.org/.

[25] Judith Warner, *Perfect Madness: Motherhood in the Age of Anxiety* (New York: Riverhead Books, 2006).

[26] Melinda Giles, *Mothering in the Age of Neoliberalism* (Bradford, Ont.: Demeter Press, 2014). Studies abound on single mothering in poverty, such as Kathryn Edin and Maria Kefalas, *Promises I Can Keep: Why Poor Women Put Motherhood before Marriage* (Berkeley: University of California Press, 2005) and Ruth Sidel, *Unsung Heroines: Single Mothers and the American Dream*, 2nd ed. (Berkeley: University of California Press, 2006). Other difficult mothering circumstances that have drawn attention in contemporary motherhood studies are Lana Marlow, *Mothers in Prison: Women's Autobiography and Activism* (Riga, Latvia: VDM Verlag, 2009); Gabriel Ricci, ed., *Mothers in Prison* (New York: Routledge, 2018); and Michelle Oberman and Cheryl L. Meyer, *When Mothers Kill: Interviews from Prison* (New York: New York University Press, 2008).

[27] Dorsía S. Silva, Lalia Malik, and Abigail L. Palko, eds., *Mothers, Mothering, and Globalization* (Bradford, Ont.: Demeter Press, 2017).

[28] Ruddick, *Maternal Thinking*; Claudia Dey, "Mothers as Makers of Death," *Paris Review*, August 14, 2018, https://www.theparisreview.org/blog/2018/08/14/mothers-as-makers-of-death/.

[29] See the numerous works on political mothering, such as Jocelyn Fenton Stitt and Pegeen Reichert Powell, eds., *Mothers Who Deliver* (Albany: SUNY Press, 2010).

Famous political movements have been led by women who identify their actions as the actions of *mothers*.[30]

Motherhood and the Christian Tradition

Motherhood has been an undeniable institution within the Christian tradition as well. Despite its universal message of eternal life and the erasure of social status in Christ, the spread of the Christian gospel did not actually break down the strong societal constructs within which most women, mothers in particular, existed. Women still faced marriage and motherhood with all the hardships that those institutions entail. In fact, a case could be made that Christianity only entrenched the institution of motherhood more deeply into the European imagination. After all, by the Middle Ages, the figure that stood at the heart of Christianity, representing its gentle, serene, nurturing, redemptive, and protective side, was none other than a mother and her child: the Virgin Mary and her Son, Jesus Christ. The Reformation codified the domesticity of mothers in its theological thought, insisting that the proper Christian mother should retain a proper Christian home, despite the rich ways that women had been living out their lives in all-female convents or as Beguines or ascetics. The European Protestant Christians who planted their lives in the new soil of North America brought with them a strong Christian imagination about motherhood as an institution. In fact, Christian colonizers on North American lands needed white Protestant motherhood to be an institution in a land where familiar European social structures did not exist.

Although the Christian theology that has been handed down through the centuries often boxes women into the notion that they are created by God and called by God to become mothers, the faith itself, in its practices and in the ways that women engage it, allows

[30] Maternal activism has a long history in modern times, most notably in the Women's Temperance Movement in early twentieth-century America, the mothers of the Plaza de Mayo, MADD, Moms for Gun Control, Mom's Clean Water Action, etc. Political action by mothers has also taken place on the far right as well. See Glen Jeansonne, *Women of the Far Right: The Mother's Movement and World War II* (Chicago: Chicago University Press, 1997). Black motherhood is also becoming a locus of activism (however, Black mothers have been forced to advocate and be politically active for centuries on behalf of their children and their communities). See Dani McClain, *We Live for the We: The Political Power of Black Motherhood* (New York: Bold Type Books, 2019).

women to mother in more ways than one. In other words, even within the Christian tradition, with its strong sense of motherhood as an institution and its grand narrative about women's bodies being meant primarily for motherhood, there *has never been a single narrative* about what a Christian mother is or how to mother as a Christian. Women have engaged the Christian tradition in numerous ways to help them both be good mothers to their children and to be the person that they seek to be.

Unfortunately, little about how mothers have previously engaged the Christian tradition has been captured in the historical record. Because history has preserved so few of women's writings about God or their own experiences, it is impossible without more historical evidence to undertake any kind of analysis about what mothers may have felt about themselves, their roles, their faith, or their families from the earliest days of the church up until the nineteenth century. White women's suffrage leader Elizabeth Cady Stanton mourned this very fact in her interpretation of the Bible, *The Woman's Bible*. There she writes: "How much satisfaction it would have been to the mothers adown the centuries had there been testimony by Mary and Elizabeth recording their experiences of motherhood. [There exists] not a statement by them, nor one about them, except what man wrote."[31] Women's voices, mother's voices about being mothers in particular, are glaringly absent from the Christian historical record.

With the rise of modern discourse around the experiences of mothering, contemporary mother-theologians have begun to think theologically from their perspectives of mothering. One such mother-theologian is Bonnie Miller-McLemore. Miller-McLemore followed in Rich's vein and wrote a book showing the gap between the discipline of doing academic theology and the disciplines needed for mothering young children. She laid bare the tensions between her academic thoughts and the imagination that she developed about God and humanity through the routines and challenges of mothering. Miller-McLemore's 1994 work *Also a Mother: Work and Family as Theological Dilemma* opens up the same kind of feminist, maternal conversation that is taking place today, only here, it is for female theologians and religious leaders. Miller-McLemore shows how

[31] Elizabeth Cady Stanton, *The Woman's Bible* (Boston: Northeastern University Press, 1993 [1895]), 164.

generativity and the work of mothering have taken a back seat to the concerns of a male-dominated church. Ignoring this maternal reality skews the power of families and the Christian community in general.

Other thinkers such as the French psychoanalytical philosopher Julia Kristeva have sought to change the discourse on God based on their experiences and practices of mothering. Kristeva was one of the first thinkers to put together feminism, mothering, and religion. Using psychoanalytical theory and a feminist critique of Freud, she pointed to the ambivalence within the Christian tradition about mothers and what she calls the "immeasurable, unconfinable maternal body."[32] She focused on the Virgin Mary to show how Christianity put the love and empathy of a mother at the center of its theology but stripped her of a maternal body. Using depictions of Mary in Western art and music, such as the fourteenth-century song attributed to Jacopone da Todi and played throughout the Baroque period "Stabat Mater" (from "stabat mater dolorosa" or "the mother who stands there grieving"), Kristeva shows how Mary and mothers have been reduced to their breast milk and their tears in the Christian imagination.[33] She sought to find a theological discourse that mothers would be able to recognize in their own reality of welcoming an "other"—a child—into their subjective, emotional, psychological space. She questioned whether Christianity had space for actual mothers in its veneration of the Virgin Mother.

Kristeva powerfully illustrated just how disconnected maternal thought patterns and discourse are from the Word-centered, abstract discourse of Christian theology by relating her academic reflections on Christian history to a punctuated, more poetic discourse about her experience as a mother to an infant son. Right in the midst of her scholarly discourse on Mary, she interrupted herself to tell the reader about the child she was carrying, who "dances in my neck, flutters with my hair, seeks a smooth shoulder . . . and finally flies away on my navel in his dream carried by my hands. My son."[34] After several paragraphs of such poetic, empathetic discourse, Kristeva returned to the scholarly discourse of her analysis. Her point was to visually show that Christian discourse, Christian *writing*—and in turn, much

[32] Julia Kristeva, "Stabat Mater," in *The Portable Kristeva*, ed. Kelly Oliver, European Perspectives (New York: Columbia University Press, 1997), 324.

[33] Kristeva, "Stabat Mater," 322.

[34] Kristeva, "Stabat Mater," 319.

of Western thought—has a blind spot when it comes to the realities of actual mothering. Spiritual and religious rhetoric about the purity of Mother Mary is disengaged from actual discourses and thought processes of women who mother. For those women who are Christian and are mothers, both discourses reside in them.

Another mother-theologian who has added her voice to the growing body of maternal feminist thought by mothers themselves is Natalie Carnes. Carnes' book, *Motherhood: A Confession,* takes its inspiration from Augustine's *Confessions*, which was written sometime around the turn of the fifth century. Like Augustine, Carnes speaks of God in the second person, drawing God's presence into her theological discourse. But she also talks to her child in the second person. Her narrative, confessional style is both God-oriented and directed towards her child. In contrast to Augustine's own beliefs, Carnes insists that the lives of women and children are sites of theological reflection.[35] Like Kristeva, Carnes seeks out new forms of theological discourse that affirm God's revelation in the lives of mothers and children. She speaks to her unborn child and describes how already, by sharing its fetal cells with her maternal body, the unborn child is practicing mercy. She tells her unborn child how much the child has in common with Jesus—who also came into the world through his mother's womb.[36] Like Miller-McLemore, Carnes wrestles with the tension that so many mothers have experienced between yearning to be with their children and being called into other types of work besides mothering.[37] These mother-theologians want to show that women who are mothers utilize a different logic about life and death based on their experiences of pregnancy, birthing, and caring for an infant than most male-authored theologies and doctrines have historically used.

About This Book

The one thing that Kristeva, Miller-McLemore, Carnes, and so many other contemporary mothers have, especially after Adrienne Rich's work, is the privilege of sharing their voices. With the exception of the voice of one lonely mother named Dhuoda from

[35] Natalie Carnes, *Motherhood: A Confession* (Redwood City, Calif.: Stanford University Press, 2020), 3.

[36] Carnes, *Motherhood*, 15.

[37] Carnes, *Motherhood*, 73.

the ninth-century Carolingian kingdom, mothers in the Christian tradition have had no voice at all. Only beginning in the seventeenth century, when Christian mother-authors such as Dorothy Leigh and Elizabeth Joscelin started writing, do we begin to get a glimpse into how women navigated their experiences of motherhood, their commitments to their children, and their Christian faiths. To understand how Christian mothers navigated these experiences during the fifteen hundred years before that, we can only piece together the way male theologians wrote about mothers and the maternal body. In such a lacuna of women's voices, this study scans the wide variety of clues, fragments, prayers, comments, actions, and attitudes towards motherhood that made their way into the Christian imagination. Through such a wide-lens investigation, we can begin to get a glimpse of what the Christian faith imagined mothers to be and how mothers themselves navigated motherhood and their faith in God.

Chapter 1, "Early Christian Skepticism of the Mother-Child Bond," examines the way that early Christian theology was skeptical of the mother-child bond. Patristic theologians such as Jerome of Stridon celebrated the way wealthy Roman mothers such as Paula (later sainted Paula of Rome) left her children for the ascetic life in the eastern desert regions of the Roman Empire. Other early thinkers such as Gregory of Nyssa, Tertullian, and Ambrose seemed to believe that motherhood was an obstacle to true commitment to God. The earliest Christian thinkers, such as Origen of Alexandria, held that resurrection would liberate women from the reproductive attributes of their female bodies, suggesting that mothering and maternal bodies had no place in God's salvific plan for humanity. Motherhood required women to have bonds to earthly things like the material needs of children, the emotional lives of families, and the management of wealth and property. Church Fathers such as Gregory of Nyssa and Augustine saw children as narcissists who distracted mothers from true devotion to God, and they celebrated the droves of women like Paula and Melania who left the social constraints of Roman family customs to remain virgins and dedicate themselves to Christ. A prime example of mothers who relinquished their roles for the sake of Christ are the martyrs Perpetua and Felicity, both of whom abandoned their newborns for the beasts' arena. Their actions, their devotion to Christ, and their relinquishment of the role of mother have been celebrated in the Christian tradition since the second century. This tradition of mother-martyrs continued in small ways throughout the Christian tradition, including right up into the seventeenth century when Marie de L'Incarnation abandoned her teenage son to become a nun, only to then travel to the New World and establish a well-known convent in Quebec. Through these numerous examples, we can see that Christianity has harbored an antagonistic attitude towards the deep bonds and commitments that mothers have for their children.

Chapter 2, "Eve's Sin and the Generosity of the Maternal Body," continues to explore the rhetoric around motherhood in the Christian imagination and, in particular, how it relates to the maternal body. Since its inception, the Christian story of Eve has been connected to the ancient Greek myth of Pandora and the chaos that this beautiful muse supposedly unleashed upon the men of the world. Theologians throughout the centuries connected the pain of childbirth to the sinfulness of women, and they struggled to make sense of how and why God chose to become incarnate in the form of a baby who was born from a woman's body. The early church Father Tertullian reversed generally negative attitudes towards the maternal body, showing how God chose the lowest, muckiest, and most shameful place—the mother's uterus—to prove God's love for humanity. Not only did centuries of church theologians believe that the maternal body was a sign of polluted humanity, they also believed that the pain of birthing labor was a metaphysical reality that reflected the sinfulness of women and connected every single woman back to the disobedient and rebellious Eve. It was not until the mid-nineteenth century that doctors and theologians began to let science lead the Christian imagination in defining the pain of labor as productive pain from which women in childbirth deserved to be free. Science also helped shape the Christian understanding of the way that the maternal body contributes to reproduction with the discovery of the egg. Even theologians like Jonathan Edwards attested to how the female egg was a tool of God's power. In the end though, the Christian imagination has struggled with the reality that the maternal body is a generous creature that gives as much of itself as the fetus can take. This maternal generosity as a sign of God's creative activity is only beginning to receive attention in the Christian tradition.

Chapter 3, "The Vulnerable Sinner's Attachment to Mother Mary," explores the rise of the mother in the Christian imagination. This chapter examines how Christianity's move into early European lands and kingdoms caused the religion to meet with northern tribal social and cultural norms that were different than Roman familial laws and codes. More liberal customs around the movement of mothers and their visibility in society contributed to the rise of Mary as the mother of not just God (as the *theotokos*) but of Jesus Christ as a human being. To thinkers like Anselm of Canterbury, Mary became the protective mother to whom sinners turned when they faced the judgment of Christ and God the wrathful Father. She became the one person between heaven and earth who could intercede for humanity to her Son, Jesus Christ. Monastic leaders such as Bernard of Clairvaux modeled his leadership after maternal values such as wisdom and empathy, even going as far as to assert that he experienced the miracle of drinking from the breast milk of Mary. Her body became the protective layer that shielded sinners from God's judgment. In many ways, the medieval devotion to Mary seems to be a form of attachment. In other words, the bond that develops between a child and its mother and the ways that the presence of the mother contributes to the survival and positive growth of the child seem to be reflected in the Christian's attachment to Mary, especially in European medieval thought. This is particularly interesting because scientists did not theorize the significance of the mother-child bond until the twentieth century, when thinkers like John Bowlby and Mary Ainsworth were conducting research. But the rise of the Christian mother also led to the rise of the Christian household in Reformation Germany, which, ironically, confined the power and wisdom of the maternal experience to the "holy household" as a contrast to the convents and monasteries that Martin Luther so despised. The mother had become domesticated in the Christian imagination.

Throughout the long centuries of Christian thought about motherhood, or its lack thereof, mothers, daughters, female neighbors, and midwives continued to do what they needed to in order to survive the life-threatening challenges and conditions of pregnancy, birth, and the postpartum period. Chapter 4, "Maternal Piety, Magic, and Sisterhood," shows how Christianity believed in the porous maternal body, which was susceptible to both physical ailments as well as spiritual evils that could penetrate the pregnant woman and affect her unborn child. Despite being faithful Christians, women also turned to ancient magic, spells, prayers, rites, rituals, and sacred tokens to get them through the perils of motherhood. The sisterhood of women who helped each other through this challenging life passage included saints such as Saint Margaret, Mary the mother of Christ, and Saint Anne, *her* mother. While there were and continue to be many more saints who have been seen as protectors of women and children, these three were especially important to women in their childbearing years. Women would take pilgrimages to shrines to Mary or Anne in order to receive healing for themselves or their children. Legends about how women were healed or saved by various saints in their times of trouble abound. Throughout the ages when the church had no official place for women, one ritual around childbirth known as "churching" was embraced by women. Although officially it was an occasion to welcome a postpartum woman back into the church space after her weeks of uncleanness, women began to see it as an opportunity to celebrate the power and vitality of their maternal bodies and their work as mothers.

Despite the power and teamwork of women throughout pregnancy and birth, mothering was hard, dirty, and deathly work. The Christian promise of resurrection could not prevent the frequent deaths of infants, children, and mothers. In other words, women throughout the centuries had to show courage and resilience as they mothered children in times of persecution, war, illness, and harsh living conditions. Chapter 5, "The Prayers and Tears of Christian Mothers," explores the heroic actions and attitudes of mothers on behalf of their children. It recounts the anecdotes of mothers such as Origen's, who saved his young life, and the commitment of Monica to her famous son, Augustine, despite his criticism of her. It shows how Birgitta of Sweden was the one medieval thinker who gave Mary her own narrative voice, which portrayed Mary as a strong mother facing the death of her son. Other mothers who faced the deaths of their children or their own deaths also left behind traces of how they used the Christian tradition to give them strength and courage. Dhuoda, the one lonely mother's voice from the ninth century, wrote a *Handbook* to her son William and his baby brother Bernard as they were taken away by their father into service to the Carolingian king, Charles the Bald. She never saw her precious sons again, but in her *Handbook*, Dhuoda tried to teach her sons the Christian theology of the Trinity and the Christian moral code of graciousness and mercy. She reminded her sons that God was on their side and that God wished them to be good men even in a highly masculine and militarized culture. The rise of the genre of "mothers' legacies" in the seventeenth century shows that Christian mothers such as Puritans Dorothy Leigh and Elizabeth Joscelin used the Christian faith to teach their children that they were loved even if they themselves were no longer around. In other words, these mothers turned to writing and the Christian faith to give their children a sense of a loving presence and the grace of God when they themselves could no longer give it.

As Christianity developed in the New World of North America, it succumbed to white supremacist cultural ideas that claimed God's providential will was for European domination of the land and the conversion of Indigenous children by means of separating them from their own Indigenous mothers. Chapter 6, "White Mothers' Theology, Black Mothers' Bible," explores how the Reformation's understanding of the holy household became an institution of the "domestic altar" in the New World and how white Protestant mothers were seen as the linchpins of civilized humanity. White mothers embraced this role wholeheartedly even if they felt ambivalent about their own mothering skills. The well-known Christian and author Harriet Beecher Stowe was one such mother who did so. The holy household ignored the way that white Protestant mothers were engaging in the workforce or in public life and instead celebrated the domesticity and self-sacrificial demands of motherwork. While white mothers witnessed the suffering, oppression, and hardships of the mothers of color around them, in particular enslaved African mothers, they still continued to support the colonizing and dominating endeavors of white men and even participated in breaking up Indigenous and enslaved families. This is an unfortunate and complex phenomenon within white Christianity and white motherhood that deserves more attention and exploration today. While the white Protestant mother was viewed as the savior of humanity in America, enslaved African mothers were fighting for their lives and the lives of their children. Enslaved African mothers utilized Christianity to help them survive the horrors of American slavery and utilized the Bible to show their commitment to their families and their people. Poets like Frances Harper Watkins are a good example of how Black mothers utilized a biblical imagination to help them endure the torture of the white Christian establishment. The complex relationship between white motherhood and Black motherhood in the American Christian imagination deserves much more exploration than can be covered in a study such as this.

While the Christian imagination embodied a very specific notion of motherhood in the figure of the Virgin Mary, this study shows that there has not been a single overarching narrative of mothers and mothering in Christian thought. Even though scholastic theology has traditionally confined the purpose and vocation of women to motherhood while dictating motherwork as subordinate to other kinds of work, mothers of all times and places throughout Christianity's long history have utilized their faith for both the benefit of their own well-being and the well-being of their children. This study is hopefully just the beginning of further research into the ways that mothers have navigated male-dominated Christian theology to develop their own ideas about how God works in their lives.

1

Early Christian Skepticism of the Mother-Child Bond

Earthly Bonds and Devotion to God

If there was one thing that the early Christian church demanded of its adherents, it was a pure and wholehearted devotion to Jesus Christ. Under Roman rule, which deemed Christianity illegal, following Jesus meant choosing between worshiping Caesar and worshiping God. To many early Christian thinkers, Caesar did not just represent the Roman government but all things earthly. This meant that worldly preoccupations like wealth, land, politics, and social status were all seen as distractions from a pure devotion to Jesus Christ. Among these worldly preoccupations was the human body. Following various philosophical ideas about human physicality from ancient Greece and Rome, early Christian theologians targeted the body's needs, desires, and attachments as obstacles to pure devotion to God.[1] Scores of early Christians showed their devotion by joining ascetic movements whereby they renounced all earthly attachments.

This was not an environment that was conducive to a positive theological view of the reproductive work of the female body or of the bonds of attachment between mothers and their children. Rather

[1] For a comprehensive treatment of early Christian attitudes towards the body, see Peter Brown, *Body and Society: Men, Women, and Sexual Renunciation in Early Christianity* (New York: Columbia University Press, 1988).

than seeing the mother-child bond as necessary for the proper development of children and the good of society, early Christian theological writers were suspicious of it. After all, the mother-child bond involved two of the most profoundly creaturely things: namely, the female body and earthly attachments. The ideal life for an early Christian woman was not motherhood but its opposite: childless virginity. As a virgin, a woman's body was untouched by sexuality and the blood of birth; without children, a woman could focus all of her attention on God. The ascetic communities that sprung up throughout the desert landscape of the eastern Roman Empire encouraged the ideal of childless virginity. Groups of women lived together to read the Bible, learn, and pray. While some of these women were already mothers who turned to the lifestyle of chastity, many women were not. Although there is no historical record of how many women chose to relinquish motherhood or detach from their earthly familial systems and their children to join such communities, early Christian thinkers celebrated a few of the women who did. Such faith communities encouraged Christian women to see themselves outside of the conventional familial identities.

Four of the greatest women from the early Christian era were all mothers who detached from or gave up their children to prove their devotion to Jesus Christ. These were namely Paula (later sainted Paula of Rome), Melania, the young martyr Perpetua, and Perpetua's slave Felicity. Paula and Melania were two of the richest Roman women in the early church. Their money and their leadership contributed to flourishing communities of ascetics in the deserts of the far eastern Roman Empire.[2] Perpetua narrated her time in custody with her slave girl Felicity and their newborns before they were martyred in the third century in Carthage at the birthday celebration of the Emperor Geta. Celebrated for their unwavering devotion to Christ above all other earthly obligations and for their stories of bravery and modesty, the legacies of these mothers have been passed down through the Christian ages.

But many open questions remain about the relationships of these women to their children and families. Did these women leave their children in order to prove their worthiness to a religious ideology

2 See Lynn H. Cohick and Amy Brown Hughes, *Christian Women in the Patristic World: Their Influence, Authority, and Legacy in the Second through Fifth Centuries* (Grand Rapids: Baker Academic, 2017).

that made no space for women and motherhood? Or did they use the new worldview of a fledgling Christianity and recent legal freedoms for Roman women to pursue ambitions outside of the role of motherhood that Roman families protected so carefully? We will never fully know how these women related to their roles as mothers in the new Christian faith, nor is there any historical record of the wide variety of reasons that mothers either detached from their children to join the Christian faith or took their children with them into the ascetic life like how Paula took her daughter Julia Eustochium with her. The myriad of narratives of mothers and their children in the new Christian faith—and the cost to them too—are lost to history. What is clear, however, is that those authors and church leaders who recorded and celebrated the actions of mothers such as Paula, Melania, Perpetua, and Felicity reduced the diverse ways of being devoted to God in the Christian faith to one single narrative of virginity and heroism.

Paula and Melania Relinquish Roman Motherhood

In the year 385 CE, Paula (347–404), who was one of the wealthiest women in the Roman Empire, stepped aboard a ship bound for Jerusalem. She was the mother of five children, some of them still young. Paula was quickly rising through the ranks of early Christian leaders after having learned about the new Christian faith in the community of ascetic women led by another well-known early church Mother, Marcella. She was eager to read the Bible, pray, and understand Christian theology. Most of all, Paula intended to live a virtuous life for the sake of herself and her family. It was the era in Christian thought when men and women flocked to Christian communities in the deserts of the eastern region of the Roman Empire in order to prove themselves worthy of salvation and bring glory and spiritual direction to the nascent Christian church. Paula would be at the forefront of this movement, becoming a powerful Desert Mother among the Christian communities in the Egyptian desert; learning Latin in order to read Scripture; and working with Jerome to produce the Vulgate, which would become the standard Latin translation of the Bible in Western Christendom for the next thousand years. She was sainted Paula of Rome only a year after her death.

The scene at the quay should have been an exciting and joyous one except that Paula was not bringing her children with her. Much to their fright and dismay, their mother was leaving them behind with extended family. Only one daughter was to accompany her, the ten-year-old Julia Eustochium, who had already vowed to live as a Christian virgin. Paula was leaving behind her older teenage daughter Rufina and her tiny son Toxotius. She would not perform the expected duties of an upper-class Roman mother at Rufina's upcoming wedding.[3] She would leave young Toxotius desperate, who "howled in terror and aching" as he watched his mother slowly depart from the shore.[4] Their emotional goodbye makes it clear that Paula had strong and loving maternal bonds with her children that were typical of Roman motherhood. Despite the system of *paterfamilias* in Roman society that gave fathers comprehensive legal rights over their children, Roman mothers developed deep and abiding bonds with their children.[5]

It would not have been too unusual for a mother like Paula to leave her children in the hands of family or the state in Roman society. Paula came from a deeply rooted Roman family and was very wealthy. Her children would have been raised in a large home with slaves and other family members playing a key part in their upbringing. From the perspective of wealthy Roman families, Paula's enterprise as a wealthy Roman mother would not have been surprising. Her children would be well taken care of. They would be raised in the upper classes of Roman society and be given every opportunity to lead good lives. Paula's entry into the world of the desert Christian communities would also have not been radical, as

[3] See Susana Reboreda Morillo, "Childhood and Motherhood in Ancient Greece: An Iconographic Look," in *Motherhood and Infancies in the Mediterranean in Antiquity*, ed. Margarita Sánchez Romero and Rosa Mª Cid López (Oxford: Oxbow Books, 2018) 135–50, esp. 144.

[4] Jerome, Letter CVIII (108) to Eustochium, point 6, quoted in Nicola Denzey Lewis, *The Bone Gatherers: The Lost Worlds of Early Christian Women* (Boston: Beacon, 2007), 187. Jerome depicts Rufina as silently sobbing on the shore and uses the word "entreaty" to describe Toxotius' reaction; http://www.tertullian.org/fathers2/NPNF2-06/Npnf2-06-03.htm#P1069_228819, accessed June 11, 2020.

[5] Iconography of ancient Greece and imperial Rome depict religious rituals of thanksgiving for the birth of a child as well as reliefs of women who suffer and die in childbirth. Historical records and art also show mothers publicly displaying deep grief at the death of a child. See Morillo, "Childhood and Motherhood in Ancient Greece."

many women of all classes were throwing off the conventions of Roman society to join Christian communities.

What is remarkable, however, is how her friend—the fiery, famous, and controversial theologian Jerome of Stridon—described for the ages the spiritual and theological significance of the rupture with her children. Years after Paula's successful spiritual career and later her death, Jerome recounted the remarkableness of her life in a letter to her daughter Eustochium. Out of all the moments of leadership and wisdom in Paula's life, Jerome pinpoints and applauds precisely Paula's decision to leave her children behind. He recounts the scene:

> Disregarding her house, her children, her servants, her property, and in a word, everything connected with the world, . . . she [Paula] went down to Portus accompanied by her brother, her kinsfolk and above all her own children eager by their demonstrations of affection to overcome their loving mother. At last, the sails were set and the strokes of the rowers carried the vessel into the deep. On the shore the little Toxotius stretched forth his hands in entreaty, while Rufina, now grown up, with silent sobs besought her mother to wait till she should be married.[6]

Jerome notes how on their way down to the quay, the children seemed to be trying to convince Paula not to go. They tried to "overcome" their "loving mother" perhaps by clinging to her, hugging her, crying, and begging her not to go.

He never tried to make the argument that it was the natural thing for a woman to have ambitions outside her role of mother or to want more than motherhood. In fact, on the contrary, Jerome specifies that what Paula was doing was unnatural for a mother because he believed that nature intended for mothers to be with their children; they are "parts of her."[7] He highlights precisely her bond with her children to demonstrate her great piety and the significance of her decision to choose the Christian ascetic life over the worldly life of a wealthy Roman mother. He notes that Paula's "greater love for God" won out over her natural attachment to her children. His letter continues:

6 Jerome, Letter CVIII (108) to Eustochium, point 6.
7 Jerome, Letter CVIII (108) to Eustochium, point 6.

> But still Paula's eyes were dry as she turned them heaven wards; and she overcame her love for her children by her love for God. She knew herself no more as a mother, that she might approve herself a handmaid of Christ. Yet her heart was rent within her, and she wrestled with her grief, as though she were being forcibly separated from parts of herself. The greatness of the affection she had to overcome made all admire her victory the more. Among the cruel hardships which attend prisoners of war in the hands of their enemies, there is none severer than the separation of parents from their children . . . But she turned away her eyes that she might not see what she could not behold without agony. No mother, it must be confessed, ever loved her children so dearly. Before setting out she gave them all that she had, disinheriting herself upon earth that she might find an inheritance in heaven.[8]

History did not record what Paula was really feeling in these moments. It leaves the modern reader of Jerome's letter to Eustochium with so many questions about Paula's motives and her intentions for herself and her children. But one thing is abundantly clear in Jerome's celebration of Paula's imminent departure: her commitment to God and the Christian cause took precedence over all that she loved dear: namely, her children and their attachment to her.

Paula's decision as a mother to detach from her children for her own ambitions of spiritual power and position within the new Christian ascetic communities was not an outlier. Another wealthy Roman mother, Melania the Elder (325–410), was celebrated by male leaders of the early church for her renunciation of motherhood. At age twenty-two, widowed and with two stillborn children in her past, Melania the Elder took her baby son Publicola and traveled to Rome to join an ascetic community, possibly until her son was ten or eleven years old.[9] She then gave him up into the hands of the state and left for Alexandria for a stricter ascetic life.[10] Her story was one of the most widely circulated accounts of Roman women who gave up earthly attachments to join a monastic

8 Jerome, Letter CVIII (108) to Eustochium, point 6.

9 See Francis X. Murphy, "Melania the Elder: A Biographical Note," *Traditio* 5 (1947): 59–77, here 65.

10 Like Perpetua, the accounts of Melania the Elder's abandonment of her preteen son show that her departure was vehemently opposed by her family.

community. She renounced motherhood and family life and became the long-standing companion and patron of the monk-theologian, Rufinus.[11] She was perhaps one of the wealthiest Roman women to do so, and she used her wealth to support many other monasteries and Christian churches.[12]

Melania's noble family vehemently opposed her plans and tried to stop her. But her relative Paulinus clearly had a Christian ambivalence towards the mother-child bond. He recounted that Melania, "strengthened beyond power of temptation, joyfully loosed the bonds of bodily kinship" in order to sail to Alexandria.[13] Paulinus commented that Melania "tore her only son from her breast and set him in Christ's bosom"; "[she] loved her son by neglecting him and kept him by relinquishing him."[14] Another account of her decision to abandon her son came from her friend Palladius who similarly remarks, "She was not drawn (from her purpose) by desire for her son, nor did yearning after her only son separate her from love towards Christ."[15] Just as in Paula's situation, it seems that early Christian attitudes saw that as a woman renounced her motherly bonds, she gained something far greater: eternal life.

The actions of these two extremely wealthy Roman mothers, Paula and Melania, suggest that they believed that their Christian faith required them to give up everything they loved dear in order to obtain standing in the Christian community and to secure salvation in Jesus Christ. We will never know how they truly felt about

11 Rufinus and Jerome were close friends until the two had a falling out about Origen's theology.

12 Elizabeth A. Clark, *The Origenist Controversy: The Cultural Construction of an Early Christian Debate* (Princeton: Princeton University Press, 1992), 21. It is important to note throughout this section that class and wealth played a big part in these women's decisions to desert their children and families for the Christian ascetic life. Deserting their children was only one piece of a larger practice of selling off land, slaves, clothing, etc., to become poor in devotion to God. Most of these women and men were aristocrats or from families of means, and their Christian practice of renunciation was a serious disruption to family lines and the carrying on of wealth.

13 Paulinus, Letter 29.10, quoted in Murphy, "Melania the Elder," 65.

14 Paulinus, Letter 29.9, quoted in Gillian Cloke, "*Mater* or Martyr: Christianity and the Alienation of Women within the Family in the Later Roman Empire," *Theology and Sexuality* 5 (1996): 37–57, here 50.

15 Palladius, *The Lausiac History of Palladius*, trans. W. K. L. Clarke, Translations of Christian Literature (London: SPCK, 1918), 54.2, 158.

their choices to relinquish their family connections and their statuses as Roman mothers. We will never know if Paula or Melania regretted their decisions to leave their children behind.[16] But one thing is clear about the Christian imagination of their era: male theologians looked down upon earthly pleasures, and the mother-child bond was one of the most profound earthly connections.

The Distracting Narcissism of Children

In early Christian thought, mothers were also seen as too distracted by the narcissistic tendencies of children and the all-consuming needs of family life. Early Christianity had a low opinion of the biological family. The Apostle Paul had his own anxieties about marriage, commitment, and family; he remained single. On several occasions, he pointed to the fact that his singleness was a positive attribute for spreading Christianity across the world. It was also a sacrifice. He wrote explicitly in his letter to the congregation at Corinth about the disadvantages of marriage and family, pointing to the anxieties of married men and women. John Chrysostom wrote of the pains of marriage, such as jealousy, and all the worries of the wife, which included the fortune or misfortune of her family members, the pains of childbirth, and the worries of raising children.[17] Other leaders such as Tertullian, Cyprian, Ambrose, and Jerome all saw marriage and childbearing as tragedies and burdens.[18] Unmarried virgins, both male and female, on the other hand, were able to focus all of their attention on the "affairs of the Lord."[19]

Motherhood was seen as a barrier to truly understanding the Gospel: women's minds and attentions were too often directed

[16] It is clear that Paula grieved deeply when her daughter Eustochium died of starvation due to her extreme practices of fasting, but we will never really know whether Paula regretted what she brought Eustochium into or whether she regretted leaving her other children behind.

[17] Amy-Jill Levine and Maria Mayo Robbins, eds., *A Feminist Companion to Patristic Literature*, Feminist Companion to the New Testament and Early Christian Writings 12 (London: T&T Clark, 2008), 78–79; John Chrysostom, *On Virginity. Against Remarriage*, ed. Elizabeth A. Clark, trans. Sally Rieger Shore, Studies in Women and Religion 9 (Lewiston, N.Y.: Edwin Mellen, 1983), 1–11, 25–50, 51–72.

[18] Jerome, cited in Levine and Robbins, *Feminist Companion to Patristic Literature*, 79.

[19] 1 Cor 7:32–34.

elsewhere or divided between God and their maternal duties. Women who bore children were seen as making poor choices about their bodies, dedicating them primarily to earthly things like sex and procreation rather than to God. Clement of Alexandria said that as long as women continued to bear children, death would continue to hold its power over humanity.[20] Wives and mothers were believed to only sometimes receive the Gospel and were therefore dubious candidates for eternal life.[21] Gregory of Nyssa criticized his own mother Emmelia for loving his deceased brother Naucratius too excessively. He mused that perhaps Naucratius died young (the only sibling to die) because Emmelia's excessive maternal affection left her and her son vulnerable to exploitation by the Devil.[22] Augustine himself, famous for his attachment to his mother Monica, believed that human attachments resulted in not enough focus on the Creator. A life of marriage and bearing children was, at best, a second-class way of being Christian.

Along with women in general, children had no place in ancient Greek or Roman academic philosophy or in early Christian theology. Children were seen as a "bitter, bitter pleasure."[23] They represented both the narcissism of earthly life and false hope in a material future. They were seen from the perspective of adults and were expected to act like adults from very young ages, their developmental needs mostly ignored. When children gave signs of need such as crying, fussing, not being able to sleep, or exhibiting the typical behaviors of young children, they were seen as both narcissistic and as performers of the original sin of human disobedience.[24] Although Augustine had more positive views about children than Jerome did, he famously interpreted his own childhood

[20] Mary T. Malone, *Women and Christianity*, vol. 1, *The First Thousand Years* (Maryknoll, N.Y.: Orbis, 2001), 153. See also Brown, *Body and Society*, 122f.

[21] Malone, *Women and Christianity*, 149.

[22] Carol Monica C. Burnett, "Mother-Child Bonding in the Fathers of the Church," in *Children in Late Ancient Christianity*, ed. Cornelia B. Horn and Robert R. Phenix (Tübingen: Mohr Siebeck, 2009), 90–91.

[23] Tertullian, *Ad Uxorem* 4, in *Ante-Nicene Fathers: The Writings of the Fathers Down to A.D. 325*, ed. Alexander Roberts, James Donaldson, and Arthur Cleveland Coxe (Peabody, Mass.: Hendrickson, 1994), 41.

[24] See Martha Ellen Stortz, "'Where or When Was Your Servant Innocent?' Augustine on Childhood," in *The Child in Christian Thought*, ed. Marcia J. Bunge (Grand Rapids: Eerdmans, 2001), 78–102.

vulnerability as selfish, narcissistic, and sinful[25] rather than as a natural attribute of being a survival artist, as babies are.[26]

Children were seen as gifts and as being in the image of God, but they were also seen as unformed and incomplete human beings. It was the parents' job to shape their morals and teach them how to be godly. This concern with godliness dominated early Christian thought about children such that their basic needs of safety, warmth, and comfort, as well as a consistently loving gaze from a trusted caregiver, were never considered positive in early church thought. Children needed discipline and shaping, not maternal affection and bonding.[27] Jerome's admiration for Paula's tearless eyes as she departed from her children may not have been simply admiration for her strong will. It was also an affirmation of her spiritual maturity. She was able to resist the sinful desires and narcissism of her young child Toxotius.

Becoming Male in the Resurrection

For the church Fathers, virginity was the most desirable Christian lifestyle for women (and men). Fathers such as Tertullian, Jerome, Ambrose, and Augustine took inspiration from all-female ascetic communities of "virgins," and they wrote lengthy scholastic treatises on virginity. Male writers rated women on the scale of their virginity. To them, virgins understood the Word of God and received the Gospel perfectly. Virgins were the women who were seen as being uniquely able to overcome female nature and ascend to something like angel status. The Fathers wove elabo-

25 Augustine, *Confessions*, vol. 1, trans. Carolyn J. B. Hammond, Loeb Classical Library (Cambridge, Mass.: Harvard University Press, 2014), 1.11, pp. 26–27.

26 See for example Alison Gopnik, Andrew Meltzoff, and Patricia Kuhl, *How Babies Think: The Science of Childhood* (London: Phoenix, 2001).

27 See Jerome's instructions to Paula's daughter-in-law, Laeta, on how to bring up her daughter (also named Paula) in his letter to her. Jerome, Letter 107 to Laeta (107.4 and 5), https://www.tertullian.org/fathers2/NPNF2-06/Npnf2-06-03.htm#P3757_1005453, accessed April 22, 2022. See the analysis of Jerome and John Chrysostom's attitudes towards child-rearing in *Childhood in History: Perceptions of Children in the Ancient and Medieval Worlds*, ed. Reidar Aasgaard, Cornelia B. Horn, and Oana Maria Cojocaru (Abingdon: Routledge, 2018), 167-172. See also Odd Magne Baake, *When Children Became People: The Birth of Childhood in Early Christianity* (Minneapolis: Fortress, 2005).

rate arguments, encouraging women to take up virginity even if it meant leaving husbands and children that they already had. Virginity functioned as a way to engage the body in the transformation of the soul. By renouncing all earthly attachments, virgins began the process of healing the soul; it put one on the road to resurrection. Renouncing motherhood and maternal bonds to earthly loves was one of the most accessible ways that women could gain power over their fates and their salvations, and stories like Paula's were convenient propagandistic narratives of a devotion to Christ that trumped all other loves.[28]

Alongside early Christian attitudes towards children by leading thinkers like Jerome, there was the widespread belief that in the resurrection, the human body would be transformed from flesh into pure spirit.[29] More specifically, all human bodies would be transformed into male bodies, since that was the gender of Jesus Christ. Masculinity was also an ideal in ancient Greek and Roman cultures: the true human being was a male human being. These beliefs can be seen already in the theology of one of the earliest theologians, Origen of Alexandria (184–253). In his work *On the Resurrection*, Origen relied heavily upon biblical passages such as Romans 8:29, which states that resurrected bodies would be conformed to "the image of the Son."[30] This transformation into the image of the Son implied just that: all humans would turn into the image of a *son*—a male. Origen's contemporary Clement of Alexandria (ca. 150–215) argued specifically that women were to shed all the qualities of their bodies that made them reproductive, such as menstruation, breastfeeding, pregnancy, and so forth. In other words, females would be resurrected to *look* like females, but they would no longer ever identify as mothers.

While it demanded that women be denied their identities as mothers, early Christianity's focus on renunciation offered women a chance to join the ranks of the saved. The women who followed

[28] See Gerontius, *The Life of Melania the Younger*, ed. and trans. Elizabeth A. Clark (Lewiston, N.Y.: Edwin Mellen, 1984), 152.

[29] See Brandon Morgan, "'We Will All Be Changed': Materiality, Resurrection, and Reaping Spiritual Bodies in Origen's *Peri Archon*," *American Theological Inquiry* 7, no. 2 (2014): 13–16.

[30] Evagrius of Pontus also made this a significant element of his thought, in particular in his "Letter to Melania" (which may actually have been written to Rufinus). See Clark, *Origenist Controversy*, 72–73.

the Christian practice of virginity and the ascetic life were seen as being healed from their sin and shame. Renouncing earthly pleasures was seen as an act of healing and redeeming corrupted human flesh. Perhaps mothers like Paula and Melania took to heart the words of Clement of Alexandria, who said that wives, like their husbands, could achieve spiritual perfection.[31] Women who embraced virginity were often called "female m[e]n of God" and "manly creature[s] in everything but body."[32] Paula's relinquishment of her role as mother to her children indicated to theologians like Jerome that she was heading into the process of shedding the attributes of her femaleness that trapped her in her maternal flesh and prevented her from salvation.

New Forms of Christian Kinship

Symbolic and theological understandings about new forms of kinship in Jesus Christ also had an influence on how early Christian theologians thought about mothers, children, and family. People from all classes, religions, and ethnicities, as well as both enslaved and free people, were beginning to worship Jesus and join the Christian community. Early Christian groups faced the task of preaching the universal message of the Gospel while trying to draw the lines of insider and outsider. Paul's writings made it clear that Jesus' ministry ushered in a new era of community that pushed beyond the boundaries of bloodlines and ancient familial bonds.[33] Early Christians pointed to Jesus' own teaching in the Sermon on the Mount where he emphasizes God the Father as the most important parent to the human race, downplaying the importance of actual, earthly parents for the

[31] Clement of Alexandria, *Stromata* IV.19–20, cited in Patricia Wilson-Kastner, *A Lost Tradition: Women Writers of the Early Church* (Washington, D.C.: University Press of America, 1981), xiii.

[32] See Palladius, *Dialogue* 56, quoted in Gillian Cloke, *This Female Man of God: Women and Spiritual Power in the Patristic Age, AD 350–450* (New York: Routledge, 1995), 214.

[33] See for example Sin-Pan Daniel Ho, *Paul and the Creation of a Counter-Cultural Community: A Rhetorical Analysis of 1 Cor. 5.1–11.1 in Light of the Social Lives of the Corinthians*, Library of New Testament Studies 509 (London: Bloomsbury T&T Clark, 2015); Jacobus Kok, Martin I. Webber, and Jermo Van Nes, eds., *Drawing and Transcending Boundaries in the New Testament and Early Christianity*, Beiträge Zum Verstehen der Bibel 38 (Zürich: Lit, 2019).

flourishing and survival of children.[34] He also preaches against the family in Matthew,[35] in Mark,[36] and in Luke.[37] In such passages, the nuclear family and the life of the household do not seem to be locations for faith formation or Christian piety but instead seem to be "potential obstacles to following God's will."[38]

In contrast to the complex and broad kinship networks of Roman imperial society, extended families were not at the core of the new Christian movement. Groups of believers who followed Jesus Christ and anticipated the possible end of the world made up the nucleus of the early Christian community, and kinship groups formed outside of Roman laws and social expectations. Those in Christ were not confined to the strict kinship laws and norms of the Roman world; they considered themselves no longer as slave or free, Jew or Greek, but rather as "adopted" children of God. The countercultural thrust of early Christian communities had an expansive nature that included all kinds of people and emphasized the concept of adopted children of God, sidelining the biological realities of maternal attachment and the necessity of mother-child bonding. Studies of the "burial clubs"[39] that were common among Roman lower classes—in which those who were of similar social class, craft, or ethnicity but had no biological family ties were buried together—show that Christians also utilized these traditions when they buried fellow Christians in one kinship-community group.[40]

The combination of attitudes towards the narcissism of children, the belief that the maternal body would be shed in resurrection, and the new forms of Christian kinship surely all factored into Jerome's belief that Paula was doing the right thing by relinquishing her duties and role as a mother to her children. To please God meant to approach all earthly relationships with *apatheia*. In his male, Christian gaze, Paula was proving her worth as a Christian.[41]

34 Matt 7:7–11, 21–23.
35 Matt 10:16–30.
36 Mark 13:9–13.
37 Luke 12:51–53.
38 Alicia Myers, *Blessed among Women? Mothers and Motherhood in the New Testament* (New York: Oxford University Press, 2017), 71.
39 Suzanne Dixon, *The Roman Mother*, Routledge Revivals (Hoboken, N.J.: Taylor and Francis, 2014), 211–17.
40 Dixon, *Roman Mother*, 211–17.
41 Malone, *Women in Christianity*, 146.

She was demonstrating to those around her that she could overcome her emotions and her desires for her children, who kept her bound to earthly cares and pleasures. She was shedding the maternal in all its femaleness. She was becoming male.

The Mother-Martyrs: Perpetua and Felicity

If there is one early account of maternal relinquishment for the sake of the new Christian faith, it is the account of the mother-martyrs Perpetua and Felicity. Perpetua, known as one of the most famous early Christian martyrs, describes in exquisite detail how she relinquished her maternity for the sake of her heroic and very public execution. One the one hand, Perpetua's narrative is unique in Christian literature for its detail and first-person perspective. On the other hand, the Christian tradition does contain other brief vignettes of mothers who sacrificed themselves or their children in brutal and horrific ways during the periods when Christians were persecuted by Romans.[42] The Christian poet Prudentius (348–405) tells the story of a mother and her toddler who were tortured during the trial of the Christian deacon Romanus, which took place in Antioch in 303. The account says the toddler laughed before he was beheaded, for the glory of Christ was his.[43] The famous

[42] Ironically, in the hagiographic treatment of several early Christian mothers in the *Acts of the Christian Martyrs*, infants and toddlers were willingly given up by mothers to be killed at the hands of the Romans for the sake of gaining eternal life. More than a few early Christian mothers apparently found the appeal to Christian spiritual perfection and glory stronger than the attachment to their children or their own maternal instinct for survival. Eusebius tells the story of the young mother, Agathonicê, who left her child in the public square and threw herself onto the flames of another Christian being burned alive under the persecutions of Marcus Aurelius (161–180). I take this from Bakke, *When Children Became People*, 267–68. He cites Eusebius for the dating of this story: Eusebius, *Historia Ecclesiastica* 4.15.48. See the account in Herbert Musurillo, ed., *The Acts of the Christian Martyrs* (Oxford: Clarendon, 1972), 27–29. Another account, the legend of Sophia, has her modeling the famous Maccabean mother who watched each one of her sons die and encouraged them to stay strong in their faith. Sophia did the same to her two daughters who were burned alive. Their torture was their liberation and salvation. See also A. S. Lewis, John Smith, and F. Crawford Burkitt, *Select Narratives of Holy Women: From the Syro-Antiochene or Sinai Palimpsest as Written above the Old Syriac Gospels*, Studia Sinaitica 9–10 (London: C.J. Clay and Sons, 1900).

[43] See the full account in Prudentius, *Peristephanon*, 10.661–664; Baake, *When Children Became People*, 271.

Golden Legend tells the story of Julitta and her small son Quiricus, both of whom were killed in the persecutions of the year 230. When Julitta saw Quiricus die, she rejoiced, proclaiming that at least her child would reach heaven before she did.[44] These horrifying tales—which have been preserved as hagiographies—may not be what actually happened, but they suggest that it was perhaps exceedingly difficult for mothers to protect their young children from the violence and anarchic forces of the late Roman Empire. They also suggest that stories of mothers sacrificing themselves or their children were circulating as heroic tales among Christians in the early centuries of the faith.

The famous Perpetua was one of these young mother-martyrs. She described in detail, and with a focus on her maternal functions, how she detached from her son in order to be sacrificed for her faith.[45] In her famous account *The Martyrdom of Perpetua and Felicity*, the two young mothers Perpetua and Felicity were part of a small group of Christians who refused to offer up sacrifices to the Emperor Geta on the occasion of his birthday on March 7, 203/204 C.E. They were taken to the Roman amphitheater to be killed by wild animals. Perpetua was twenty-two years old and hailed from a well-regarded family. At first, she was thrown in prison without her infant who was still nursing at the breast. Perpetua indicates that she was deeply bonded with him. She narrates that when she was thrown into prison, she was "tortured with worry" about him. When he was brought back to her prison cell so that she could nurse him, the place "had suddenly become a palace" to her.[46]

Competing with her bond to him, though, was the promise of the glory of Jesus Christ, the Lord. Early Christian piety celebrated dying for one's faith, and the group of Christians that accompanied Perpetua and Felicity was a group that would not waver in their

44 "Saint Quiricus and His Mother Saint Julitta," in Jacobus de Voragine, *The Golden Legend: Readings on the Saints*, trans. William Granger Ryan (Princeton: Princeton University Press, 2012), 323–33.

45 It is now accepted that an editor put together the text of the martyrdom, or "passion," of Perpetua and Felicity. Most likely a male editor, he included parts of the text that have been attributed to Perpetua herself. See Eric Rebillard, ed., *Greek and Latin Narratives about the Ancient Martyrs*, Oxford Early Christian Texts (Oxford: Oxford University Press, 2017), 295–96.

46 *The Martyrdom of Perpetua and Felicity*, 3, in Musurillo, *Acts of the Christian Martyrs*, 109.

disobedience to the emperor or in their confessions to identify with the illegal faith of Christianity. As the terrible day of her death sentence drew closer, Perpetua made it a point to note that her baby was choosing to detach from her. She had left him temporarily with her family. They had been pleading with her to change her mind and come home. The fact that her Roman father pleaded with her to change her mind, begging her to "have pity on your baby!" suggests that both of them knew the child was likely to die without Perpetua's maternal nourishment.[47] However, much to Perpetua's relief, her newborn no longer wanted to feed at her breast. He had detached from her. Perhaps as a way to show the reader that God was taking care of her, she noted in the narrative that her breasts did not suffer any inflammation despite the abrupt end to nursing. The addition of such a detail suggests that Perpetua wanted the reader to know that God approved of this mother-child detachment.

Perpetua's account does not say what happened to her baby. Perhaps he lived; perhaps he died. She was relieved, however, that he would not need her body anymore. It was now ready to be fully prepared as a sacrifice to Jesus Christ. Perpetua's slave, Felicity, had not yet given birth as the day of their deaths drew closer. Felicity was afraid she would *not* be killed with her friends if she were pregnant, so this group of young Christians prayed together with her for a preterm birth for her child.[48] And God apparently answered this mother's prayer for a preterm birth. The account describes Felicity giving birth to her daughter at eight months. Once the baby was born, Felicity promptly gave up the infant girl for someone else to raise. The reader has even less reason than in the case of Perpetua's son to have confidence that Felicity's newborn would live. It is unclear how a slave woman's baby would have found a wet nurse. In any case, the narrative of these two young mother-martyrs is not concerned about the fate of their children—or about how these two young women would navigate motherhood. It is concerned about portraying these two mothers' undying devotion to Jesus Christ. Felicity is said to have

[47] Perpetua's father twice pleads with Perpetua to "have pity" on her baby. He also declared that the child may not live without Perpetua: *Martyrdom of Perpetua and Felicity*, 3, 5, in Musurillo, *Acts of the Christian Martyrs*, 109, 113.
[48] *Martyrdom of Perpetua and Felicity*, 15, in Musurillo, *Acts of the Christian Martyrs*, 123.

declared that as she went from birthing a child to being killed, she went "from one blood bath to another, from the midwife to the gladiator, ready to wash after childbirth in a second baptism."[49] Her decision affirms a Christian theology of fatality rather than a theology of natality.[50]

One more detail in the narrative points to the early Christian idea of all people being resurrected as male. In an extended vision, Perpetua saw how she would be transformed into the glory of Christ after her death. She saw her clothes being ripped off, and when they were, she saw that suddenly she "was a man."[51] Perpetua envisioned her own transformation from mother to man. Her actions illustrate the "sex-change" soteriology that was present in early Christian theology.[52] It is unclear whether this part of the narrative was written by Perpetua herself or by a male co-author. Therefore, we cannot judge whether Perpetua had internalized the Origenist imagination of a sex-change in resurrection or whether this part of her narrative is a product of the male gaze upon her actions. What is clear, though, is that Perpetua's narration of her transformation from mother to martyr was also a celebration of her transformation from mother to male.

Christianity's Other Mother-Martyrs

The tradition of renouncing the role of mother and detaching from one's children remained a part of Christian piety long after theologians like Jerome stopped celebrating it. Throughout the Middle

49 *Martyrdom of Perpetua and Felicity*, 18, in Musurillo, *Acts of the Christian Martyrs*, 127.

50 See Grace Jantzen, "Flourishing: Towards an Ethic of Natality," *Feminist Theory* 2, no. 2 (2001): 219–32.

51 *Martyrdom of Perpetua and Felicity*, 10, in Musurillo, *Acts of the Christian Martyrs*, 119.

52 Kari Vogt, "'Becoming Male': A Gnostic and Early Christian Metaphor," in *The Image of God: Gender Models in Judaeo-Christian Tradition*, ed. Kari Elisabeth Bøerresen (Minneapolis: Fortress, 1995), 170–86. Vogt traces the origins of the sex-change metaphor to the Logion 114 of the *Gospel of Thomas*, a Valentinian gnostic text that was widely circulated in the first and second centuries of the church. In Logion 114, Simon Peter says, "For every woman who makes herself male (*hout*) will enter the Kingdom of Heaven." Evagrius of Pontus also made this a significant element of his thought, in particular in his "Letter to Melania" (which may actually have been written to Rufinus). See Clark, *Origenist Controversy*, 72–73.

Ages, mothers pursued spiritual power by renouncing their roles as biological mothers. This practice was particularly common among medieval Italian mothers, who often joined Franciscan communities in order to live in poverty. To them, the lack of children and the denial of maternal affection was a special kind of poverty that could bring these women sainthood.[53]

Other mothers, such as Ivette of Huy from Belgium (1157-1228) gave her two young boys to their grandfather to be raised. Child-free, she then let herself become enclosed as an anchoress next to a leper colony where she had worked. Her position as an anchoress brought her tremendous power in the region, and scores of young women traveled to Belgium to join her.[54] Elizabeth of Thuringia (aka Elizabeth of Hungary, 1207–1231) deserted her own biological children and devoted the rest of her life to caring for the children of *others*. This piety came "only after God had sufficiently hardened her heart towards her own" children.[55] In the hagiographic account of her life as given in the *Golden Legend* (*Legenda aurea*), it is clear that Elizabeth adhered to a common medieval view of children as *earthly* riches that tempted her attention away from devotion to God.[56] They were a form of worldly wealth who needed to be renounced—in effect, deserted—in order to live a life of poverty worthy of Christ.

Another young mother, Marie de L'Incarnation (1599–1672), carried this tradition all the way into the seventeenth century. She abandoned her son in order to become a nun at the Ursuline Monastery in Tours, France. She too believed that the renunciation of her motherhood and the desertion of her son was obedience to God's will and a true *imitatio Christi*.[57] Marie ended up traveling to New France (Quebec) and establishing a convent

53 Barbara Newman, *From Virile Woman to WomanChrist: Studies in Medieval Religion and Literature* (Philadelphia: University of Pennsylvania Press, 1995), 87.

54 Brenda Bolton, "*Vitae Matrum*: A Further Aspect of the *Frauenfrage*," in *Medieval Women: Studies in Church History*, Subsidia I, ed. Derek Baker (Oxford: Basil Blackwell, 1978), 258. Bolton relies on the *Vita Ivettae Reclusae Huyi*, written by a younger contemporary of hers in 1230, Hugh of Floreffe. The *Vita* was edited by G. Henschenius, *ASB* January 1 (Antwerp, 1643), 863–87.

55 Newman, *Virile Woman*, 87.

56 See the hagiographic account of Elizabeth of Thuringa (Hungary) in de Voragine, *Golden Legend*, 688–704.

57 See Mary Dunn, *The Cruelest of All Mothers: Marie de L'Incarnation, Motherhood, and Christian Tradition* (New York: Fordham University Press, 2016): 43–62.

there. Marie regretted her decision for the rest of her life, even calling herself "the cruelest of all mothers." In her correspondence with her estranged son, Marie continually justified her choice to leave him and enter a convent.[58] The choice may have been a painful one, but she believed it was the only way to be properly committed to God.

Victims or Beneficiaries?

The tradition of renouncing motherhood within the Christian faith has been seen by some historians as "insidious."[59] Such acts of maternal renunciation in the early church do not appear from a modern vantage point to be some kind of quasi-feminist statement against the cultural institution of motherhood in the way modern feminists like Adrienne Rich expressed it. Instead, Christian mother-martyrs and mother-ascetics believed that their own mothering was distracting them from being proper followers of Jesus.[60] Leading Christian theologians of the late Roman Empire celebrated and encouraged these women and perhaps many others to untangle themselves from children and family in the name of proper dedication to God. If the modern science of attachment theory—as grounded and developed by researchers such as John Bowlby[61] and Mary Ainsworth[62]—is correct, then these mothers were renouncing a role that was of central, existential importance to their children: namely, the role of a loving and consistent caregiver.[63] From the modern perspective of attachment, it is widely understood that attachment to a mother or other consistent caregiver is optimal for human well-being and perhaps even a factor in a more peaceful society.[64]

58 Dunn, *Cruelest of All Mothers*, 47–49.

59 Dunn, *Cruelest of All Mothers*, 45–47

60 Newman, *Virile Woman*, 84. See also the example of Angela of Foligno, the mystic who rejoiced in being free from her husband and children once they all died young, in Shulamith Shahar, *The Fourth Estate: A History of Women in the Middle Ages* (New York: Methuen, 1983), 105.

61 See John Bowlby, *Attachment*, vol. 1, 2nd ed. (New York: Basic Books, 1982).

62 Mary D. Salter Ainsworth, Mary C. Blehar, Everett Waters, and Sally N. Wall, *Patterns of Attachment: A Psychological Study of the Strange Situation* (New York: Routledge, 2015).

63 Susan Hart, *The Impact of Attachment: Developmental Neuroaffective Psychology* (New York: W. W. Norton, 2011).

64 See Jeremy Rifkin, *The Empathic Civilization: The Race to Global Consciousness in a World in Crisis* (New York: J. P. Tarcher/Penguin, 2009).

But modern motherhood studies also tell another story. Many women who bear children have an ambivalent relationship to their role as mother. For centuries, women have struggled with their own ambitions and the demands of motherhood. Giving birth and caring for children is such a transformative experience that many women often express feeling like they have lost themselves and no longer know who they are. Could it be that wealthy women like Melania and Paula experienced their own ambivalence towards mothering? We will never know. But clearly, they were agents in their own decisions. Each woman seems to have kept in touch with her children, and each one acquired high status and power within the Christian community. These wealthy mothers were surely committed to their families. Both Melania and Paula brought their children into the new communities that they had founded at a later date; neither one ever stopped trying to influence the lives of their children, even from afar. It could be that wealthy mothers such as Melania and Paula left their children and the rigid conventions of Roman motherhood because they wanted to.

Historians argue that this may have been a part of Perpetua's choice as well. Perpetua's martyrdom may have been pure rebellion against the strict Roman norms for daughters in the houses of their fathers.[65] Hers was quite an extreme rebellion if that was the case, but the emphasis on her father's anguish and pleas suggests that Perpetua was motivated by a chance to make her own decision and rebel against his rule. These mothers, all in their own ways, exhibited a kind of freedom from domesticity and maternity that had not existed for Roman women of their classes in earlier decades, and they laid the groundwork for women to take on new roles within the Christian faith that did not require motherhood to obtain status.

We will never know what Paula, Melania, Perpetua, or Felicity was thinking as they left their children in the hands of family or the state to pursue Christian holiness and pure devotion to Christ in the early church. We will never know how deeply their children

65 M. R. Lefkowitz notes that Perpetua's rejection of her father in his apparent desperation shows how a generation of young Roman women were rejecting the strong culture of the *paterfamilias* in which the father alone determines who lives and dies in his household. See M. R. Lefkowitz, "The Motivations for St. Perpetua's Martyrdom," *Journal of the American Academy of Religion* 44, no. 3 (1976): 417–21.

resented them or whether their decisions placed a great strain on their familial relationships. We will never know if they regretted their decisions or if they left their children because they fully bought into the call of early Christian theology to leave all earthly loves behind. What we can probably safely say from the vantage point of modern motherhood is that each woman had her own particular reasons to pursue her spiritual ambitions and that the spiritual lionizing of these famous women is only one small piece of a larger, lost narrative about mothering in the Christian faith.

2

Eve's Sin and the Generosity of the Maternal Body

Early Christianity's uneasiness with earthly attachments and its skepticism of the mother-child bond seems to have supported many women as they followed their own spiritual ambitions along with, or despite, their roles as mothers. Yet, besides the spiritual successes of mother-martyrs like Perpetua or mother-ascetics such as Paula and Melania, there remained a vexing problem within the Christian imagination: namely, what to do about the earthliness of the maternal body. Putting it aside was not quite so easy. After all, early Christians defended their confession that Jesus Christ was truly divine *and* truly human with a human body. And every single human being shares one thing in common: we all come from the body of a woman. Jesus Christ, too, was born from the body of a woman. One of the earliest theologians of the church, Tertullian of Carthage (155–220), found himself facing precisely this conundrum.

Christ's Descent into Shame

For all of its life-giving properties, the maternal body has been regarded as a site of fatality. For Tertullian and many other early Christian thinkers, as well as for early modern theologians like Martin Luther who relied upon the early church Fathers for his own Reformation theology, Christ was born for one purpose: to die. Tertullian noted that "there is a shared debt between birth and death" and, further, that "the project of dying is the reason for being born."[1] Gregory of Nyssa commented that at the moment of birth, "it is not the birth of the child but the presence of death that is thought of, and the death of the mother anticipated."[2] *The project of dying is the reason for being born.* This is quite a radical sentiment that overlooks all the life-sustaining ways that human bodies help one another survive and live on earth. For centuries upon centuries, the tight connection between birth and death shaped the way the Christian imagination saw the maternal body. It was caught in the paradox and ambivalence of Jesus Christ's appearance on earth and his fate on the cross.

Early Christianity did not lack ideas about how Jesus Christ appeared on earth. Many stripes of Gnostic Christianity, a popular form of early Christian faith, affirmed his presence on earth as an appearance of the divine who had come to show his followers the secret escape from the trials of the flesh into an existence of pure spirituality. One of the more powerful and popular Gnostic thinkers was Marcion of Sinope (85–160).[3] Marcion hated the human body and argued for an extreme spirit-body split. Marcion's views about the incorruptibility and superiority of God over and against the lowliness and shame of human flesh found resonance among early Christians and pagans far and wide.

Marcion's ideas about the lofty deity of Christ and his purity penetrated parts of Latin Christianity. This had Tertullian deeply worried. If Christ did not participate in the struggles of the flesh, how could his actions on earth actually touch humanity? Marcion insisted that Paul was the only true witness to Jesus Christ rather than the Gospel accounts. He also disparaged the embodied anthropology of the Hebrew Bible. The popularity of his ideas helped deepen the Hellenistic anthropology of the spirit-body split and came to dominate many Christian groups throughout the region.

1 Tertullian, *On the Flesh of Christ* 6.25. See also Carly Daniel-Hughes, *The Salvation of the Flesh in Tertullian of Carthage: Dressing for the Resurrection* (New York: Palgrave Macmillan, 2011), 70.

2 Gregory of Nyssa, *On Virginity*, in *St. Gregory: Ascetical Works*, trans. Virginia Wood Callahan (Washington, D.C.: Catholic University Press, 1967), 15–16, quoted in Caroline T. Schroeder, *Melania: Early Christianity through the Life of One Family* (Berkeley: University of California Press, 2018), 72.

3 Sebastian Moll, *The Arch-Heretic Marcion*, Wissenschaftliche Untersuchungen Zum Neuen Testament 250 (Tübingen: Mohr Siebeck, 2010), 25ff.

Marcion preached that God was so utterly removed from the created order that the thought of Jesus Christ being born and nursed from a woman and her shameful human flesh—uterus, placenta, blood, breasts, and so forth—was repulsive, heretical even.[4] Everything having to do with maternity was gross and dirty in Marcion's theological system. There was no way the maternal body could possibly be a site of the deity's incarnation. That would fatally compromise the divine. His Christology was docetic; Jesus was a spirit who appeared as a human, but he had no contact with anything fleshly.

Tertullian was concerned about all this. He did not accept the way Marcion elevated the person of Christ to such heights that he was only a deity and not truly human. If Marcion were right, it meant that the Incarnation was simply not true and that salvation was not actually enacted among real, physical humans on earth. The logical conclusion to such a deified Jesus was that the God of heaven did not display God's mercy and love for humanity in any real or actual way. In order to contradict Marcion's powerful logic of a God who was so superior that God was not touched by the grunge of human existence, Tertullian turned to the corporal and fleshly aspects of Christ's earthly existence. He wanted to ensure that Christianity had an imagination for the saving power of the flesh.[5] And so, Tertullian turned to none other than the maternal body to make his theological point. The uterus was ground zero.

But Tertullian's view faced headwinds. The early church Fathers inherited their understanding of female physiology from a long and robust history of gynecology in ancient Greek culture. Hippocrates and his many followers (the Hippocratic school) studied the uterus closely and observed how it mysteriously expanded and contracted like an independent organism within the female body. It could "breathe" in the male sperm just as nostrils breathe in air.[6] Many

4 Hans Jonas, *The Gnostic Religion: The Message of the Alien God and the Beginnings of Christianity*, 3rd ed. (Boston: Beacon, 2001), 142–45.

5 Charlotte Radler, "The Dirty Physician: Necessary Dishonor and Fleshly Solidarity in Tertullian's Writings," *Vigiliae Christianae* 63 (2009): 345–68, here 354. See also p. 359, where Radler notes the Stoic influences on Tertullian, who believed that all things have some form of corporeality. Hence bodily-ness could potentially be a site for salvation.

6 Helen King, *Hippocrates' Woman: Reading the Female Body in Ancient Greece* (London: Routledge, 1998), 31.

thinkers believed that the uterus was made up of more than one section that was connected to a system of tubes and channels throughout the body that led in and out of it.[7] The uterus was also seen as a wayward and unpredictable female organ. This meant to Tertullian and others that women themselves were morally suspect. The uterus could become untethered from its original position and move about a woman's body causing all kinds of mental illness and poor judgment, so the theory went. The ancient physician Aretaeus of Cappadocia even called the uterus "an animal within an animal" because it seemed to be so troublesome.[8] The uterus was also a dangerous location. The Hippocratic school believed that the onset of labor happened when the child began thrashing about trying to get out.[9] If the child did not break out of the uterus in a timely fashion, it would die in there. Early Christians sometimes even invoked "uterine magic"[10] to coax the child out. A spell from the fifth century apparently intended to make sure that the womb did not trap

[7] Some thinkers believed the uterus had two compartments, while others believed it had more; medieval doctors relied on illustrations of the uterus that showed seven compartments. See Danielle Jacquart and Claude Thomasset, *Sexuality and Medicine in the Middle Ages* (Princeton: Princeton University Press, 1988), 21.

[8] Although ancient autopsies showed that the uterus was not connected to other organs via a *hodos*, and despite the fact that other ancient physicians such as Soranus and Galen doubted the mobility of the uterus, this view of the wayward uterus stuck in the Western imagination for millennia. Plato in his *Timaeus* propagated the view of the wandering uterus, and because the *Timaeus* was one of the first and most widely read Greek texts that got transmitted into medieval Europe, the school of the "wandering womb" did not really die out until early modern medicine finally put it to rest. Clarissa Atkinson, *The Oldest Vocation: Christian Motherhood in the Middle Ages* (Ithaca, N.Y.: Cornell University Press, 1991), 31. The "hysteria" of Sigmund Freud's female patients was called such because of the belief that uniquely "female" mental health issues came from the fact that the "race" of women, the classification of which lived with the label *hysterê*, had a sexual and reproductive system that could turn problematic.

[9] Hippocrates, *De natura pueri* [On the Nature of the Child] 30.1–9 (7.530.20–532.9 L), cited in Nancy Demand, "Monuments, Midwives, and Gynecology," in *Ancient Medicine in Its Socio-Cultural Context*, vol. 1, ed. H. F. J. Horstmanshoff, Philip J. van der Eijk, and P. H. Schrijvers (Amsterdam and Atlanta: Editions Rodopi, 1995), 284–85.

[10] Jean-Jacques Aubert, "Threatened Wombs: Aspects of Ancient Uterine Magic," *Greek, Roman, and Byzantine Studies* 30, no. 3 (2005): 421–49. See also Nancy Demand, *Birth, Death, and Motherhood in Classical Greece* (Baltimore: Johns Hopkins University Press, 1994), 87–101. Men who were afraid

the baby inside. It went: "Come out of your tomb, Christ is calling you . . ."[11] In other words, in the imagination of Tertullian and other church Fathers, the uterus could turn quickly from womb to tomb.

Another headwind against Tertullian's argument that Christ was both perfect *and* truly human was the general Roman attitude towards the maternal body. Because of its mysterious nature and unpredictability, Roman philosophy saw the female body as a defective form of humanity. For centuries, ancient Greek and Roman anthropology held up the male as the truest and most well-formed human being. Males were considered the highest form of humanity. Men in the classical world were afraid of losing their strength and virility and becoming "womanish."[12] Women's bodies were seen as more primitive, wetter, colder, more disorganized, and spongier. They were generally passive, especially in intelligence and in reproduction. Female fetuses were seen as under-formed in the womb, not receiving enough heat to become a more complete person (i.e., a male).

The rise of Christianity did not change these perceptions about gender difference. The Christian thinker Hieronymus states it most clearly based on Ephesians 4:1. He writes that "so long as woman is subject to childbirth and the care of children, she is different from man, like the body is different from the soul."[13] Romans believed that the ancient Roman gods and goddesses were too dignified and too perfect to have anything to do with shameful, fleshly occupations such as birthing, nursing, and human bodily care. In the Roman imagination, there was nothing generative about a woman giving birth. The maternal labor of birthing was not just unclean and animalistic, it was *shameful*.[14] So, when early Christians in the Roman Empire preached that God was born—actually *born*—through a woman, they were saying something quite controversial. By the

---

that their wives might be unfaithful would cast a spell on her uterus so that she could not get pregnant by anyone but him.

11 Aubert, "Threatened Wombs," 439.

12 Peter Brown, *Body and Society: Men, Women, and Sexual Renunciation in Early Christianity* (New York: Columbia University Press, 1988), 10–11.

13 Hieronymus, Patrologia Latina 26, p. 567, quoted in Kari Vogt, "'Becoming Male': A Gnostic and Early Christian Metaphor," in *The Image of God: Gender Models in Judaeo-Christian Tradition*, ed. Kari Elisabeth Bøerresen (Minneapolis: Fortress, 1995), 180.

14 See Virginia Burrus, *Saving Shame: Martyrs, Saints, and Other Abject Subjects* (Philadelphia: University of Pennsylvania Press, 2008), 53.

mid-second century, the idea of a deity who willed to enter into the dirt, death, and decay of human life did not seem like a deity at all.

In order to refute Marcion, Tertullian turned the theological and cultural distaste for the maternal body into an argument for God's deep love. Along with most early Christians, Tertullian assumed that due to the Fall, the human condition was defined by "muck."[15] The epitome of this human experience of "muck" was none other than the uterus in the female body. Its movement, the way it expands and contracts, and the way it fills up with blood and tissue and other fluids during pregnancy exhibits precisely the dirtiest and most shameful of human muck. Tertullian argued that despite this muck and shame, Christ loves humanity. In fact, Christ loves humanity so much that he was willing to be "curdled in the uncleanness of the womb."[16] Tertullian used such disgusting imagery to make his point against Marcion's disembodied Christ. He argued against Marcion, saying:

> [Marcion's Christ] was not conceived in a womb . . . [H]e was not set free after ten months' torture [*cruciate*], nor was he split upon the ground through the sewer of a body, with a sudden attack of pains along with the uncleanness of all those months, nor did he greet the daylight with tears or suffer his first wound at the severing of his cord . . . no question thereafter of his wallowing in uncleanness in a mother's lap.[17]

Because Jesus Christ experienced the shame and dirt of Mary, her maternal body became a witness to the "therapeutic foulness" of his true human nature.[18] This was an important element in Tertullian's view of who God was. Tertullian believed that God was a *healer*.[19] God was not a distant, supreme being but a

15 Jennifer Glancy, "The Law of the Opened Body: Tertullian on the Nativity," *Henoch* 30 no. 2 (2008): 267–88, esp. 275.

16 Radler, "Dirty Physician," 361; Tertullian, *On the Flesh of Christ*, 4.1–3.

17 Tertullian, *Marcion*, 4.21, quoted in Glancy, "Law of the Opened Body," 275–77. Ironically, Tertullian bases his reflections on the Gospel of John, which actually lacks an account of the Nativity (in contrast to Luke and Matthew who both describe the birth of Christ). He uses John 3:6 to uphold his logic that "what is born of flesh is flesh." See also Glancy, "Law of the Opened Body," 342–44.

18 Radler, "Dirty Physician," 362.

19 Radler, "Dirty Physician," 345.

divine physician who stuck God's hands into the illness and vulnerability of a sick human community. Salvation meant that the human was healed from its corruptibility, dirtiness, and putridity. The only way the Healer could heal was if God intimately understood the morally sick condition and suffering of humanity. The polluted maternal body was the perfect entry of God into such a state. Tertullian's affirmation of the uterine filth of the Incarnation was an effective contrast to Marcion's loveless, airless, apathetic God.

The Pain of Eve in Labor

The lack of understanding about the female reproductive system was not the only negative influence on Christianity's imagination about the maternal body. The Bible itself seemed to suggest that pregnancy and labor were events to be suffered because of the sin of Eve. In the account of the Creation in Genesis chapter 3, God curses Eve and promises pain in human reproduction. As the saga goes, once God discovered that Eve had taken the fruit from the tree in the Garden, the author has God saying to Eve: "I will greatly increase your pangs in childbearing; in pain you shall bring forth children."[20] These words have cast a long shadow over women throughout the centuries. Birth has been associated with sin, and women in labor have been tied to Eve's pain and fear in childbirth. Christian women were encouraged to remember that they were Eve's sisters in both sin and in furthering the human race. The idea of laboring pain as the punishment for Eve's sin has been a constant throughout the history of Christian thought.

It was not difficult for early Christians to interpret the Genesis account in a way that disproportionately blamed Eve for humanity's fall into sin. There was already a woman responsible for the ills of humanity within the ancient world's social imaginary, and her name was Pandora. The early Christian imagination connected Eve closely with the ancient Greek myth in which Pandora opened the box of the world's beautiful evils. She became the framework for interpreting the Genesis account of Eve and the fate of the world through Eve's actions in the Garden of Eden. According to the Greek author Hesiod, Pandora was the first woman of the female race.

20 Gen 3:16 (NRSV).

She was a *parthenon*: a beautiful virgin. However, this was only her appearance. The inside of her body was actually that of a sensuous adult woman of reproductive age—a *gyne*. Her body was like a "jar"[21] because it was both capable of holding something inside of it and was fashioned out of earth and water. But Pandora also had a dangerous side. Her insides were not neutral but in fact "ravenous," and when it opened up, Pandora's body unleashed death and destruction upon the race of men. The vagina was represented as Pandora's box: it was outwardly something of beauty and pleasure, but what came out of it was evil, chaotic, and corrupt.[22] The fascination with Pandora and the moral turpitude of the uterus and vagina continued into modernity. Famous twentieth-century artists such as Max Beckman and Paul Klee depicted Pandora's box as a woman's vagina.[23] The field of gynecology still holds its name from the ancient word *gyne*, which has been forever associated with Pandora's dangerous and mysterious insides.

Although church Fathers like Tertullian, Chrysostom, Gregory of Nazianzus, Origen, Gregory of Nyssa, and even Augustine dismissed the story of Pandora as just a story, each one of these Christian thinkers alluded to her somehow in their interpretations of Eve.[24] Eve was a creature derived from the male and fashioned out of dirt and water. She too was beautiful on the outside but had a lethal curiosity on the inside. Like Pandora, Eve's insides were not neutral either. Eve, like Pandora and all women, held a fatal secret: the secret pleasures of sexuality and the power of human reproduction. Eve too was regarded as "beautiful evil."[25] She too unleashed sin and suffering in the world by reaching for forbidden fruit in the Garden of Eden.

Like many other Christian thinkers, Martin Luther compared the birthing body to Eve, but he put a positive Christological twist on it: he told women to wear their birth pangs like a badge, encouraging women in labor to power through the pain and fear just as Jesus

21 Hesiod, *Works and Days: A Translation and Commentary for the Social Sciences*, ed. and trans. Walter C. Neale and David W. Tandy (Berkeley: University of California Press, 1996), 65, para. 90.

22 J. A. Philips, *Eve: The History of an Idea* (New York: Harper and Row, 1984), 23.

23 Philips, *Eve*, 23, 44.

24 Philips, *Eve*, 21–22.

25 Philips, *Eve*, 22.

Christ powered through the crucifixion. But such positive Christological views did not stick as the theology of Eve's curse traveled with Christianity into the New World. It was spread among Christian colonists through famous American Puritan preachers like Cotton Mather, who wrote a manual for midwives.[26] Rather than being full of useful, new medical information, however, it instructed midwives to remind their patients to reflect on their painful and cursed connection to Eve.[27] Among the humanitarian advancements of the nineteenth century, social reformers like John Stuart Mill and Jeremy Bentham argued that pain was not necessary for the physical or spiritual well-being of women.

However, there continued to be scores of Christian leaders who insisted that pain in labor was both a means of God's continuing punishment on women for Eve's sin *and* a moral lesson for women. Some Christians even argued that it was necessary for mother-child bonding.[28] Eve's connection to ancient attitudes that women have unleashed all that is wrong in the world misinformed how the fields of gynecology and obstetrics developed for modern times even though her explicit relationship to Pandora had been long forgotten. As obstetrical advances like breathing techniques came around, Christians in America debated whether such techniques were even moral: did they go against Scripture's prescription of pain in the memory of Eve for laboring women?[29] American doctors such as Benjamin Rush wrote in 1802 that even though the pain of childbirth did hearken back to the sin of Eve, her curse had been partly taken away in the modern world. Therefore, there was no reason for medicine to withhold pain-reducing practices for birthing and laboring women.[30] Other Christian doctors argued that God

[26] Cotton Mather, *Elizabeth in Her Holy Retirement: An Essay to Prepare a Pious Woman for Her Lying In. Or, Maxims and Methods of Piety, to Direct and Support a Handmaid of the Lord, Who Expects a Time of Travail* (Boston: B. Green, 1710).

[27] Linda S. Schearing, "Parturition (Childbirth), Pain, and Piety: Physicians and Genesis 3:16a," in *Mother Goose, Mother Jones, Mommie Dearest: Biblical Mothers and Their Children*, ed. Cheryl Kirk-Duggan and Tina Pippin (Atlanta: SBL Press, 2009), 95.

[28] R. Meyer and S. P. Desai, "Accepting Pain over Comfort: Resistance to the Use of Anesthesia in the Mid-Nineteenth Century," *Journal of Anesthesia History* 1 (2015): 115–21.

[29] Schearing, "Parturition (Childbirth), Pain, and Piety," 92.

[30] Schearing, "Parturition (Childbirth), Pain, and Piety," 88.

did not continue to punish women for Eve's ancient sin and that, in fact, it was a matter of justice to give birthing women the same kind of pain alleviation that they would to other suffering patients.[31]

In the mid-nineteenth century, it began to be generally accepted that alleviating the pain of birth was appropriate. However, it is striking that doctors and social reformers had to make winding arguments about Christian theology, biblical interpretation, and the well-being of women in order to release laboring women from the curse of Eve. Sadly, no Christian theologians of this time period were able to invalidate this theme in the Christian imagination. It would take modern scientific views of the female body and how it functions to vanquish the ongoing theology of God's curse upon women.

Mary's Closed Body

By the fourth century, an entrenched theological ambivalence towards the maternal body was already part of Christianity's mental furniture. Whereas Tertullian had argued that Mary was morally qualified as a human mother to bear the Incarnation precisely because of her uterine *immorality*, Ambrose, the Bishop of Milan, took another view. He argued that it was Mary's *virginal* body[32]—or the fact that her body was never "opened" or penetrated by a man—that made her morally qualified to bear God in Jesus Christ.

Cultural and religious norms in ancient Greece believed that the dignity of a human body was based on whether it was "opened" or "closed." Ancient Greeks believed that bodies kept their integrity as long as they remained "closed": that is, as long as they were not penetrated or opened in any way. It was, in fact, illegal to do autopsies on dead bodies or cut them open; hence, doctors had little knowledge of what female insides looked like or how they operated. However, when it came to the maternal body and fertility, ancient

[31] Carolyn Corretti and Sukumar P. Desai, "The Legacy of Eve's Curse: Religion, Childbirth Pain, and the Rise of Anesthesia in Europe: c. 1200–1800s," *Journal of Anesthesia History* 4 (2018): 182–90, here 188.

[32] Ambrose, *On Virginity* 2.2.6, in *Nicene and Post-Nicene Fathers*, Second Series, vol. 10, ed. Philip Schaff and Henry Wace, trans. H. de Romestin, E. de Romestin, and H. T. F. Duckworth (Buffalo, N.Y.: Christian Literature Publishing Co., 1896); rev. and ed. for New Advent by Kevin Knight, http://www.newadvent.org/fathers/34072.htm.

medical models admitted that the opening and closing of the uterus was a good thing: it let in sperm for reproduction, and it let out old blood and poisons. In other words, ancient medicine did not believe that an opened uterus made the female body any more undignified than it already was. Early Christian thinkers like Origen believed that Mary's "opened," fertile body made her receptive to the Word of God and the work of God within her to bear Jesus Christ. To Origen, the opening up of her virginal body did not compromise her virginity or her sinless state because fertility and the dynamism of the uterus had little to do with virginity or a girl's purity.

Beginning with Ambrose of Milan in the fourth century (ca. 340–397), the opposite came to be imagined. Mary's opened body did not suggest fertility and an openness to God's salvation but rather that her body had been morally compromised by sexuality and a man. It was precisely her *closed*, virginal body that qualified Mary to bear Christ. She was *theotokos* because she was virginal, and because she was virginal, she was sinless. And because she was sinless, she was *morally* worthy to carry God. In the Christian imagination since Ambrose, "Mary's moral consent to be the mother of Christ is of greater worth than her physical conception of God incarnate in her womb."[33] Under Ambrose's pen, rhetoric about Mary went from calling her the "mother of God" to the "Virgin Mary."

Ambrose went even further to establish a theology of the *perpetual* nature of Mary's virginity. Mary's perpetual virginity meant that she originated from a sinless place and that her own body remained closed and sinless before, during, and after the birth of Christ. By insisting on her perpetual virginity, Ambrose almost single-handedly turned Mary into the perfect image of the Christian woman as sinless, silent, and obedient to male authority. She perfectly obeyed God the Father; she was always submissive. Her state of virginity was perfect: she had a perfectly intact body before, during, and after giving birth to Jesus Christ. Moreover, she never lusted.[34]

[33] Sarah Jane Boss, "Francisco Suarez and Modern Mariology," in *Mary: The Complete Resource*, ed. Sarah Jane Boss (Oxford: Oxford University Press, 2007), 259.

[34] Although women did relate to Mary and Mary's sorrow as a mother who experienced all normal maternal functions such as pregnancy, childbirth, and poverty, Catholic teaching and preaching almost always pointed out the

The notion that Mary's body needed to stay "intact" and "closed" throughout the conception and birth of Jesus Christ remained an entrenched tradition within Christianity. Hildegard of Bingen believed that Mary's labor and birthing were not in the general manner of normal women. She argued that Christ came out of Mary's "side—not from the opening of the womb—without her knowledge and without pain, corruption, or filth."[35] Other women writers such as Birgitta of Sweden believed that Mary did give birth to a child but in a highly irregular manner. To Birgitta, Christ's birth happened "in the twinkling of an eye," the light of his newborn body so bright and splendorous that his actual exit from Mary's body could not even be seen properly.[36] Other hagiographies of the lives of saints followed this ancient logic of the opened and closed body. Some hagiographies of saints portrayed the saint being born through the appearance of a bright light or being conceived in extra-vaginal ways, such as a star or moon falling into the saint's mother's mouth at the time of conception.[37]

In some cases, Christian theology would bypass the uterus and its mysteries entirely. Instead, God's enlivening, spermatic Word entered Mary's body through her innocent ear. After all, Jesus was God's incarnate *Word*. Mary listened to the voice of the angel Gabriel and the command of God in the Annunciation, therefore indicating her obedience and her moral worthiness to carry God's own child. The conception of Christ did not penetrate any of her

---

differences between Mary's perfection and the "sinful daughters of Eve." See Bridget Heal, *The Cult of the Virgin Mary in Early Modern Germany: Protestant and Catholic Piety, 1500–1648* (New York: Cambridge University Press, 2007), 268.

[35] Hildegard of Bingen, "Ein unveröffentlichtes Hildegard-Fragment," ed. Heinrich Scipperges, *Sudhoffs Archiv für Geschichte der Medizin* 40 (1956): 41–77, quoted in Barbara Newman, *Sister of Wisdom: St. Hildegard's Theology of the Feminine* (Berkeley: University of California Press, 1987), 176.

[36] Birgitta of Sweden, *Revelations* 7.21, in *Birgitta of Sweden: Life and Selected Revelations*, ed. Marguerite Tjader Harris, trans. Albert R. Kezel, Classics of Western Spirituality (Mahwah, N.J.: Paulist Press, 1990), 203. See also Sarah Jane Boss, *Mary*, New Century Theology (London: Continuum, 2004), 103.

[37] Jane Tibbetts Schulenburg, *Forgetful of Their Sex: Female Sanctity and Society, ca. 500–1100* (Chicago: University of Chicago Press, 1998), 221–28. One instance of extra-vaginal conception can be seen in the life of Saint Maedoc of Ferns. Other stories like this can be found in the hagiographic accounts of the lives of Irish Saints.

Fig. 2.1 North Portal, Marienkapelle, Würzburg, 14th century Gothic

membranes and therefore did not "open" her body. Even Tertullian alludes to this possibility. He writes: "As Eve had believed the serpent, so Mary believed the angel."[38]

The fourth-century theologian, Ephrem the Syrian wrote,

> Just as from the small womb of Eve's ear
> Death entered in and was poured out
> so through a new ear, that was Mary's
> Life entered and was poured out.[39]

Yet another fourth-century preacher, the Bishop of Brescia, referred in a sermon to the Son of God as "he who having slipped in through his mother's ear, then filled the womb of the virgin."[40] A

[38] Tertullian, *On the Flesh of Christ*, 17, quoted in Tina Beattie, "Mary in Patristic Theology," in Boss, *Mary: The Complete Resource*, 88.

[39] Ephrem the Syrian, *Hymns on the Church*, 49.7, quoted in Beattie, "Mary in Patristic Theology," 89.

[40] Gaudentius, Bishop of Brescia, Sermon 13, in Jacques-Paul Migne, ed., *Patrologia Latina*, vol. 20 (Paris: Garnier, 1958 [1844–1866]), 20:934a; cited in Maurizio Bettini, *Women and Weasels: Mythologies of Birth in Ancient Greece and Rome* (Chicago: University of Chicago Press, 2013), 115.

depiction of the Annunciation on the tympanum of the Würzburg city cathedral shows Mary sitting peacefully as the tiny Jesus slides down from God's mouth (the Word) into Mary's ear. The medieval hymn "Gaude virgo, Mater Christi" also celebrates Christ's conception through Mary's ear:

> Rejoice, O Virgin, Mother of Christ
> Who conceived through the ear
> At Gabriel's announcement
> Rejoice, for filled with the Godhead
> You gave birth without pain.[41]

Certainly, this tradition had much to offer to the Christian belief in Mary's virginity. It affirmed her obedience to God's Word in contrast to the disobedience of Eve, and it conveniently avoided thorny questions about Mary's body and sexuality. It integrated Christian commitments to preaching and the Incarnation, and yet, it completely obscured the work of a singular mother and her body in God's entry into human existence.

The Maternal Character of Jesus Christ

The efforts of thinkers across centuries to explain the conception and birth of Jesus Christ while maintaining Mary's virginity are remarkable. Clearly, the purity and "intactness" of Mary's body was a touchy subject in the Christian imagination. As theological rhetoric and imagery of Jesus *himself* as a mother became more popular in medieval Christianity through the writings of Anselm and others, so did an imagination about the generosity of Christ's body. In the imaginations of these thinkers, Jesus was like a mother who nurtures believers. He gathered them like a hen gathers her chicks and fed them from his own breast. Jesus consoled and comforted believers like a mother. Anselm asked in a prayer: "But you, Jesus, good lord, are you also not a mother? . . . Truly master, you are a mother."[42] William of Saint Thierry described Jesus's breasts as feeding believers with the milk of his

[41] *Horae Eboracenses*, 63–64, quoted in Eamon Duffy, *Royal Books and Holy Bones: Essays in Medieval Christianity* (New York: Bloomsbury Continuum, 2018), 228.

[42] Anselm, Prayer 10 to St. Paul, *Opera omnia* 3:33, 39–41, quoted in Caroline Walker Bynum, *Jesus as Mother: Studies in the Spirituality of the High*

"little ones."[43] In many other medieval depictions of the Trinity, Jesus is offering his blood and his broken body next to Mary who is offering her breast milk.[44]

One thinker, an unnamed anchoress who had the chance to write her original and radical thoughts in the privacy of an enclosed space next to the Church of Saint Julian in Norwich, took the generosity of the maternal body to a whole new level. Rather than fretting about the sexual status or bodily state of Mary, this anchoress, now famously known as Julian of Norwich, turned to Jesus himself and the way he opened up his body for the sake of the world. Julian had vivid visions of Jesus bleeding the fresh, life-giving blood of a mother and of God reaching down to help vulnerable sinners like herself. No one knew about these radically maternal views of God by Julian at the time. Or, if those around her did read her writing, they certainly did not share it with the church authorities, for Julian presents a vision of a caring God who is infinitely patient with sinners, just as a mother is patient with a child.[45] Because Julian's theology is pervaded by such intimate knowledge of the mother-child bond and knowledge of how the female body works, scholars speculate that she herself likely had been a mother. Nothing is known of what happened to her child or her children; it is likely that they succumbed to the bubonic plague, which swept through Europe several times during Julian's lifetime.

During her own battle with an unknown acute illness, during which Julian was convinced that she was going to die, she saw a series of visions of Christ. The local priest and his acolyte had come to give her the last rites. As she was staring at the crucifix, she had the most amazing visions, which she wrote down once she miraculously recovered. In her visions, Julian saw the blood trickling down from Christ's head under the crown of thorns: "the

---

Middle Ages, Publications of the Center for Medieval and Renaissance Studies 16 (Berkeley: University of California Press, 1982), 113–15.

43 William of St. Thierry, "Sur le Cantique," ch. 38, 122–124, in *The Works of William of St. Thierry 2: Exposition on the Song of Songs*, trans. Mother Columba Hart, Cistercian Fathers Series 6 (Spencer, Mass.: Cistercian Publications, 1970), 30, quoted in Bynum, *Jesus as Mother*, 119.

44 See Barbara Newman, *God and the Goddesses: Vision, Poetry, and Belief in the Middle Ages* (Philadelphia: University of Pennsylvania Press, 2003), 261–66.

45 Julian of Norwich, "Long Text," ch. 61, in *Showings*, trans. Edmund Colledge, Classics of Western Spirituality (Mahwah, N.J.: Paulist Press, 1978), 300.

red blood flowing down from under his crown, hot and flowing freely and copiously, a living stream, just as it was at the time when the crown of thorns was pressed on his blessed head."[46] Julian made a point to describe Christ's blood as abundant and fresh. Her descriptions of its freshness suggest she saw it as a source of life and joy, similar to the way that the blood that accompanies birth and female fertility is fresh and part of the life-giving process. In Julian's visions, the blood she saw is often associated with life, and in particular, love.[47]

Julian connected Jesus' blood to our salvation. The imagery resembled more closely the fresh, generative blood of the female menstrual cycle or the uterus than it did the blood spilled in sacrifice or warfare. Her visions suggested that the blood coming from Jesus' head was actually the maternal, uterine blood that accompanies life rather than death. The fact that salvation came for Julian in Christ's blood suggests that she may have been alluding to how fetuses develop inside the generative blood of their mother's uteruses. Julian wrote, "we truly know our God, who has enclosed us all in himself."[48] God does not just tolerate the filth of the maternal body, God *is* the maternal body shedding life-giving uterine blood out of love and the promise of life.

Julian does not restrict the motherhood of Jesus to his human nature. Even as a divine being, as *God,* Jesus is like a mother to Christians. As God, Jesus Christ incarnate comes to us in our deepest physical needs. God "comes down to us to our humblest needs," Julian writes.[49] Whereas ancient thinkers such as Tertullian spoke about human neediness in terms of shame, Julian speaks of the neediness of humanity in terms of our vulnerabilities. We are creatures who need to be clothed, fed, and kept safe. God does not judge our human condition. Instead, God holds us close in it.

[46] Julian, "Long Text," ch. 4, in Colledge, *Showings,* 181. As Caroline Walker Bynum points out, when Julian speaks of blood in her visions, it is often bright red, flowing blood, the kind that is like uterine blood or birthing blood. Julian calls Christ's flowing blood here a "living stream."

[47] See Caroline Walker Bynum, *Wonderful Blood: Theology and Practice in Late Medieval Northern Germany and Beyond,* The Middle Ages (Philadelphia: University of Pennsylvania Press, 2007), 207; Julian of Norwich, "Long Text," ch. 86, in Colledge, *Showings,* 342.

[48] Julian of Norwich, "Long Text," ch. 6, in Colledge, *Showings,* 186.

[49] Julian of Norwich, "Long Text," ch. 6, in Colledge, *Showings,* 184.

God and the Egg

For almost its entire history, the Christian imagination believed that the single most important spiritual and enlivening element of human reproduction was the male sperm. The ancient world's preference for the male as the energy and spirit of all life, with the female as the bearer and giver of substance, dominated the Christian conception of the maternal body all the way until the nineteenth century. Aristotle believed that the *father* was the active, sensing, and rational parent for Greek children.[50] In his *De Formatione Corporis Humani in Utero* (1276), the scholastic theologian Giles of Rome (1247–1316) compared male spermatic energy to God's divine energy of creation, likening the sperm to an almost transcendent force that works upon the dead material of the mother. Because the sperm is so complex and "intelligent," it contains the capabilities to design the bones, organs, and other parts of the body *in utero*.[51] In other words, most medieval thinkers like Giles of Rome adhered to the ancient biology of Aristotle, in which the mother was only ever the laborer in the work of producing a child.[52] Her body would do its task, but the father would be the one to form the child, to give the energy and impetus to the child's movement through life, and to decide whether the child got to live or die.[53]

But the faint idea of a female egg had hovered at the margins of the scientific and Christian imagination for a very long time. It originated in second-century Greece with the famous and widely-read physician Galen of Pergamum (129–200). He theorized that there must be a "female seed." Galen believed that the female reproductive system was the inverse and mirror image of the male: the ovaries were inverted, internal testicles, and the uterus was an inverted,

50 Maryanne Cline Horowitz, "Aristotle and Women," *Journal of the History of Biology* 9, no. 2 (1976): 197.

51 Jacquart and Thomasset, *Sexuality and Medicine in the Middle Ages*, 59.

52 Even in his day, Aristotle's extreme view of the passivity of the maternal body was disputed. He could not explain how or why children looked like their mothers if the mother truly did not contribute anything to their production. The Hippocratic school, by contrast, also believed in the passivity of the maternal body, but it hypothesized that she contributed *something*, some kind of female "seed," to the embryo.

53 Turid Kralsen Seim, "Motherhood and the Making of Fathers in Antiquity," in *Women and Gender in Ancient Religions*, ed. Stephen P. Ahearne-Kroll, Paul A. Holloway, and James A. Kelhoffer (Tübingen: Mohr Siebeck, 2010), 121.

internal penis. Although he believed in the natural inferiority of the female body, he disagreed with Aristotle that the maternal body only contributed space and blood to the embryo. Galen's paradigm was called the two-seed hypothesis, meaning that the woman had *something* vivifying to offer the embryo, but what it was remained a mystery.[54] Indeed, the male seed was the performing agent in conception; if the female had a seed, it was the weaker of the two.[55]

The scholastic theologian Duns Scotus, a Scottish priest and Franciscan friar (1266–1308), believed the mother contributed an active seed. Thomas Aquinas adhered to Galen's idea that the mother contributed something to the embryo; some kind of semen or seed.[56] With the lack of ability to *see* precisely what the maternal body offered in conception, Galen's theories were only ever theories, and Christian thinkers preferred Aristotle's paradigm of the spongy, cold, passive female body.[57] Aristotle's paradigm for the passive female body reigned in the Christian imagination for well over *a thousand years* despite Christianity's familiarity with Galen's hypothesis of a female egg.

By the seventeenth century, things began to drastically change. It was an era of scientific discovery and advancement, much of which was done by scientists who were Christian and who were seeking to unlock the secrets of God and God's creation. Thinkers like Gabriele Falloppio, who discovered the workings of the fallopian tubes and wrote about them in his 1561 work *Observationes anatomicae*, changed the game for both the science of the female body and theology. Like many of his fellow scientists, he

54 Galen, *On the Usefulness of the Parts of the Body*, vol. 1, trans. and ed. Margaret Tallmadge May, Cornell Publications in the History of Science (Ithaca, N.Y.: Cornell University Press, 1968), 299–300.

55 Galen, *On the Usefulness of the Parts of the Body*, 1:299–300.

56 Eric Johnston goes so far as to argue that Aquinas believed that the mother contributed something like the DNA of the child, even though Aquinas clearly did not have any conception of DNA. But this is conjecture on Johnston's part. In the Thomistic scheme of causes, Aquinas saw the maternal body as the efficient cause. See Eric Johnston, "The Biology of Woman in Thomas Aquinas," *The Thomist: A Speculative Quarterly Review* 77, no. 4 (2013): 577–616, esp. 598, 602.

57 As Roberto Lo Presti notes, the dialectic between the hypothesis of Aristotle's passive female and Galen's female seed defined much of the ancient understanding of conception. See Roberto Lo Presti, "Informing Matter and Enmattered Formes: Aristotle and Galen on the 'Power' of the Seed," *British Journal for the History of Philosophy* 22, no. 5 (2014): 929–50, here 930.

was a Christian seeking to understand God's creation. His ideas and observations were able to be tested once the microscope was developed and scientists were able to see smaller and smaller particles of mammalian bodies. But what they thought they were seeing and what they were actually seeing were two different things. There was no scientific or philosophical paradigm for genes, proteins, or other building blocks of embryos in the way we understand them today. Leading scientists like Charles Bonnet and Albrecht von Haller argued that what scientists saw under microscopes were miniatures of fully formed creatures which have existed since the creation of the universe. These tiny but fully complete organisms were stored within the bodies of adults and passed down from one generation to the other.[58] This became known as the "preformationist" or "preexistence" theory.

The "preexistence" theory of tiny but complete organisms contained within the human body was a decisive turning point in understanding the maternal body. It confirmed the theories that claimed there truly *was* an active female component to reproduction. The mother's body was not simply a workshop or incubator for a fetus that was only enlivened by an intelligent male sperm. It became more widely accepted that embryos develop from some kind of female egg with contributions from the male sperm; the question was, "How?" Scientists were not sure whether the miniature creatures they thought they saw under the microscope developed in the male sperm or the female egg. Many scientists educated in the Aristotelian paradigm of the passive female body believed that what they saw under the microscope were miniature creatures folded up in the male sperm. Even Antonie von Leeuwenhoek, who was famous for developing the microscope and seeing tiny protozoa under it, believed he was seeing tiny creatures encapsulated within individual spermatozoa because of his anachronistic Aristotelian assumptions about the passivity of the female body.[59] Von Leeuwenhoek believed that male sperm were *animalcules* or protozoa that contained the entire fetus, about which he wrote in 1677. The famous image of the "homunculus" drawn by Nicolaas Hartsoeker

[58] Peter J. Bowler, "Preformation and Pre-Existence in the Seventeenth Century: A Brief Analysis," *Journal of the History of Biology* 4 (1971): 221–44.

[59] Sarah Blaffer Hrdy, *Mother Nature: Maternal Instincts and How They Shape the Human Species* (New York: Ballantine, 2000), 70–71.

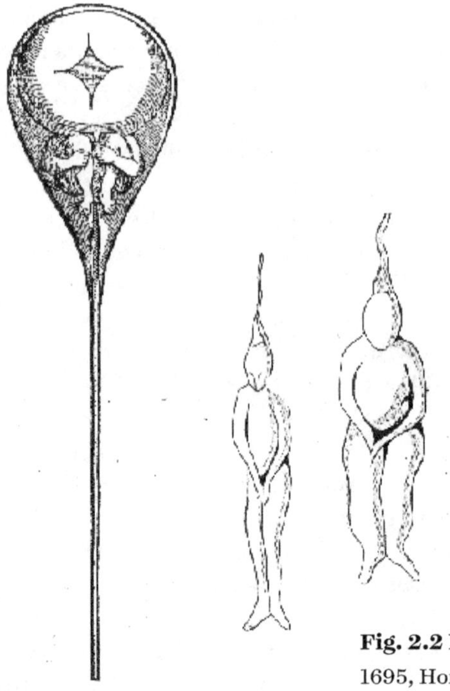

Fig. 2.2 Nicolaas Hartsoeker, 1695, Homounculi in sperm

in his *Essai de Dioptrique* from 1694 also popularized the belief that the male sperm contained tiny, complete fetuses.

On the other side of the debate were scientists who dared to think that maybe the female egg itself held the entire miniature life. But could a miniature fetus really be seen folded up inside a female egg? After thousands of years of believing in the passivity of the maternal body, this was a difficult one for scientists to reconcile. But many scientists were slowly coming around to the idea that maybe the female egg had the capacity to contain the entirety of embryonic life inside itself after all. They were becoming "ovists" of one kind or another. Scientists like the Dutch thinker Jan Swammerdam turned to the Bible to make their cases. Swammerdam argued in his 1672 pamphlet *Miraculum Naturae* that the ovist hypothesis was the biblically accurate, scientific viewpoint. He argued that all humans actually have their origins in the eggs which were enclosed in the first mother: Eve herself. These eggs have continued to be passed down through generations of women. Once the eggs are used up, he argued, the human race will go extinct.[60] Although Swammerdam's argument was pro-egg, it was, ironically, also anti-maternal. He still held on to the false theology of Eve's sin. His reasoning went thus: precisely because all humanity is enclosed in the eggs of the shameful and disobedient maternal body of Eve, humanity would consistently be born into sin.

Even the preeminent Puritan theologian Jonathan Edwards chimed in on the debates over egg and sperm.[61] He took the ovist side of the preformation debate, accepting the hypothesis that God formed all embryos at creation and encased them inside one another, starting with Eve.[62] Like any good Calvinist adhering to the doctrine of election, Edwards even mused that God *chose* the exact egg in Mary's ovaries from which the divine fetus of Jesus Christ would be formed.[63] Like so many other theologians and scientists of his day, Jonathan Edwards was not interested in maternal bodies for their own sake. He argued that Christ is truly from Mary's flesh, not because human generativity is a creative force but rather because God's election is truly arbitrary and not dependent upon anything in creation. Mary's lowly status and anonymity only proved Edwards' point about God's divine activity in election. The ovist view upheld the Calvinist theology of God's sovereignty: the smallness of Mary's egg showed the power and vastness of God. God elects those to be God's servants solely out of God's own mysterious will and not out of any bondedness to creation. Further, the ovist view upheld Edwards' theological commitments to human depravity. The fact that Mary was of shameful status like her foremothers in Christ's lineage, Tamar, Rahab, Ruth, and Bathsheba, highlighted God's goodness

60 Jan Swammerdam, *Miraculum Naturae*, 21–22, cited in Bowler, "Preformation and Pre-Existence in the Seventeenth Century," 238.

61 Edwards wrote about embryology in no. 769 of his "Miscellanies," which are still unpublished. See Ava Chamberlain, "The Immaculate Ovum: Jonathan Edwards and the Construction of the Female Body," *William and Mary Quarterly*, 3rd ser., 57, no. 2 (2000): 289–322, here 289, and n. 1.

62 Edwards clearly took his cues from John Calvin himself. John Calvin also accepted earlier ovist hypotheses that were circulating in the sixteenth century in order to maintain Christ's true flesh; if Mary was completely passive in the conception of Christ, how was his flesh real? Mary's flesh itself had to contribute something for Christ's humanity to be authentic. See John Calvin, *Institutes of the Christian Religion*, vol. 1, ed. John T. McNeill, trans. Ford Lewis Battles (Philadelphia: Westminster, 1960), bk. 2, ch. 13, pp. 474–81.

63 Chamberlain, "Immaculate Ovum," 289.

over human sinfulness. In a similar view that hearkens back to Tertullian's stance, Edwards argued that Mary's womb represented the lowest and most shameful places to which God could go.[64] In this way, Edwards brought two of Puritan America's core theological beliefs—the sovereignty of God and the sinfulness of humanity—to bear upon the scientific debates about the body of the mother.

But the debate would start to turn on how God brings forth creation in the first place. Eventually, more and more microscopic observations of human cells demonstrated that neither male nor female cells contain entire miniature creatures. They only contain particles or more cells; there were no fully created creatures placed into the male or female body waiting to spring to life in human reproduction. But many scientists living in Christian Europe were slow to move away from the preformationist paradigm of egg and sperm, in particular the idea that the sperm held fully formed tiny creatures.

One reason for this was that seventeenth-century scientific thinkers were deeply influenced by Descartes' view of the universe as mechanical and dead except when animated by God. They held that everything that ever existed was patterned after a specific, preset paradigm designed by God alone. As the Scottish minister and physician George Garden wrote, "it seems most probable that the stamina of all the plants and animals that have been, or ever shall be in the world, have been formed *ab origine mundi* by the Almighty Creator within the first of each respective kind."[65] In other words, God did not create in an evolutionary way. Rather, through the method of polygenesis, God directly molded each thing in its kind in a way that kept every creature static in its own set being. Every creature on earth was created exactly that way and was not the result of any natural or evolutionary process.

This theological view meant that scientists, despite the evidence before their eyes, did not believe that the created universe could bring forth any new living being *out of nothing*. Only God could create out of nothing. Hence, the maternal body could not be creative in its own right and bring into existence a new human being

[64] Chamberlain, "Immaculate Ovum," 303.

[65] George Garden, "A Discourse Concerning the Modern Theory of Generation," *Philosophical Transactions of the Royal Society of London* 16, no. 192 (1691): 474–83, here 476–77; see also Bowler, "Preformation and Pre-Existence in the Seventeenth Century," 242.

out of seemingly nothing. An embryo either had to be animated by a force like the sperm or it had to contain tiny but fully developed living creatures inside itself that traced their origin back to the first human beings. Every single living organism, past, present, and future, was believed by scientists to be here as a direct result of God's original creation of the universe.[66]

Maternal Generosity

And then it finally happened. The mammalian egg was actually seen. It was observed under a microscope in 1827 by the Prussian scientist Karl Ernst von Baer (1792–1876). Von Baer's discovery settled decades of scientific dispute over the actual existence of the female egg, but his observation also held profound philosophical import. It empirically demonstrated what both scientists and theologians had suspected for a long time: namely, that women were active contributors in the creation of new life. The maternal body was *generative*. This discovery would open up entirely new paradigms for both the fields of medicine and theology. Unfortunately, even after von Baer's accurate description of the maternal egg, it would take a long time for scientists to shake off the assumptions that maternal bodies are essentially passive in human reproduction. For about another one hundred years after von Baer described the mammalian egg—that is, even into the twentieth century—scientists believed the egg only contributed passive cells to the formation of an embryo. The egg continued to be seen as a passive vessel for the agency and life force of the sperm.[67]

While modern science has enjoyed profound and happy advancements regarding the female contribution to reproduction, it is more difficult to say how Christian theology has adjusted to the new base of knowledge about maternal agency and female generativity. Not one single twentieth-century theologian—from Karl Barth to Jürgen Moltmann, Hans Küng to Wolfhart Pannenberg, or Reinhold Niebuhr to James Cone—has thematized the maternal body in their theological work. Even white feminist theologians have hardly touched the subject. Instead (and not wrongly), they have

66 A renewed interest in the theology of Augustine, who argued this view, also influenced seventeenth- and eighteenth-century thought on embryology. See Bowler, "Preformation and Pre-Existence in the Seventeenth Century," 236–37.

67 Hrdy, *Mother Nature*, 70.

been occupied with advancing the political positions and authority of women in the church. Many other feminist and LGBTQ theologians have focused on female agency and sexuality.[68] But where has the theological meaning of the maternal body gone?

Modern science has given the Christian imagination a wealth of knowledge about the human body and the workings of the natural world. When it comes to the maternal body, science and the field of genetics have shown that it is a profoundly active organism within God's creative and generative activity. Science has shown that mothers invest in their children down to the molecular level. Today, we know that when a female child is just a tiny fetus in her own mother's uterus, she already has all the eggs she would need to bear her own children—and millions more.[69] A single cell in her body—actually, the largest cell in any human body—the egg, has the right amount of genetic and cellular materials to build another human being.[70] Even before the egg meets the sperm, it already starts dividing into sixteen cells. The outer layer of the egg, the "zona pellucida," wraps itself around the approaching sperm engulfing it. Then the female egg produces chemicals that allow the sperm's genetic material to merge with it and "fertilize" it. The female body, in other words, unbeknownst to the mother or anyone else, selects *both* the egg that is available to be fertilized *and* the sperm that does the fertilizing. Once one of those cells is fertilized, other cells in the egg "nurse" it, providing nutrients and other important chemicals to the embryo.

From the moment the embryo attaches to the uterine wall, a mother's body is no longer fully her own. The mother grows an entirely new organ, the placenta, which stands as a border zone between her own bodily needs and the hunger and "greed" of the growing embryo. The work the placenta does to regulate the competition between the fetus and the mother for nutrients

[68] See for instance Marcella Althaus-Reid and Lisa Isherwood, *Controversies in Feminist Theology*, Controversies in Contextual Theology (London: SCM Press, 2007).

[69] Hrdy, *Mother Nature*, 419–20. Scientists still do not understand why this abundance is present in the maternal body.

[70] For an account of the beauty and capacities of the human female egg, see Natalie Angier, *Woman: An Intimate Geography*, rev. ed. (Boston: Mariner Books/Houghton Mifflin Harcourt, 2014), 14f.

and other essential elements of life is evidence of just how *costly* the creation of a new human being really is. The maternal body is a resource for the hungry fetus, and she is invested in its survival—sometimes well beyond her own physical means.[71] For the first nine months of a person's life, they live off of the mother's "uterine generosity."[72] This maternal generosity protects the human fetus and allows it to develop a larger and more complex brain than other animals; it even dictates some of the structures and composition of the fetal brain.[73] Evolutionary science has shown that the female uterus in particular is partly responsible for humans becoming the unique species of *Homo sapiens* that we are.[74]

As the famous feminist philosopher Julia Kristeva has pointed out, so many Christian doctrines have historically depended upon a divine *Father* rather than a real human mother.[75] The reality of uterine generosity that has been observed by scientific exploration of the female body is a long way from the ancient Greek notions of a mysterious or wayward uterus and Christian ideas about it as a filthy and shameful place. The modern understanding of the maternal body as an active organism that contributes to the creation of human life is also a long way from ancient Christian and Greek ideas of the maternal body as a passive jar that merely receives and holds a place for the male-directed embryo to grow. It takes us far away from ancient but deeply entrenched notions that women are more deformed, unformed, or lesser beings than men.

The science of the female egg and the maternal body in all of its biological and evolutionary contexts suggests that women, as well as men and every gender in between, are deeply intertwined with the rest of the building blocks and processes of the

71 Hrdy, *Mother Nature*, 434–36. Large placentas might mean famine; gestational diabetes results in the placenta signaling for sugar-rich blood; poorly nourished fetuses may raise a mother's blood pressure, causing preeclampsia.

72 Angier, *Woman*, 84.

73 Gretchen Reynolds, "Mother's Exercise May Boost Baby's Brain," *New York Times*, "Well," November 20, 2013, https://well.blogs.nytimes.com/2013/11/20/mothers-exercise-may-boost-babys-brain.

74 Angier, *Woman*, 7.

75 Julia Kristeva, "Stabat Mater," in *The Kristeva Reader*, trans. León S. Roudiez, ed. Toril Moi (New York: Columbia University Press, 1986), 175.

natural world. This reality can ripple throughout and inform other aspects of the Christian imagination. Knowing what we know now about the generativity and hospitality of the maternal body, the Christian imagination can begin to stretch itself and bring the "bio-maternal" realities of actual human motherhood to bear upon teachings like salvation, creation, and even resurrection. Such an understanding of the mothering process pushes back against long-standing sentiments of disgust and confusion regarding the female body. It reaffirms the mother's central and esteemed role in the core tenet of Christian faith: the Incarnation. Far from being a site of disgrace and inferiority, the uterine generosity of the maternal body is a force that contributes to God's creative processes in the natural world in ways that no other organ, or organism, can.

3

The Vulnerable Sinner's Attachment to Mother Mary

The Rise of the Mother in the Christian Imagination

Although it took modern science's discovery of the female ovum to settle the question of maternal agency in human reproduction, medieval European Christians were already beginning to intuit and understand the importance of the maternal body for the survival of infants and children. So much so, in fact, that during the deep anxieties of the tenth and eleventh centuries, when Christians anticipated the Second Coming of Jesus Christ as an awe-inspiring Judge, they saw themselves as sinful children in the eyes of an angry God. So, they reached towards the one mother they knew might be able to help: Mary the Virgin Mother. As Roman Christianity moved north into modern-day European lands, Mary's significance for Christians morphed from being the ideal virgin to being the protective, loving mother.

Mary's role as mother was centuries in the making. By the fifth century, the wheels were coming off the cart of Roman Christianity as the Empire crumbled and was attacked by Gothic, Barbarian, and Visigoth invaders. The old, sprawling yet rigid *paterfamilias* system that reigned in the Mediterranean region of the Empire disintegrated as Romans migrated into the Germanic territories, Spanish lands, and Gaul. The Romans encountered in those places a wider variety of marital and family forms than what had been sanctioned in the old empire. They met clans and dynasties that were generally more flexible in terms of class and gender. Many cultures such as the Franks and the Merovingians gave women more legal rights and more freedom from male tutelage than they had experienced under Roman rule. Barbarian women were not expected to remain behind the walls of large villas or hidden from public view. They were out and about in public life and were even seen on the battlefield tending to their warrior husbands and sons.[1] Among the culturally and linguistically diverse barbarian kingdoms, the public, political, economic, and familial positions of mothers were more widely recognized. Childbearing and birth were highly valued.[2] Powerful women in dynastic lines were not always the legal wives of male heads of households, and it seems that many women and mothers were the sole managers of dynasties and family wealth since their men were often out to war for months or years on end.

Despite the cultural and societal variations of early medieval European kingdoms and dynasties, the fundamental tasks of mothering would have looked remarkably similar. Women faced danger in giving birth, breast milk was still the only way that babies could survive, and mothers would have invested what they could into making sure that their offspring reached the age of sexual maturity. Undoubtedly, mothering styles and rituals would have looked different depending upon the mother's tribe or kingdom, but the historical record has left no clear data about the variety of early European constructs of motherhood. We do not know how women felt about themselves under the cultural norms of early medieval Frankish, Merovingian, or barbarian kingdoms.

What historians do know is that the period between the eighth and tenth centuries was a violent period full of tribal wars. It was

1 See Tacitus, *The Germany and the Agricola of Tacitus: The Oxford Translation Revised, with Notes*, produced by Anne Soulard, Charles Aldarondo, Tiffany Vergon, Eric Casteleijn, and the Online Distributed Proofreading Team, Project Gutenberg, May 17, 2013, point 7. Tacitus describes the "Germans" as a people dominated by the natural world, uncivilized, simple, and pagan. On the one hand, he seems to admire them, and on the other, he was probably trying to show how uncultured the barbarian kingdoms were north of Rome; the women did not stay inside the households in the private, familial sphere as was "natural" for women but were out in public doing men's work. Their dress often revealed their arms and breasts, and they engaged in all kinds of activities inappropriate for true women.

2 See Valerie L. Garver, "Childbearing and Infancy in the Carolingian World," *Journal of the History of Sexuality* 21, no. 2 (2012): 208–44.

dominated by male politics and male concerns. Most of the information that historians have about the lives of women in these early European centuries comes from legal codes, penitential writings, instructions to clerics, and other administrative writings left behind by men in the ruling classes. Hence, only very general patterns can be sketched regarding mothering and the status of women in these early medieval European cultures. For instance, kingdoms such as the Burgundian and Visigoth had laws that allowed women to retain the rights over their property. It gave them wide economic freedoms over the household, which they were expected to manage. Barbarian legal codes also placed an *economic* value on mothers. Although violence would have been a quotidian part of life, if a mother or a woman of reproductive age got killed or injured, her family would be entitled to monetary recompense, or *wehrgeld*.[3] In fact, the monetary value of a woman's life was relatively high. This indicates that such societies valued the work of women bearing and raising children. Germanic law codes tried to deter violence upon mothers and their children, offering up valuable reparations for the killing or harm of mothers and children.

Another social development that was relatively protective of mothers and children was the growing religious and moral meaning of monogamous marriages that were not abusive to the woman. Husbands and wives were expected to honor the marital bond and monogamous sexuality. The moral and cultural value of monogamy was supported by Carolingian laws around the sanctity of the marriage bond. In one typical marriage of the ninth century, the bride and groom signed a contract stating that God did not intend marriage to be an agreement through which "men might licentiously abuse all the women they might desire, but rather that the fidelity of marriage be preserved between man and woman . . . not to several women, but only to one."[4] The official sanctioning of monogamy shed new light on women's worth in the Christian imagination as well. Carolingian theologians such as Haimo of Auxerre suggested that Paul never meant for women to become ascetics: abstinence

3 Jane Tibbetts Schulenburg, *Forgetful of Their Sex: Female Sanctity and Society, ca. 500–1100* (Chicago: University of Chicago Press, 1998), 218.

4 Ines Weber, "The Reception of Biblical Texts and Their Normative Effect Upon Marriage, Adultery, and Divorce from the Seventh to the Eleventh Century," in *The Early Middle Ages*, ed. Franca Ela Consolino and Judith Herrin, The Bible and Women (Atlanta: SBL Press, 2020), 321–22.

in marriage could be interpreted as rebellion against the husband's authority and honor.[5] The poet Notker wrote a poem about the ladder to heaven that had steps for every kind of women's work, including mothering.[6]

Wives of powerful men were recognized for their status as the *mothers* of future kings. Many Frankish and Germanic mothers also became queen regents until their sons were old enough to rule; in such relationships, there seems to have been deep loyalties to the "uterine line."[7] Such was the case with famous mothers in the Merovingian dynasty such as Brunhild (543–613) and Plectrude (650–717). The powerful king of the Carolingian dynasty Charles the Bald (823–877) was often known as the son of his mother Judith, who was a famous woman in her own right.[8] These mothers, like many other powerful mothers in the dynasties of the barbarian kingdoms, brought large dowries to their marriages and retained power and influence through their status as mothers to future kings.

These powerful women incorporated the new Christian faith into their own pagan spirituality. Some wealthy mothers began insisting that their warrior sons be educated in Christian theology. They wanted their warrior sons to model Christian values and worship

5 Suzanne Fonay Wemple, *Women in Frankish Society: Marriage and the Cloister, 500 to 900*, Middle Ages (Philadelphia: University of Pennsylvania Press, 1981), 103.

6 Notker, "In natale sanctarum feminarum" [The Festival of Holy Women], in *Poetry of the Carolingian Renaissance*, ed. Peter Godman (Norman: University of Oklahoma Press, 1985), 318–20.

7 Wemple, *Women in Frankish Society*, 60.

8 It is important to note here that indeed, matronymics, or the practice of naming children the son/daughter of a mother rather than a father (suggesting *matrilineages*) in ancient Europe, did occur and appeared in several early medieval European charters. But these charters are not evidence of any kind of true matriarchies or strong matrilineal dynasties in northern Europe or the British Isles. Several historians in the nineteenth and twentieth centuries were convinced that matriarchies could be found among the ancient Europeans, but there is little evidence to suggest genuinely established European matriarchal societies. Even though the Romans encountered barbarian women who were unusually liberated compared to Roman women, men still officially ruled over the laws, politics, and households. For studies in historical matriarchies, see Heide Göttner-Abendroth, *Die Göttin und ihr Heros: Die Matriarchalen Religionen in Mythos, Märchen und Dichtung* (Munich: Frauenoffensive, 1980) and Henrich Zimmer, "Das Mutterrecht der Pikten," *Zeitschrift der Savigny-Stiftung für Rechtsgeschichte, Romanische Abteilung* 15 (1894): 219–40.

the Christian God. One very unique piece of evidence of this trend among early European Christian mothers is the *Handbook*, written by the ninth-century Christian mother Dhuoda to her son William. The *Handbook* contains her instructions to him on how to be a successful man in the Merovingian kingdom so that he would rise in the ranks as a warrior and an aristocrat. To Dhuoda, that meant teaching her son the Christian virtues of patience, mercy, humility, and self-control—as well as the identity of God as Triune and as the one who would secure eternal life for him.[9] In another example, Armentaria, the mother of Gregory of Tours (who was bishop of Tours from 573–594), insisted that he get an education in Christian theology and values; this was at a time when paganism abounded and a quasi-secular education was popular in Gaul.[10]

Granted, the statuses of powerful mothers in Merovingian or Carolingian dynasties did not guarantee their voices being respected in the all-masculine politics and internecine skirmishes of the day. The statuses of early medieval mothers and the more flexible views of women did not approximate any kind of feminist movement in the modern definition of the word. Early European societies placed value on women for their childbearing capacities, not because women were seen as rational agents in the political sphere. Even though it is likely that such powerful mothers had a deep self-awareness of their agency in society and in the lives of their menfolk, the notion that women had interests or dignity as full human beings was a long way off, but such societal dynamics were the beginning of an understanding of the woman as a mother in a monogamous household. They indicate that the religious and spiritual understanding of women in early medieval Europe, and the importance of women's roles in dynastic politics, was fertile ground for the Christian ideology to develop its own appreciation of mothers and maternal work.

It was during this period of time that the church as a nascent governing institution with a long spiritual history became more involved in women's lives. As Christianity moved into European

[9] See Dhuoda, *Handbook for William: A Carolingian Woman's Counsel for Her Son*, ed. and trans. Carol Neel, Medieval Texts in Translation (Washington, D.C.: Catholic University of America Press, 1991). I will analyze Dhuoda's *Handbook* further in the following chapter.

[10] See Pauline Stafford and Anneke B. Mulder-Bakker, *Gendering the Middle Ages* (Oxford: Blackwell, 2001), 33.

territories, it brought with it both a Roman legacy of organized society with institutionalized public administration and a unified religious message of the Christian God. Thinkers like Boethius (480–525) spread a standard Catholic theology based on the Nicene Creed. It provided a blueprint for spirituality, theology, religiosity, and ethics for the early European peoples who were adopting Christianity into their own pagan values and ideas. He and other thinkers were committed to several key doctrines of the Christian faith. First, God was one divinity in three persons; second, God took on human flesh in Jesus Christ; third, Jesus was a God-man, and not just a man, as many barbarian Arians held; fourth, God was born of a human mother, the body of whom contributed to God's human flesh. Eternal life and rescue from the perils of hell were promised through this one supreme, triune God and God's Son, the God-man. This unified religious message and the Christian encouragement of sexual discipline offered new lifestyle options for men and women alike. Both socially and economically, the Roman Christian Church became a kind of centralized administrative power throughout Europe. This meant that across the diverse cultures and constructs of motherhood, the Christian imagination both transformed ideas of mothers and was itself transformed by the practices and cultural norms of barbarian mothers.

Mothers looked to Christianity to help them guard their daughters' virginity. Girls were trained to be obedient, disciplined, and totally in control of their feelings and passions. Mothers worried about the fates of their daughters if they were not married off to honorable men, and many mothers and daughters entered convents for safety and community.[11] Large numbers of women who were biological mothers became foundresses of monasteries or abbesses.[12] Monasteries, convents, and parishes were helpful to mothers trying to raise good daughters and sons. Friendships and alliances with influential churchmen were sought out by mothers both for their own sakes if their husbands died or divorced them as well as for the sake of their children. Friendships with monks and ecclesiastical leaders gave mothers a sense of "supernatural help" in their everyday lives.[13] Ecclesiastical connections gave

11 Wemple, *Women in Frankish Society*, 60–61.

12 Schulenburg, *Forgetful of Their Sex*, 218.

13 Wemple, *Women in Frankish Society*, 61.

mothers assurances that should their families meet demise, there would be support for them or their children. For these reasons, and perhaps many others, mothers forged relationships with the Christian church.

Alliances and friendships aside, the church also began to more heavily regulate the behaviors of mothers when it came to child endangerment, infant death, and self-induced abortions. Prominent churchmen such as Caesarius of Arles (470–542) preached against abortion and infanticide as early as the sixth century. Penitential writings such as the ninth-century *Canons of Theodore*[14] imposed penalties and punishments upon people who intentionally or accidently caused the death of their child, had an abortion, suffocated an infant during co-sleeping, or harmed their children in any way.[15] The *Canons* also contained penalties for those who sold their children into slavery.[16] They even had different penalties for different cases of maternal violence. For instance, impoverished mothers who killed their infants out of economic desperation were subject to lesser fines and punishments than wealthier mothers who committed the same act.[17] By the ninth century, the city of Trier (in modern day Germany) had a marble basin by the church where mothers could abandon their infants. If these infants did not die, they would be raised by monks and nuns.[18] This was the beginning of a long (and somewhat inglorious) history of the Christian Church taking in abandoned babies and children.[19] It also points to a widespread experience of mothering that has been completely lost to history: the experience of mothering as nuns. This is an entire field of study in how women

14 These *Canons* were most likely not written by Archbishop of Canterbury, Theodore of Tarsus, but rather after his death.

15 *The Canons of Theodore,* B78.01.02, accessed September 29, 2021, https://archive.org/details/EarlyPenitentialsTheCanonsOfTheodore.

16 *Canons of Theodore*, YY44.21.01.

17 *Canons of Theodore*, B77.04.12–B77.04.13. See also Garver, "Childbearing and Infancy in the Carolingian World," 238; and Ronald C. Finucane, *The Rescue of the Innocents: Endangered Children in Medieval Miracles* (New York: St. Martin's Press, 2000), 48–49.

18 Schulenburg, *Forgetful of Their Sex*, 247–48.

19 Most famous among Christian orphanages is the Hospital of the Innocents, built in fourteenth-century Florence, Italy, in response to a baby boom in the city. Sadly, the care there was not stellar. Up to 90 percent of the children and infants abandoned there died.

engaged the Christian faith as mothers that has yet to be investigated. What was it like to mother the children of others, often in all-female communities, without husbands, after taking vows of chastity? It is an experience of mothering that has left vanishingly thin evidence in the history of Christian thought.

Although the church tried to regulate mothers' behaviors towards pregnancies and births, self-induced abortions, infant abandonment, and infanticide were widespread in European societies—just as they were in the Roman Empire.[20] Church regulations for maternal violence and child abandonment in this time period, along with religiously sanctioned solutions for mothers who engaged such in acts, illustrate some beliefs about mothering that are widely held today by modern anthropologists and sociologists. Firstly, these sanctions illustrate that the human species is very successful at reproducing itself, but humans do not always have compassionate ways of taking care of the youngest of their species, especially if children are abandoned by their biological mothers. The cities of Florence and Paris in the thirteenth century put a fine point on this human reality. Descriptions of the foundling hospitals that arose in these cities describe how babies were being abandoned just about "everywhere:"[21] in public places and "along the streets of the city."[22] These church regulations also illustrate how *women* were targeted as perpetrators of inhumane or dispassionate treatment of infants. It has been women who have consistently faced the agonizing decision about whether to allow a pregnancy to move forward and to raise a child (or yet another child). Poignant historical records of child abandonment show that babies were left with jewelry, coins, or written prayers expressing hopes

[20] See John Boswell, *The Kindness of Strangers: The Abandonment of Children in Western Europe from Late Antiquity to the Renaissance* (New York: Vintage Books, 1990).

[21] See an *Atlas Obscura* article about the building of the Hospital of Innocents in Florence, Italy in response to its population boom in the fourteenth century: https://www.atlasobscura.com/places/ospedale-degli-innocenti-hospice-innocent.

[22] On the extent of child abandonment and the establishment of French Christian orphanages, see Anne E. Lester, "Lost but Not Yet Found: Medieval Foundlings and Their Care in Northern France, 1200–1500," *Journal of the Western Society for French History* 35 (2007), https://quod.lib.umich.edu/w/wsfh/0642292.0035.001/-lost-but-not-yet-found-medieval-foundlings-and-their-care?rgn=main;view=fulltext.

that the mother would find them again and that God would protect them and save them from death.[23]

In the church's attempt to curb infant abandonment, neglect, and infanticide, it labeled all types of maternal violence as sin. Although children were also seen as natural-born sinners, it was always the *mother's* fault—and no one else's—when things went wrong with infants and toddlers. The focus of the church was always on the guilt of the woman. Such views lasted well into the nineteenth century. It was the mother's fault if she gave birth to a child she could not afford or handle.[24] For such sins, the church imposed acts of penance on mothers. On one level, this fact points to the church's attempt to enact grace and mercy upon women who found themselves in difficult situations; mothers could find absolution for maternal crimes. Yet, the church has never officially recognized the widespread reality of maternal struggle in strategizing around the life and death of infants. The church has not shown a curiosity about how such agonizing decisions around infant survival and care have shaped women's imaginations about God or their uses of ecclesiastical support structures. This kind of religious and social disinterest about the internal lives and thought processes of mothers informs modern debates in the United States about access to reproductive services and legal abortions.[25]

Surely there were many other factors in the historical churn of Christianity's move into Europe that contributed to evolving ideas about mothers and mothering. Along with the laws, powerful mothers, and women's use of the institutional church as well

[23] Maria Zytaruk, "Artifacts of Elegy: The Foundling Hospital Tokens," *Journal of British Studies* 54, no. 2 (2015): 320–48.

[24] See Rachel G. Fuchs, *Poor and Pregnant in Paris: Strategies for Survival in the Nineteenth Century* (New Brunswick, N.J.: Rutgers University Press, 1992), 77–98.

[25] For just two examples out of a sea of writings on the decision-making processes of women and their offspring, see, in popular culture, the film "I Had an Abortion," dir. Gillian Aldrich and Jennifer Baumgardner, 2005, https://www.wmm.com/catalog/film/i-had-an-abortion/; and the story about the Eipo mother in Papua New Guinea who decided that she would abandon her child if it was another daughter. Once the baby daughter was born, the mother left the newborn in the forest, as was custom, but she returned to retrieve and raise her because she saw that the child was too strong to abandon. Sarah Blaffer Hrdy, *Mother Nature: Maternal Instincts and How They Shape the Human Species* (New York: Ballantine, 1999), 455–56.

Fig. 3.1 Ambrosius Benson, Madonna and Child, 16th century

as the church's willingness to address issues of mothering, early European art began reflecting a new consciousness of mothers and mothering. Rising to the top of Christianity's understanding of mothers was none other than Mary, the mother of Christ. In Carolingian art, Mary was adored as a queen, just as mothers were often queen regents.[26] She was a seen as a strong, impassible mother who could shield sinners from the male violence of God's fatherly wrath. Depictions of her in early medieval art reflect views of the strong mother in charge of dynasty and wealth.

The adoration of Mary's queenliness eventually softened into a deep intimacy with and attachment to her. Christians' deepening attachment to Mary as a mother is reflected through prayers and liturgies that appeal to Mary as a loving, comforting mother who is emotionally available to needy Christians. Thinkers like Hrabanus Maurus (d. 856) started praying to Mary as a suffering mother who witnessed the death of her son. In another prayer from around

[26] See, for example, *Plaque with the Virgin Mary as a Personification of the Church*, ca. 800–825, Aachen, Germany, Metropolitan Museum of Art, Gallery 304, Item 17.190.49, accessed October 7, 2021, https://www.metmuseum.org/art/collection/search/464454.

the same time (author unknown), the sinner tells Mary that she is the only one who can help him because she is the "mother of our Savior."[27] And a certain Maurilius of Rouen (d. 1067) begged Mary to take him back after he strayed from the pious life, asking her: "To whom should I go, in whose presence should I lament my grief?" He returns to her "breasts" of "consolation" as a prodigal son.[28] Just as Mary suffered with her own Son, sinners believed she would understand and empathize with their suffering too.

Medieval Christian art also overflows with the theme of Mary as loving mother in the countless artistic renditions of the Madonna and Child. Mary and her baby Jesus were adored for their intimate and loving connection. In depiction after depiction, Mary offers Jesus upon her lap for the world to see. She bares her breast from which the infant Jesus suckles.[29] She holds her child close to her.[30] She stands upon the moon;[31] she comes to the world with her infant in her hands.[32] She sits in lovely European landscapes playing with her sweet child.[33] She looks out to the viewer with kindness, affection, power, and love. Italian Christian art in particular focused on the theme of mother-child love, especially in the thirteenth and fourteenth centuries. In such depictions, Jesus is often seen as a baby gently touching Mary's veil or her face as only a baby can do.[34]

[27] See this unknown author's prayer in Rachel Fulton, *From Judgment to Passion: Devotion to Christ and the Virgin Mary, 800–1200* (New York: Columbia University Press, 2002), 223.

[28] Fulton, *From Judgment to Passion*, 223.

[29] See Van Eyck, *Lucca Madonna*, 1436, Städelsches Kunstinstitut, Frankfurt, Germany, accessed February 22, 2022, https://www.jan-van-eyck.com/lucca-madonna/.

[30] See Sandro Botticelli, *Madonna della loggia*, ca. 1466/67, Florence, Uffizi Gallery, accessed October 7, 2021, https://www.uffizi.it/en/artworks/madonna-loggia-en.

[31] See Niklaus Weckmann, *Madonna Enthroned with Her Child on a Crescent Moon*, ca. 1510–1520, Kunsthistorisches Museum, Vienna, accessed October 6, 2021, https://www.khm.at/objektdb/detail/86229/.

[32] See Raphael, *Sistine Madonna*, ca. 1513/14, Gemäldegalerie Alte Meister, Dresden, accessed October 7, 2021, https://en.wikipedia.org/wiki/Sistine_Madonna.

[33] See Lucas Cranach the Elder, *Madonna under the Fir Tree*, 1510, Archdiocese of Wrocław, accessed October 7, 2021, https://commons.wikimedia.org/wiki/File:Cranach_Madonna_under_the_fir_tree.jpg.

[34] See *Madonna and Child* by Ambrosius Benson, ca. 1495/1500–1550, Milan, Flanders. See also Dorothy C. Shorr, *The Christ Child in Devotional Images in Italy during the XIV Century* (New York: G. Wittenborn, 1954).

Turning to Mother Mary for Protection

The Christian's attachment to Mary as a mother blossomed throughout medieval Western Christianity, especially because many thought that the end of the world was near. Right around the turn of the millennium, Christians were getting restless because the year 1000—or maybe the year 1033, they could not be certain—would be the year that Jesus Christ would come back to judge the world and begin a new thousand-year reign.[35] A series of frightening weather events and natural occurrences around that time solidified in people's minds that the end of the world was coming. There were local droughts and floods, which then led to famines. There were plagues and celestial occurrences such as solar and lunar eclipses. Rivers dried out. Leading thinkers of the day enacted church and liturgical reforms as ways to get the Christian house in order, so to speak, for the Second Coming of Christ. They persecuted Jews and executed bishops accused of heresy. Many people believed that they saw Jesus Christ weeping in the sky. It was a terrifying time.

In this age of unpredictable weather and apocalyptic anxiety, Christians hesitated to turn directly to Jesus Christ. They were wary of him. In the imagination of the Franks and Carolingians, Jesus Christ was the suffering warrior, the solider who laid down his body and spilled his blood for the fight. Seen as the Final Judge in his Second Coming, Christ was not expected to *protect* sinners from the wrath of God. Rather, he was going to *execute* the wrath of God upon them. This apocalyptic expectation instilled fear into the hearts of European Christians and drove them into the protective, maternal arms of Mother Mary. She became the holy mother who protected believers from God's paternal wrath. Sinners could hide in her oversized and flowing maternal cloak. This depiction of Mary shielding sinners under her cloak became known in German piety as the *Schutzmantelmadonna*. Her maternal power stood between an angry God and fearful sinners.

The Christian imagination during this era seems to have intuited what modern psychology has called attachment. Leading twentieth-century researchers such as John Bowlby and Mary Ainsworth have shown that attachment to a caregiver, usually the mother, is vital for

[35] See for instance Rev 20:1–3; 4:1.

Fig. 3.2 Ravensburger *Schutzmantelmadonna* ca. 1480 Bode-Museum Berlin

the survival and growth of children.[36] In modern theories of attachment, mothers are intercessors and mediators between the world and their vulnerable children, but both mother and child are active agents in the relationship of attachment.[37] Children seek out every opportunity to be close to their mothers and are exquisitely attuned to their mother's voice, behaviors, and emotional states. They look to the mother or caregiver when stressed or afraid, and they work to remain in close proximity to their mothers. Mothers, in turn, become attached to their children as well and behave in ways to provide comfort, protection, and nourishment. This intimate relationship

[36] See John Bowlby, *Attachment*, vol. 1, 2nd ed. (New York: Basic Books, 1982) and Mary D. Salter Ainsworth, Mary C. Blehar, Everett Waters, and Sally N. Wall, *Patterns of Attachment: A Psychological Study of the Strange Situation* (New York: Routledge, 2015).

[37] Susan Hart, *The Impact of Attachment: Developmental Neuroaffective Psychology* (New York: W. W. Norton, 2011), Kindle edition, locations 1474 and 1502.

of comfort between mother and child functions to give children the building blocks they need to grow into fully functioning and empathic adults. The mother becomes a buffer and a guide for the child against an often confusing, harsh, and overwhelming world. The principles of attachment still influence how we study young children today.

Christians seem to have imagined that Mary would act like other human mothers who could provide food, comfort, compassion, protection, and other kinds of aid that children might need. The general criteria that define modern understandings of attachment are easily applied to the medieval Christian's attitude towards Mother Mary. She is the caregiver to whom a child looks, especially when fearful or stressed. She protects her children, the fearful sinners. She provides them security with her clothes, her love, and her body. Finally, medieval Christian prayers show that vulnerable Christians were distressed at the thought of Mary not responding to their prayers, reflecting modern understandings of attachment that show that the loss of the caregiver causes grief and sorrow.[38]

A theology of attachment to Mary was not just popular among the laity in medieval Europe: it rose up to the top of scholastic thinking. Powerful theologians such as Anselm Bishop of Canterbury turned to Mary and utilized a rhetoric of attachment in his prayers to her. He called upon Mary to protect him, not with her spiritual authority, her virginity, or her status as Queen of heaven, but as a *mother*. Only in the maternal role could Mary offer the comfort, physical protection, and intercession that a sinner like Anselm craved. She is the "Mother dear to the human race."[39] His "Prayer to St. Mary (2)" showcases the Christian imagination of Mary as a mother and her protection in a powerful way. Anselm prays,

> Blessed assurance, safe refuge,
> the mother of God is our mother.
> The mother of him in whom alone we have hope,
> is our mother.
> The mother of him who alone saves and condemns
> is our mother.[40]

[38] Lee A. Kirkpatrick, *Attachment, Evolution, and the Psychology of Religion* (New York: Guilford, 2005), 61–85.

[39] Anselm, *The Prayers and Meditations of Saint Anselm with the Proslogion*, trans. and ed. Sister Benedicta Ward (New York: Penguin, 1973), 110.

[40] Anselm, *Prayers and Meditations*, 122.

Anselm cries out to Mary in prayer the way a child might cry out to his mother in the face of a wrathful father:

> Lady [Mary], it seems to me as if I were already
> before the all-powerful justice of the stern judge
> facing the intolerable vehemence of His wrath,
> while hanging over me is the enormity of my sins,
> and the huge torments they deserve.
> Most gentle Lady,
> whose intercession should I implore
> when I am troubled with horror, and shake with fear,
> but hers, whose womb embraced
> the reconciliation of the world?[41]

He continues his supplication of Mary as mother in his third prayer, "Prayer to St. Mary (3)," throwing himself at her, saying,

> I desire to venerate you in my understanding,
> I love to pray to you from my deepest being,
> I commit myself wholly to your protection.[42]

He figures himself the child, loving his mother, and needing her protection. His prayers illustrate that a sense of vulnerable, child-like attachment to Mary had taken hold in the Christian imagination.

What makes Anselm's prayers even more significant is the fact that he himself was saved as a child from an abusive and terrifying male teacher. As the story goes, Anselm's own mother Ermenberga committed him to an educator who locked little Anselm in a house for years. When Ermenberga found out what was happening, she went to retrieve him and took him back. All this happened when Anselm was yet a very young boy. When Anselm was finally returned to his mother, probably sometime in his elementary school years, she very intentionally set out to rehabilitate him from his trauma and from his profoundly low self-esteem. For this, Anselm was forever grateful to his mother and admired her greatly. She also protected him from an abusive and unpredictable father and taught him about God as a supreme being who knows and understands all things. After all of this, Anselm's teaching and

41 Anselm, *Prayers and Meditations*, 110.
42 Anselm, *Prayers and Meditations*, 115.

mentoring of his subordinates was self-consciously modeled after the way his mother brought him up and facilitated healing from his traumatic childhood experiences.[43]

Anselm was not the only one who adored Mary as a mother. Throughout the twelfth through the fifteenth centuries, Mary's maternal presence was ubiquitous. Christians everywhere turned to her in times of need and in times of joy. Women carried around with them tiny books of prayers to her, as seen by examples in *The Hours of the Virgin Mary* and *The Mirror of Our Lady*.[44] Illiterate women carried rosaries so that they could pray to her. All kinds of miracles were attributed to her on behalf of mothers and their family members. The Benedictine monk William of Malmesbury (ca. 1090–1143) collected as many of the stories that circulated during his life about the miracles of Mary as he could. He compiled them in a book entitled *Miracles of the Blessed Virgin Mary*. Among these miracles are healing stories, stories of her visiting people in prison, and stories of her bringing estranged family members back together, among many others. In one poignant miracle story, Mary saved a pregnant woman who was caught by an incoming tide at the famous cloister of Mont Saint Michel. Others caught with her by the tide were able to escape, but because the woman was pregnant and could not run fast, she was trapped by the waves. The crowd feared her dead, but when the water receded, there she was with a newborn baby who had been born in the waves, protected by the holy sleeve of Mary.[45] Mothers across European Christendom nurtured their devotion to Mary in the hopes that when their time came to face pregnancy and birth, she would be there to protect them and empathize with them.

Mary's Eucharistic Body

Mary's maternity did not stop at her emotional closeness with sinners and her protection of them. Aligned with modern attachment

[43] Sally N. Vaughn, *St. Anselm and the Handmaidens of God: A Study of Anselm's Correspondence with Women* (Turnhout, Belgium: Brepols, 2002), 78–81.

[44] Rachel Fulton Brown, *Mary and the Art of Prayer: The Hours of the Virgin in Medieval Christian Life and Thought* (New York: Columbia University Press, 2018).

[45] William of Malmesbury, *Miracles of the Blessed Virgin Mary*, ed. and trans. R. M. Thomson and M. Winterbottom (Rochester, N.Y.: Boydell Press, 2015), 119–20.

theory, the presence of her *body* also became a significant source of comfort and grace for sinners. This aspect of attachment to Mary played out especially in medieval theologies of the Eucharist. In Carolingian Christianity, the Christian sacrament of the Eucharist was evolving as a church ritual. It was used in significant ways as Charlemagne forced the Saxons to convert, and it subsequently only grew in importance as the central Christian ritual. But, in fact, the notion that Christ's body and blood were "substantially" present in the eucharistic elements was a fairly new development in the Christian imagination. Earlier thinkers such as Augustine and Ambrose believed in the power of the Eucharist as a ritual, but they did not see it necessary to ponder the nuances of *how* Christ's body and blood were present. As the Eucharist grew in importance, so did the questions about Christ's substantial and physical presence in it.[46]

The famous dispute that has come to be called the Carolingian Eucharistic Controversy began between two ninth-century theologians, Paschasius Radbertus and Ratramnus, at the famous monastery at Corbie in Amiens, France.[47] Although the men debated how Christ's flesh was present in the Eucharist, one thing united them: both men agreed that Jesus' human body and nature came from the flesh of his mother. With Mary's body being shared with Christ, she was connected to every divine action from salvation, to supplication, to the Eucharist.[48] Mary's maternal flesh was the "original source of sacramental grace."[49] No other kind of human could have played the role that Mary plays in attaching humans to God.

[46] Fulton, *From Judgment to Passion*, 53–60.

[47] Celia Chazelle, "Figure, Character, and the Glorified Body in the Carolingian Eucharistic Controversy," *Traditio* 47 (1992): 1–36. Their debate over *how* Christ's body and blood are present in the Eucharist was a precursor to the Roman Catholic Church's adoption of the doctrine of transubstantiation. By the eleventh century, the idea of "transubstantiation" was widespread. It was officially named as a doctrine in the Fourth Lateran Council in 1215. It specified that the bread and the wine of the Eucharist turn into the body and blood of Christ in their substance but retain their "accidental" outward optics of bread and wine.

[48] See Hilda Graef, *Mary: A History of Doctrine and Devotion*, 2 vols. (New York: Sheed and Ward, 1964), 1:62, 313. See also Donna Spivey Ellington, *From Sacred Body to Angelic Soul: Understanding Mary in Late Medieval and Early Modern Europe* (Washington, D.C.: Catholic University of America Press, 2001), 102–41.

[49] Sarah Jane Boss, *Mary*, New Century Theology (London: Continuum, 2004), 48.

No other human except a mother could give them access to God's grace. Only with the historicity and physicality of Mary's humanity could Christ's own humanity be guaranteed.

The theological affirmation that Christ himself received his body from his mother opened up a new vista of imagination for Christian women in particular. Mary's pure, life-giving blood, her flesh, her actions of giving birth, and her suffering the trials of parenting gave women a feeling of intimacy with her. Since they were shut out of the male world of systematic theology, Mary became the key for many women to feel a new sense of intimacy with God.[50] These developments around Mary as a mother and protector took the Christian imagination far away from the theologies of her maternal filth and shame. She was seen as a powerful mother who had access to God. Her body, which brought forth the Incarnation, was a *hospitable* place in which God formed an intimate connection to humanity. God became incarnate not despite the maternal body or because God merely *tolerated* the maternal body. Rather, God became incarnate out of the hospitality and capacity of the maternal body.

The Milk of Salvation and Wisdom

Along with her protective nature, the shield of her cloak, and the tender relationship that she had with sinners, one other aspect of Mary's maternal body also became central in the Christian imagination: namely, her nursing breasts. In medieval European Christianity, Mary's nursing breasts and the milk which her maternal body produced became a central part of various Marian cults and Christian piety. Her breasts were seen as giving life to the world; they even secured forgiveness and resurrection for humanity. Numerous statuettes and a multitude of Christian artistic pieces emphasized her nursing breasts. Saint Bernard of Clairvaux's biographer, Arnold of Bonneval (d. 1156), gave one of the first explicit depictions of Mary's breast milk as an element in the salvation of humanity. He stated that in her suffering for the death of her son, she turned her bared, milking breast towards God, just as Christ turned and held his wounded side towards God:

[50] See Caroline Walker Bynum, *Holy Feast and Holy Fast: The Religious Significance of Food to Medieval Women* (Berkeley: University of California Press, 1987), 260–69. See also Ellington, *From Sacred Body to Angelic Soul*, 50.

Fig. 3.3 The Intercession of Christ and the Virgin attributed to Lorenzo Monaco, 14th century

> [Jesus'] flank exposed, shows the Father His side and wounds; Mary shows Christ her heart and breasts; and nor is it possible in any way, when [Christ and Mary] come together and plead very eloquently in every tongue, for these monuments of mercy and signs of charity to be repulsed.[51]

In other words, *both* Mary in her maternal sorrow and Jesus in his crucified suffering secured salvation for all of humanity. While Jesus was crucified in the flesh, Mary was crucified in her spirit. Arnold claimed that in the bond of Jesus and Mary, there could be seen "two altars, the one in the breast of Mary, the other in the body of Christ."[52] By the mid-fifteenth century, artistic pieces were making visual analogies between her breast milk and the blood from Christ's wound. This has been called the "double intercession" of Christ and Mary for the salvation of the world. In a work from the fourteenth

[51] Arnold of Bonneval, aka Ernaldus of Chartres, *Libellus de Laudibus B. Mariae Virgini*, quoted in Beth Williamson, "The *Virgin Lactans* as Second Eve: Image of the Salvatrix," *Studies in Iconography* 19 (1998): 105–38, here 111–12.

[52] Arnold of Bonneval, *Libellus de Laudibus B. Mariae Virgini*, quoted in Fulton, *From Judgment to Passion*, 425.

century attributed to Lorenzo Monaco, Christ holds up his wound to the Father while Mary holds out her breast to Christ. Mary's blood, turned to milk in her pregnancy with Christ, and Christ's own suffering blood are given as the gifts of salvation. Both Mother and Son show compassion for humanity in its suffering and need.[53]

When it came to a theology of Mary's salvific breast milk, the Christian imagination relied upon ancient Greek thought. Physiological theories from the Greek physician Soranus of Ephesus (96–138) about the blood and milk of the maternal body supported the theology of Mary's breast milk as salvific. He taught that the menstrual blood of the mother helped form the fetus in the uterus. This uterine blood went through a special vein into the mother's breast and formed into milk that could feed the newborn. Mary's maternal blood then turned into the breast milk that Jesus drank: milk and blood were two different forms of the same substance.[54] Soranus' ancient physiological paradigm was widely accepted among medieval centers of learning. Hence, it was easy for Christians to tie Mary's milk to Jesus' own blood. Her body never stopped being physically connected to his in the Christian imagination. This physiological theory supported the theology that Mary intercedes for sinners through offering her breast to the world. Her milk was as effective as his blood.

Another way that Mary's nursing body filled the Christian imagination was through the remarkable rhetoric of abbots and monastic leaders. Monastic leaders of all-male Christian communities were particularly fond of using maternal imagery to refer to themselves and their positions. Historical studies suggest that male abbots utilized maternal imagery to cement themselves not just in their positions of leadership but also to communicate that their style of leadership would not be masculinized—i.e., they would not be combative or violent, which were traits typical of male leadership at the time. Bernard of Clairvaux's older contemporary, Rupert of Deutz (near Cologne, b. 1075), used the imagery of Mary conceiving and birthing the Living Word to describe his spiritual experiences.[55] He noted the deep attachment that Mary had with her Son because of the ways she carried him in her body and nursed him at her breasts. This kind of physical intimacy gave her the foresight and foreknowledge to see that he would die on

53 Bynum, *Holy Feast and Holy Fast*, 272.
54 Williamson, "*Virgin Lactans* as Second Eve."
55 Fulton, *From Judgment to Passion*, 326.

a cross. He noted that her bodily, maternal experiences with her Son Jesus—her shared flesh with God—put her in a position to inherit the kingdom of heaven on behalf of all humanity.[56] Adam, Abbot of Perseigne (d. 1221), wrote that Christians nurse at Mary's breast next to their brother, Jesus Christ. Thus, he noted that God had chosen Mary precisely "for his mother so that she may be the nurse of the humble."[57]

Bernard of Clairvaux (1090–1153) is perhaps the most famous example of male monastic leaders utilizing maternal imagery to define themselves as holy men.[58] He especially focused on Mary's breast milk. Bernard identified himself as the blessed receiver of drops of Mary's very own breast milk, an image that was rare in his day. As the legend goes, Saint Bernard was praying the prayer "Ave Maria Stella" in front of a statue of the Virgin Mary. When he came to the phrase "show yourself to be a mother" (*monstra te esse matrem*), the statue came to life and let her breast drop three drops of milk into Bernard's mouth.[59] After Bernard shared his experience of this miracle, depictions of Mary breastfeeding proliferated throughout European Christian art.[60]

For Bernard, this intimacy with Mary was meant to communicate to the male charges in his care that he was a wise and empathetic leader.[61] Mary's milk was the source of his spiritual wisdom to lead his charges. Bernard also preached about how Mary's breasts are a symbol of her maternal capacity to feel with and for

56 Fulton, *From Judgment to Passion*, 329–30.

57 Caroline Walker Bynum, *Jesus as Mother: Studies in the Spirituality of the High Middle Ages*, Publications of the Center for Medieval and Renaissance Studies 16 (Berkeley: University of California Press, 1982), 125.

58 In Bernard's sermon on the festival of Mary's Nativity from September 8, he calls her an "aqueduct." Cited in Ellington, *From Sacred Body to Angelic Soul*, 128.

59 Jutta Sperling, "Squeezing, Squirting, Spilling Milk: The Lactation of Saint Bernard and the Flemish *Madonna Lactans* (ca. 1430–1530)," *Renaissance Quarterly* 71, no. 3 (2018): 868–918, here 894. See also James France, *Medieval Images of Saint Bernard of Clairvaux* (Kalamazoo, Mich.: Cistercian Publications, 2007).

60 For how artistic depictions of Mary proliferated, see Sperling, "Squeezing, Squirting, Spilling Milk," 895–900. Bernard was not the only one who believed that he had had a true physical intimacy with Mary. Many other medieval theologians also tried to establish physical intimacy with her by doing things like licking artwork of Mary or licking a crucifix in order to taste the divine milk of Mary or the blood of Christ.

61 See Bynum, *Jesus as Mother*, 119–20.

Fig. 3.4 Alonso Cano, St. Bernard and the Virgin, ca. 1650

others. He stated, "There is no pretense about a true mother, the breasts that she displays are full for the taking. She knows how to rejoice with those who rejoice, and to be sad with those who sorrow [Romans 12:15], pressing the milk of encouragement without intermission from the breast of joyful sympathy, the milk of consolation from the breast of compassion."[62] In one depiction of the lactation, Bernard is seen ignoring Jesus Christ's offer of his own blood out of the wound in his side, and instead praying to Mary who bares her breast for him.[63]

62 Bernard of Clairvaux, Sermon 10, quoted in Bynum, *Jesus as Mother*, 118.

63 See *The Lactation of Saint Bernard with Man of Sorrows*, found in *Book of Hours of the Virgin* (French), folio 62v, Beinecke Rare Book and Manuscript Library, New Haven, MS 411, cited in Jutta Sperling, "Squeezing, Squirting, Spilling Milk," 874–75. Whereas the Italian images distort and disfigure Mary's breast in order to avoid any connection between her feeding the world and female sexuality, the Flemish and French depictions of Mary breastfeeding have an erotic dimension. The eroticism of Mary's bare breast in Flemish art was meant to pull the viewer into a spiritual and perhaps physical experience of the image. In contemporary motherhood studies, women have written about

Domesticating the Mother

Depictions of Mary breastfeeding Jesus became more domesticated by the fifteenth century, but they also became more eroticized, entangling her purely salvific maternal body in precisely the sexuality that seemed to start the whole cycle of sin in the first place.[64] Reformers like Erasmus of Rotterdam and Saint Bernardino of Siena criticized the "milk cult" that had developed around Mary's breasts. It seems that the Christian imagination did not yet have a nuanced understanding of the distinction between the sexualized female body as a product of the male gaze and the maternal body given for anxious sinners. Reformers did not tolerate the sexualized mother figure of Mary that began appearing in Christian art. In fact, Reformers like Martin Luther wanted to direct Christians away from Mary entirely. They wanted to direct Christians directly to Christ. He was the adult man who would save them; they did not need the milk of his mother.[65]

Following Martin Luther's lead, more and more Protestant Reformers started taking wives and getting married. Although these Protestant marriages were complicated affairs involving kinship ties, economics, and private and public interests, they in many ways symbolized and solidified the trends that accompanied the rise of the mother in the Christian imagination. Reformation wives were seen as tied to the household: they were the ones to keep the family together. They were expected to be the loving maternal presence in the household, just as Mary was the loving and comforting presence in a Christian's life. Gender roles were strictly defined in Reformation Germany, and women were seen as having been created by God to be empathetic, good with children, obedient to their husbands, and skilled at housekeeping.[66] While they had power, it was limited to the domestic sphere. Protestant pastors' wives additionally had strong ties to the institutional church. They

---

the erotic, sexual side of breastfeeding, but modern perspectives are less about an external gaze on the mother's breast and more of a profound experience of mothering and sexuality by the mother herself.

64 Such as those produced by the workshop of Rogier van der Weyden in the 1460s. See Sperling, "Squeezing, Squirting, Spilling Milk," 883.

65 Sperling, "Squeezing, Squirting, Spilling Milk," 892.

66 See Lyndal Roper, *The Holy Household: Women and Morals in Reformation Augsburg*, Oxford Studies in Social History (Oxford: Clarendon, 1989), 133–37.

were given the role of passing down the faith to children, and they were expected to maintain family wealth and protect the interests of the household. In other words, many of the trends that made the lives of women and mothers more visible to the church and in the Christian imagination converged on the Protestant wife in a monogamous Christian household.

As the Reformation solidified the roles of mothers as partners in monogamous marriages and the hearts of their households, Christian ideas about Mary's maternal body and its saving power began to wane. Protestant Reformers insisted on centering Jesus as a male who was accessible to the prayers of sinners, and so the need of sinners to feel attached to a powerful protective figure was transferred from Mary to Jesus Christ himself. Perhaps the attachment to Mary had become too strong, too earthly, and too physically intimate for the Christian imagination, which still harbored a deep discomfort with the female body.

4

Maternal Piety, Magic, and Sisterhood

Strategies for Survival

Even though Christianity promised eternal life, it did not guarantee the material improvement of life here on earth. Babies continued to be born and to die or never make it out of the womb alive. Children needed the protection and nurturing of their mothers, and the maternal body itself needed protection as it went through the rigors of pregnancy and the dangers of childbirth. Even women in the modern era have spoken of the profound sense of mother-thinking present among pregnant and birthing women that leaves them feeling that they are solely responsible for their survival and for the survival of their children. In her 1979 memoir *With Child*, mother-author Phyllis Chesler called these kinds of thoughts "delusions of omnipotence" when reflecting on her pregnancy and the birth of her son. She remarked, "Even the Virgin Mary couldn't do it."[1] Short on promises of survival by Christianity, mothers throughout the ages have turned to any kind of power or promise available to them in order to ensure their own survival and the survival of their children.

In the absence of robust medical systems in the eras before modern medical treatments, women utilized any and every tool in their toolboxes to help them through the perils of motherhood.

1 Phyllis Chesler, *With Child: A Diary of Motherhood* (New York: Penguin, 1981), 216.

Alongside herbs, concoctions, and foods that were thought to help women get through the physical ailments of pregnancy, they also utilized spells, charms, and magic—as well as religion and support from the church. Women gathered in large groups made up of midwives, servants, mothers, sisters, aunts, grandmothers, and friends to survive birth and the postpartum period. It was the role of daughters, sisters, midwives, and other mothers to the care for and protect the maternal body. These groups of women offered support, education, and solace. They traveled to shrines and prayed to female saints, especially the highly revered Saint Anne, mother of Mary and grandmother of Jesus. They prayed to Mary herself, and they prayed to the virginal dragon-slayer Saint Margaret. They turned rituals such as churching from a rite of purification to a celebration of maternal survival.

Protecting the Porous Maternal Body

Throughout history, the pregnant body has occupied a liminal space. People believed that the pregnant body had no fixed boundaries and was a fairly amorphous form compared to other forms of the natural world. It was open to the whims and dangers of nature and was thus prone to being corrupted or cursed. Mother and fetus were considered one single unit, united by the mother's blood.[2] With the average women bearing a child almost every year or every other year, mothers faced almost constant danger to their bodies and their offspring.

Yet, while women were surely not passive, they primarily understood what was happening in their bodies through the spiritual and metaphysical paradigms of ancient Greek biology. They believed that the maternal body was spongy and porous. It was associated not just with earth and water but with air and wind as well. This made it particularly vulnerable to the malevolent spirits that lurked among the earthly elements.[3] There was constant concern about how the porous maternal body could accidentally release good humors—the

[2] Sarah Jane Boss, *Mary*, New Century Theology (London: Continuum, 2004), 46.

[3] Avicenna's works, translated from the Arabic into Western European languages, brought with them the connection of the maternal body to wind and air. Danielle Jacquart and Claude Thomasset, *Sexuality and Medicine in the Middle Ages* (Princeton: Princeton University Press, 1988), 47.

energies and spirits that promoted health—and let in bad humors. At issue was the belief that any kind of harmful spirit or humor that entered the mother's porous body would damage or injure the baby and affect its growth. Envy, malice, greed, and any other kind of negative moral impulse could damage the baby or cause illness or deformity.[4] Hildegard of Bingen wrote that the "evil spirits of the air" were always ready to attack the fetus. She insisted that pregnant women continually hold the mineral jasper in their hands throughout pregnancy to protect them from evil spirits.[5]

The maternal body was also everybody's business. In a time when infant and maternal mortality were high, with little possibility for medical intervention, threats to a pregnant woman's body and to her uterus were a threat to the community. Widespread belief in the evil eye meant that the gaze of others—especially strangers in the community, elderly people, and anyone out of the ordinary—was particularly dangerous to pregnant women. The evil eye could cause nausea and morning sickness, for which a black hen consequently needed to be sacrificed.[6] It could even cause a miscarriage or a stillbirth.[7] Witches were also a standing threat to pregnant mothers[8] and to babies in particular.[9] Unfortunately, many midwives were suspected of being witches.[10] Newly postpartum mothers were always wary of a witch stealing their child to devour it or offer it to the devil.[11]

[4] Stephen Wilson, *The Magical Universe: Everyday Ritual and Magic in Pre-Modern Europe* (London: Hambledon and London, 2000), 151.

[5] Beryl Rowland, trans., *Medieval Woman's Guide to Health: The First English Gynecological Handbook* (Kent, Ohio: Kent State University Press, 1981), 34; Hildegard of Bingen, *De operatione Dei*, Patrologia Latina 197, col. 1257.

[6] Wilson, *Magical Universe*, 157.

[7] Wilson, *Magical Universe*, 151.

[8] One of the most popular manuals against witchcraft in the Middle Ages was Heinrich Kramer's and Jacob Sprenger's 1487 *Malleus Maleficarum* [Hammer of Witches]. See Alan Charles Kors and Edward Peters, eds., *Witchcraft in Europe, 400–1700: A Documentary History* (Philadelphia: University of Pennsylvania Press, 2001), 181.

[9] Lyndal Roper, *The Witch in the Western Imagination*, Richard Lectures 1998 (Charlottesville: University of Virginia Press, 1998), 134ff.

[10] See Gerhild Scholz Williams, ed. and trans., *Mothering Baby: On Being a Woman in Early Modern Germany. Johannes Praetorius' Apocalypsis Mysterorum Cybeles. Das ist Eine Schnakische Wochen-Comedie (1662)* (Tempe: Arizona Center for Medieval and Renaissance Studies, 2010), 20–21.

[11] Kors and Peters, *Witchcraft in Europe, 400–1700*, 188, 193.

Pregnant women were scrutinized for what they ate, where they went, and what they witnessed. Because their bodies were so porous, anything they saw or ate could affect the baby inside them. The baby would take on the qualities or traits of whatever the mother consumed, both as food and by way of her vision. For instance, if a pregnant woman ate octopus or lamprey, her child might be born with no bones. If a pregnant woman accidentally tripped over a drunken person on the street, her child might become an alcoholic. If she got spooked by a mouse, her child might be born with tufts of mouse hair; if she became involved in a quarrel, the child might be born rebellious and mean-spirited.[12] Joyful intercourse and sexual exploits during festivals were encouraged so that a couple would have a happy, joyful, and healthy baby. Men were encouraged to not get distracted by ordinary things or disturbing thoughts while ejaculating so as to not introduce any psychic dangers to the conception of his child.[13]

The medieval church condemned many forms of magic and paganism for women who were pregnant, in labor, or postpartum (also known as the "lying-in" period). Yet the church did not shy away from participating in many of these practices either. It simply combined pagan rituals with Scripture, Christian liturgy, or church teaching—off the official record, of course. Magic incantations, spells, charms, and beliefs were as prolific and kooky as the human imagination would let itself be. Sachets containing relics from saints, the True Cross, or even the rope of the parish's bell were often placed over the birthing mother's belly.[14] Little cloth bags were worn around a pregnant woman's neck, often with words of a charm or the Bible contained in them.[15] The famous manual on women's medicine, the *Trotula*, combined scientific knowledge of female physiology and remedies for pain with magical charms. Frequently, women were told to eat the paper that holy words were written on. Words such as the magical palindrome *sator arepo tenant opera rotas* (The sower with his plough holds the wheels with care) were carved into cheese or butter and then fed to the

12 Wilson, *Magical Universe*, 156.

13 Wilson, *Magical Universe*, 149ff.

14 Wilson, *Magical Universe*, 174–75.

15 Nadia Maria Filippini, *Pregnancy, Delivery, Childbirth: A Gender and Cultural History from Antiquity to the Test Tube in Europe* (New York: Routledge, 2021), 61.

laboring woman. Ritual words were often based on ones that Jesus Christ was thought to have spoken in the Gospels. Other guttural sounds would be combined with words from biblical stories, in particular the story of Lazarus coming out from the tomb. These words were often connected to wax or a strip or cloth that was tied to the laboring woman's foot.[16]

Most of these rituals were performed by women for women. Pregnancy, childbirth, and the early postpartum days were mostly a women's affair, often to the total exclusion of men. The church tolerated a wide variety of practices used to soothe, comfort, and encourage women in labor. Without full knowledge of how the female reproductive system worked, society at large both respected the maternal body and saw it as a mysterious way of being in the world. It needed protection but was also seen as being more intimately in touch with the invisible forces of the spiritual world. Ultimately, however, male church leaders were suspicious of mothers and the maternal body. They were always on the lookout for how mothers would trick their husbands or deceive those around them for evil reasons. They associated the maternal body in its unpredictability with Eve and her disobedience towards God. If Eve could pull down the whole human race with her strong will and agency, what could a mother do?

The Companionship of Saints Margaret, Anne, and Mary

The myriad of religious rites and magical accessories that were utilized by women to keep themselves safe through pregnancy, birth, and the postpartum period was accompanied by the communion of female saints. Women called upon these saints as part of their strategy to get through pregnancy and birth alive. Saint Anne, the grandmother of Jesus, and Saint Margaret, the virgin dragon-slayer, were central figures in these maternal survival strategies, as was the Virgin Mother herself.

The Christian saints made up a particularly powerful spiritual community upon whom mothers called for all kinds of help. As Peter Brown shows in his work on the rise of the Christian saints, the saints were a group of ancestors who gave a vision of hope

16 See Peter Murray Jones and Lea T. Olsan, "Performative Rituals for Conception and Childbirth in England, 900–1500," *Bulletin of the History of Medicine* 89, no. 3 (2015): 406–33.

for resurrection and heaven for ordinary people who were suffering the pain and tedium of life on earth.[17] Unlike the political and social systems of late antiquity, which cared little for the struggles of the poor or everyday people, the saints offered solace and hope to those who were forgotten or who were oppressed by Roman imperial society. Attention from the saints bestowed importance and meaning onto the ordinary lives of people and onto women's lives in particular. Christians built elaborate shrines to saints, and they went on pilgrimages to them. These pilgrimages were seen as special, beautiful, and meaningful trips. The saints were mediators between earthly mothers and the powerful, caring God. The gaze of a saint represented the gaze of the divine onto women's maternal struggles. While the popularity of many male saints gave rise to the notion of the "holy man," who became a prominent figure in the Christian imagination, mothers turned most often to female saints for support and divine connection.

Numerous women undertook the arduous task of going on a pilgrimage to a saint's shrine because of pregnancies or the fear of difficult births, as well as out of hope for a cure for sick or disabled children. Mothers in the Carolingian era frequented the grave of Waldburga in Eichstätt.[18] Her reliquary at the Monheim convent became a popular pilgrimage site for pregnant women due to the legend that two women who were at risk of death in childbirth were brought to Waldburga's grave. Although they both endured difficult births, they did not die.[19] Saint Vulfram was another popular Carolingian saint. As the story goes, Saint Vulfram, an eighth-century missionary to the Frisians, caused the abdomen of a mother carrying a dead fetus to swell and split open, ejecting it. After praying, the woman's body healed. The scar that was left was a reminder of

17 Peter Brown, *The Cult of the Saints: Its Rise and Function in Latin Christianity* (Chicago: University of Chicago Press, 2009), 86ff.

18 Also known as Walburga or Walpurga, she was an Anglo-Saxon missionary to the Frankish kingdom. Her body was originally buried in Heidenheim, then moved to Eichstätt, where it remains today, in the Benedictine Abbey of St. Waldburga. Soon after her death, her relics were moved to the Monheim convent, which became an important pilgrimage site, especially for women. Today, the parish of St. Waldburga sits on that site, See Katrien Heene, *The Legacy of Paradise: Marriage, Motherhood, and Woman in Carolingian Edifying Literature* (New York: Peter Lang, 1997), 146.

19 Heene, *Legacy of Paradise*, 146.

Vulfram's virtues and godliness.[20] Another miracle story involved Saint Ludger, who was bishop of Münster in the ninth century. A woman who was disabled after a difficult birth visited his grave and was healed.[21] These stories show that mothers felt a visceral, bodily connection to the saints they prayed to. They would hug, touch, and kiss statues or relics of the saints. The bodily connection between mother and saint gave women a sense of belonging and solidarity with the saint's own suffering—and hopefully, the saint's favor.

One of the most famous saints of the maternal experience, despite clerical disapproval of her, was Saint Margaret. Margaret of Antioch supposedly lived in the third century and died in 304, but her story did not really emerge and take hold of the Christian imagination until the ninth century in Carolingian Christianity. Margaret of Antioch's legend follows similar storylines of other early church virgins who resisted arranged marriages. As the story goes, Margaret's mother died in childbirth. Margaret was raised by her wet nurse who converted her to Christianity. When the Roman administrator Olibrius insisted on marrying Margaret, she denied him because she was a virginal girl and planned on dedicating herself as a bride of Christ. This is not the answer Olibrius wanted to hear, so Margaret was thrown into prison. There, she was eaten by a dragon. But while she was in the belly of the dragon, she gave the sign of the cross, and its body split open to eject her, fully alive and fully intact. Unfortunately, she was then beheaded after she forced yet another dragon-demon to confess his sins to Christ. At her execution, she asked God to protect women and children.[22]

It seems that Margaret's triumph over the dragon, which might symbolize sexual temptation or violence, gave women hope that they, too, would survive the consequences of their sexuality.[23]

20 Valerie L. Garver, "Childbearing and Infancy in the Carolingian World," *Journal of the History of Sexuality* 21, no. 2 (2012): 234.

21 Garver, "Childbearing and Infancy in the Carolingian World," 234.

22 Wendy Larson, "Who Is the Master of This Narrative? Maternal Patronage of the Cult of St. Margaret," in *Gendering the Master Narrative*, ed. Mary C. Erler and Maryanne Kowaleski (Ithaca, N.Y.: Cornell University Press, 1990), 94–95. The cult of Saint Margaret was in full force by the twelfth century. See also Jane Tibbetts Schulenburg, *Forgetful of Their Sex: Female Sanctity and Society, ca. 500–1100* (Chicago: University of Chicago Press, 1998), 230. Images of Saint Margaret always have a piece of her dress hanging from the dragon's mouth.

23 Michael E. Heyes, *Margaret's Monsters: Women, Identity, and the Life of St. Margaret in Medieval England* (New York: Routledge, 2020), 33.

Virginity and chastity were always the priorities for young women, and throughout Christendom, women struggled to balance the sexual desires that came naturally to them with threats of male sexual violence and compulsion to engage in sexual intercourse. Perhaps women held on so fervently to Margaret because of their own moral ambivalence about sexual intercourse and its consequences of pregnancy.[24] Margaret's fight against the dragon and her triumph over her executioner, Olibrius, gave women hope that they too would triumph in a world of profound sexual politics and sexual violence. Other interpreters suggest that the dragon was seen by medieval women to be the serpent upon which Eve stomped in Genesis: Margaret's triumph over the dragon was the virtuous Christian woman triumphing over the weakness of Eve.[25] Women wore Saint Margaret belts to promote safe deliveries and prayed to Saint Margaret both for forgiveness from falling into sexual temptation and to protect them from its consequences. Margaret became the patron saint of laboring mothers out of her own tormented "labor" to survive. Her struggles were productive, just as pregnancy and birth could bring forth something triumphant.

Another important protector saint for mothers was Saint Anne or Anna, the mother of Mary. Anne is not actually a biblical figure. It seems that stories and legends of her arose from readings of the popular second-century apocryphal works the *Pseudo-Gospel of Matthew* and the *Protoevangelium of James*.[26] The *Protoevangelium of James* connected Anne to the Old Testament mother Hannah, who experienced infertility and then gave birth to Samuel in her old age. Like Hannah, Anne conceived miraculously. Like

[24] Heyes argues that, in fact, there is nothing inherent in the stories of the life of Saint Margaret to suggest that she was particularly concerned with laboring women, except for her last words. Rather, it was women throughout the Middle Ages who pressed her into being the patron saint of both women who were sexually active and laboring women in childbirth. They offered votives to her, erected shrines and chapels to her, carried amulets of her, prayed to her, and called upon her in their need. They saw her as their advocate and retold her story over and over. Their imaginations about Margaret as protector of women in childbirth and their infants influenced the written tradition of her life as it was handed down through the centuries. See Heyes, *Margaret's Monsters*, 108–31.

[25] Heyes, *Margaret's Monsters*, 126.

[26] Virginia Nixon, *Mary's Mother: Saint Anne in Late Medieval Europe* (University Park: Pennsylvania State University Press, 2004), 12, and nn. 4 and 5.

Hannah, who dedicated Samuel to the Temple, Anne dedicated her daughter Mary to spend her childhood in the Temple. In her connection to Hannah's fertility miracle and her devotion to God, Anne became the patron saint of pregnant women, laboring women, and women who wanted to become pregnant.[27]

The legend of Saint Anne has some eyebrow-raising twists though. Much to the chagrin of the church Fathers, legend has it that Anne was married three times. With her first husband, Joachim, she bore Mary, the mother of Jesus. With her second husband, Clopas, she bore Mary of Clopas, and with her third husband, she bore Mary Salome.[28] Because of her questionable marital status and therefore questionable morals, Saint Anne was always held both in adoration and somewhat dismay by church Fathers. Perhaps this is why women loved her so much; the twists and turns of her life reflected the ups and downs of their own.

By the sixth century, Anne already had a cult of her own. Emperor Justinian even had a chapel built around 550 in Constantinople in her honor. Her cult reached a zenith in Europe between the twelfth and fourteenth centuries. It was most likely transmitted into the European Christian imagination by Hroswitha of Gandersheim from her use of a Latin version of the *Protoevangelium*.[29] Once introduced into Latin Christianity, depictions of Anne, Mary, and the baby Jesus proliferated throughout European Christendom, with the most depictions of her in Germany, France, and Flanders. This intimate threesome of grandmother, mother, and baby became known as the *Anna Selbdritt*.[30] The infant Jesus is often held in between the two women. Being held in such an intimate space illustrated Jesus Christ's deep attachment to both of them. Sometimes he would be depicted as being held in Mary's arms but gazing and reaching towards his grandmother.[31] He might

27 Anne served as the patron saint for numerous other classes of people, such as sailors, miners, educators, cabinet-makers, grandmothers, and horseback riders. See https://en.wikipedia.org/wiki/Saint_Anne.

28 This legend has been disputed for centuries upon centuries.

29 See *The Nondramatic Works of Hrosvitha*, trans. Sister M. Gonsalva Wiegand (Saint Meinrad, Ind.: Abbey Press, 1936), xviii.

30 *Selbdritt* is an old German word for "one of three"; alternatively, *zu dritt*, "the three of them," or "in a group of three."

31 See the image *Anna Selbdritt*, stained glass, 1510–1530, Workshop of Cologne, Wilhelm-Hack-Museum, Ludwigshafen, accessed October 7,

Fig. 4.1 Veit Stoss, *Anna Selbdritt*, St. Jakob, Nürnberg, 1505

be reaching for a lamb, symbolizing his own sacrifice, or grapes, to signify the Eucharist. The image or figure of Anne is usually bigger than Mary; Mary is often seen sitting in her mother's lap or next to her mother in similar size to the infant Jesus. The *Anna Selbdritt* images and figures often form a triangle shape, with Anne's figure over and above the figures of Mary and the infant Christ, making a kind of trinity of figures. It was a Trinity of mother, daughter, and son: a matrilineal Trinity of the Incarnation.[32]

2021, https://commons.wikimedia.org/wiki/File:Anna_selbdritt_Koelner_Werkstatt_WHML.jpg.

[32] Pamela Sheingorn, "'The Wise Mother': The Image of St. Anne Teaching the Virgin Mary," in *Gendering the Master Narrative*, ed. Erler and Kowaleski, 105–34, here 113.

There is one other very important image of Anne and Mary, which depicts Anne teaching her daughter to read. Many images of the Annunciation show Mary reading. Others show Anne teaching Mary how to read or Mary, Anne, and Jesus with a book. These images became very important to mothers in medieval Christianity. They affirmed what medieval European cultural constructs said about motherhood: namely, that mothers were the truest and best teachers of all kinds of knowledge to their young children—if they were lucky enough to have that knowledge themselves. As historians point out, earlier images of Mary have her spinning or weaving, but by the eleventh century, she was reading.[33] Mary being depicted as literate in an age when illiteracy was the norm showed that not only was she spiritually gifted and chosen by God but also intellectually gifted. This was truly a radical notion about a woman in the Middle Ages, when only the few very privileged and wealthy daughters were taught to read and write. Such depictions of Mary's own mother teaching her daughter to read gives a nod to the subterranean belief that women—specifically *mothers*—could be as intellectually strong as men. Such unspoken ideas were true subversions of the prevailing neo-Aristotelian and Scriptural constructs of the Middle Ages that made women physically softer, morally weaker, and intellectually duller than men.

The images of *Anna Selbdritt* often had Mary as a smaller figure than her mother or in a lower position than her.[34] These images suggest the respect that medieval Christians had for the grandmother of Jesus and the depth of their veneration of her. The popular imagination about *Anna Selbdritt* or about Anne teaching Mary how to read suggests that Christians believed Anne to be the strong female protector of women, children, mothers, and many others. Although leading theologians debated about her sinlessness (or sinfulness: three husbands!), she was heroic among lay people.[35] Innumerable

33 Sheingorn, "'The Wise Mother,'" 113.

34 See, for example, the image by Lucas Cranach the Elder, *Anna Selbdritt*, ca. 1515, Gemäldegallerie, Berlin, accessed October 7, 2021, https://commons.wikimedia.org/wiki/File:Die_Heilige_Anna_Selbdritt.jpg.

35 See Anselm of Canterbury, *The Virgin Conception and Original Sin*, chapter 18 in *Anselm of Canterbury: Complete Philosophical and Theological Treatises*, trans. Jasper Hopkins and Herbert Richardson (Jackson, Mich.: Ex Fontibus Company, 2016), 450. See also Kati Ihnat, *Mother of Mercy, Bane of the Jews: Devotion to the Virgin Mary in Anglo-Norman England* (Princeton: Princeton University Press, 2016), 62–64; and Nixon, *Mary's Mother*, 14–15.

prayers were made to her. Women from Flanders to Jerusalem went on pilgrimages to pray at shrines to Saint Anne.[36] There are paintings, altars, church furniture, and a myriad of statues dedicated to Saint Anne and *Anna Selbdritt*. She was the grandmother of humanity. The cult of Saint Anne allowed both women and men to call upon her as protector. Martin Luther famously cried out to Saint Anne in a severe lightning storm to spare his life.[37]

In many ways, the stories of Saint Anne, the Christian trust in her protection, and the depictions of her with her daughter and her grandson are all non-textual reflections of the lived lives of mothers. Like Anne, many women endured more than one marriage. Most women bore children with all its danger and joy. Most birthing and nursing mothers need *othermothers*, like their own mother or sisters, to help them raise their children. In fact, the banding together of women in the life events of birthing and raising children is a trait unique to human mothers.[38] With *Anna Selbdritt*, the Christian imagination seems to have tacitly acknowledged the way mothers, grandmothers, and othermothers all are necessary for the well-being and survival of the human race. Saint Anne can be considered Christianity's answer to popular (albeit controversial) interest in the "grandmother hypothesis" of evolutionary anthropology.[39] She bore and raised her own her child, Mary, successfully and thus had the knowledge and resources to help the young Mary raise Jesus Christ. Christians clearly believed that Anne's grandmotherly presence in the lives of her daughter and grandson contributed to their survival and well-being.

[36] A simple Google search reveals that the industry of pilgrimages to Saint Anne shrines still flourishes today.

[37] Martin Luther, *D. Martin Luthers Werke: Weimarer Ausgabe. Abteilung 1. Tischreden. Sonderedition Der Kritischen Gesamtausgabe, Gesamtwerk in 4 Abteilungen*, ed. Ulrich Köpf (Weimar: Böhlaus Nachfolger, 2000), 4:440, no. 4707.

[38] See Sarah Blaffer Hrdy, *Mothers and Others: The Evolutionary Origins of Mutual Understanding* (Cambridge, Mass.: Belknap Press, 2009), 33–109.

[39] Hrdy, *Mothers and Others*, 272. The grandmother hypothesis is currently in the spotlight of mainstream media. See for instance Joseph Stromberg, "New Evidence That Grandmothers Were Crucial for Human Evolution," *Smithsonian Magazine*, October 23, 2012, https://www.smithsonianmag.com/science-nature/new-evidence-that-grandmothers-were-crucial-for-human-evolution-88972191/; and Elizabeth Landau, "How Much Did Grandmothers Influence Human Evolution?" *Smithsonian Magazine*, January 4, 2021, https://www.smithsonianmag.com/science-nature/how-much-did-grandmothers-influence-human-evolution-180976665/.

The only female who loomed larger than the popular and beloved Saint Anne was the Virgin Mother herself. The cult of Mary that flowered between the twelfth and fifteenth centuries in Europe has its own rich and complex history that cannot be fully analyzed here. In many ways, as we have seen in the previous chapter, Mary the mother of Jesus Christ became the mother of all people: she loved them, protected them, and fed them with her body—the body of her son—and with her breast milk.[40] Women throughout Christendom thought of Mary as their own divine mother. Out of all the figures, saints, and even Christ himself, it was she who connected most intimately and knowingly with the perils of motherhood.

Scholars have argued for decades about whether Mary has been a helpful figure for average women or not.[41] After all, according to many ideas in Christian piety, Mary did not have to face the biological necessities of the human female body. She avoided the sexual politics of marriage in her perpetual virginity; she avoided the blood, fear, and pain of birth; and despite all that happened in her life, she was forever under the favor of God and the guardian of God's own Son. Although she endured earthly trials, she had access to divine power and perfections that regular women never have during their own trials of motherhood.

One aspect of Mary's life that was particularly connected to the lives of average mothers was her sorrow and pain over the death of her Son Jesus.[42] By the fourteenth and fifteenth centuries, Mary's maternal suffering and sorrow dominated Christian devotion to her. She was the mother who had witnessed the worst nightmare

[40] See Rachel Fulton, *From Judgment to Passion: Devotion to Christ and the Virgin Mary, 800–1200* (New York: Columbia University Press, 2002), 204–44 for an extended tracing and analysis of theme. See the previous chapter in this book for more detailed exposition of Mary's maternal body and protection of sinners.

[41] As examples of this debate, see the criticisms of Elizabeth Johnson, "The Marian Tradition and the Reality of Women," *Horizons* 12, no. 1 (1985):116–35. Joelle Mellon discusses the modern, second-wave feminist critiques of Mary in *The Virgin Mary in the Perceptions of Women* (Jefferson, N.C.: McFarland & Company, 2008), 6–8. The debate has raged in Germany too. See Elisabeth Gössmann and Dieter R. Bauer, eds., *Maria, für alle Frauen oder über allen Frauen?* Reihe Frauenforum (Freiburg im Breisgau: Herder, 1989); Hedwig Röckelein, Claudia Opitz, and Dieter R. Bauer, eds., *Maria, Abbild Oder Vorbild? Zur Sozialgeschichte Mittelalterlicher Marienverehrung* (Tübingen: Edition Diskord, 1990).

[42] Margaret Miles, *Image as Insight: Visual Understanding in Western Christianity and Secular Culture* (Boston: Beacon, 1985), 83.

Fig. 4.2 Michelangelo, *Pietà*, St. Peter's Basilica, 1497

of motherhood: the death of her child. She was a mother who had lost her beloved son. She was the universal and eternally suffering mother. She was the *mater dolorosa*. As many historians have argued, a robust Christian imagination about Mary's maternal suffering coincided with the onset of the plague in the terrible fourteenth century. The plague cycled throughout Europe for almost one hundred years. During this century, images and statues of Mary holding her dying Son began populating churches and other spaces. Prayers and devotionals that focused on Mary's sorrow and suffering at Christ's death circulated widely.

Deeply emotional hymns of grief and loss proliferated at this time. One instance of this is the well-known "Donna del Paradiso" by the Franciscan monk Jacopone da Todi (ca. 1230–1306) that has Jesus' mother witnessing his journey of suffering on the Cross. Mystery plays that took place throughout Europe depicted the major biblical stories tinged with loss and grief.[43] It was the era

[43] Vittoria Colonna, Chiara Matraini, and Lucrezia Marinella, *Who Is Mary? Three Early Modern Women on the Idea of the Virgin Mary*, ed. and trans. Susan Haskins (Chicago: University of Chicago Press, 2008), 29.

Fig. 4.3 Käthe Kollwitz, *Mother with Her Dead Son*, Neue Wache, Berlin, 1938, enlarged by Harald Haacke

of the Pietà: the suffering mother, the *mater dolorosa*. During the Black Death in Germany (1347–1350), miniatures of Mary were particularly morbid and gruesome.[44] Perhaps these disturbing images were an attempt to depict the distortion of maternal love by grief and the damage mothers endured by the destruction of the plague. While depictions of the Pietà can be found all over Europe, the theme of the suffering mother holding her son became especially poignant among parents of fallen young men in World War I. The sculpture of a "Mother with her Dead Son" by German artist Käthe Kollwitz shows how Mary, as the mother of Christ, and suffering mothers everywhere had one terrible and intimate connection: they witnessed the deaths of their children. Recently, photographer Jon Henry has depicted Black mothers holding their sons in Pietà-like fashion in order to illustrate the grief and terror of police violence against young Black men.

Because of her capacity to suffer for her Son and her ability to intercede with God, Christian men and women, lay and clerical alike, saw Mary as someone who cared deeply for them. They

[44] Maria Warner, *Alone of All Her Sex: The Myth and the Cult of the Virgin Mary* (New York: Knopf, 1976), 217.

Fig. 4.4 Jon Henry, *Untitled #35*, North Minneapolis, 2019

spent no small amount of energy praying to her, worshiping her, and carrying tokens and images of her in their daily lives. Church buildings were full of her images, chapels were named after her, and her shrines decorate the European landscape to this day. Despite the Roman Catholic Church's statements about Mary in Vatican II, which downplayed her importance and suggested that she and her maternal power were relics of the past that were quickly fading, innumerable Roman Catholic women today still pray to Mary, venerate her, and look to her for both comfort and guidance in mothering.[45] Therefore, Mary must be seen as a "polyvalent symbol" in any discussion of women's

[45] See the document *Lumen Gentium* from Vatican II, where Mary is treated as one of many teachings of the church rather than as a saint and co-redemptrix along with Christ. See also John Cavadini and Danielle M. Peters,

attachment and devotion to her.[46] One thing is certain: mothers wanted her presence and comfort throughout the long centuries of Christianity.

The celebration of saints, including a cheerful economy of pilgrimages, shrines, and mementos of the saints, continued up until the sixteenth century, when the German and Swiss Reformations sought to purge from Christian piety anything that distracted from Christ himself. Luther and his fellow Reformers believed that the veneration of the saints was stirring up superstition and disorder among lay people.[47] The mostly male Reformers tried to focus the layperson's gaze on Christ alone, but women continued to pray to the saints during childbirth and pregnancy.[48] More so than even the story of Jesus Christ, the various stories of the saints and their earthly, physical trials affirmed women in their own very earthly, physical sufferings. The flesh of the saints connected to the fleshly experiences of mothers and their children.[49] Female saints and their stories of survival encouraged women to keep on mothering despite life's obstacles and perils. What the male-dominated Reformation overlooked was the simple and basic needs of mothers in the Christian faith. Mothers needed divine reassurance and care. They needed to feel that the female saints heard their prayers and tears. These saints offered comfort, community, and encouragement to mothers. They connected women to the gaze of God's own Being.

---

eds., *Mary on the Eve of the Second Vatican Council* (Notre Dame, Ind.: University of Notre Dame Press, 2017), 31–78.

46 Bridget Heal, *The Cult of the Virgin Mary in Early Modern Germany: Protestant and Catholic Piety, 1500–1648* (Cambridge: Cambridge University Press, 2007), 302.

47 The Lutheran Johannes Brenz called the veneration of saints *Totenfresserei*, or "feeding on the dead." Johannes Brenz, *Ein Sermon von den Heiligen*, Aii^{v}, cited in Carol Piper Heming, *Protestants and the Cult of the Saints in German Speaking Europe, 1517–1531* (Kirksville, Mo.: Truman State University Press, 2003), 36.

48 See Merry E. Wiesner, "Studies of Women, the Family, and Gender," in *Reformation Europe: A Guide to Research II*, ed. William S. Maltby (St. Louis: Center for Reformation Research, 1992), 165. See also Lyndal Roper, *The Holy Household: Women and Morals in Reformation Augsburg*, Oxford Studies in Social History (Oxford: Clarendon, 1989), 261.

49 See Warner, *Alone of All Her Sex*, 273–84.

Churching as a Celebration of Maternal Power

Amidst all the serious maternal and sisterly strategizing to get women through the dangers of birthing and the postpartum period, there needed to be a time to celebrate the work of the maternal body. At least, that is how it seems women viewed the wildly popular ritual of churching:[50] the ritual that welcomed postpartum women back into the worshiping community and the church building.[51] It seems that Greek Christians began this ritual at least by the late fourth century.[52] This ritual was an event that took place about forty days after the mother had given birth, as it was rooted in ancient ideas about the "uncleanness" of pregnancy and delivery. Churching was based on the biblical story told in Luke 2:22–40 of Mary entering the Temple to present the infant Jesus. Christian scholastics read this event in Mary's life alongside the Levitical codes about blood and purification seen in Leviticus chapter 12. Just as Mary entered the Temple with Jesus forty days after his birth, so were new mothers allowed to enter the church forty days after giving birth. Some scholars believe that the churching ritual also reflected widespread superstitions about the porous body of the mother and how pregnant and birthing women were subject to the influence of demons and other evil spirits.[53]

As historians point out, this ritual was governed mostly by the male clerical class who proscribed how churching functioned and what its rules were. The basic order of the ritual was as follows: The new mother would come with her female entourage—such as midwife, sisters, mother, female friends, and other female neighbors—to the door of the church. The priest would meet her

[50] Germany is a good example of the popularity of this ritual. In some German territories, the clerics and rulers had to limit the number of women who could accompany the new mother back into the church because this rite was so popular among women. See Eva Labouvie, *Andere Umstände* (Cologne: Böhlau Verlag 1998), 253–54.

[51] One of the earliest Christian sources of this ritual is the fourth-century document entitled *Canons of Hippolytus*. See Joanne M. Pierce, "'Green Women' and Blood Pollution: Some Medieval Rituals for the Churching of Women after Childbirth," *Studia Liturgica* 29, no. 2 (1999): 191–215, here 194.

[52] Susan C. Karant-Nunn, *The Reformation of Ritual: An Interpretation of Early Modern Germany* (New York: Routledge, 1997), 72–90.

[53] See Walter von Arx, "The Churching of Women after Childbirth: History and Significance," in *Liturgy and Human Passage*, ed. David Power and Luis Maldonado (New York: Seabury Press, 1979), 63–71.

at the threshold and recite a Psalm, typically Psalms 112/113 and 127/128, which refer to wives and children. Then, some petitions would be read, including the first chapter of the Gospel of John. The priest would then take the new mother's hand and lead her into the church while saying a prayer. The new mother would lie down prostrate in front of the altar while the priest continued the liturgy. He then would sprinkle her with holy water and wave incense over her; in some versions of the churching ritual, the new mother was asked to confess her sins and was then offered the eucharistic bread. In France, the women would bring the bread themselves as a symbol of the placenta and the fertility of the woman.[54]

While Church leaders like Pope Gregory the Great (d. 604) maintained the official position that churching was a ceremony of thanksgiving rather than a cleansing per se,[55] clearly much of this ritual reflected the priest taking back control over the maternal body and making a public demonstration that the postpartum mother was once again under the control of the church and her husband.[56] There are even records of new mothers who asked to be ritually purified earlier than planned or in secret because they broke the lying-in code of abstinence and had already resumed sexual relations with their husbands. Many bishops would take advantage of their fear, charging women extra for such on-demand services.[57]

However, as some scholars point out, the ritual of churching was not driven solely by the male clerical class but also by women themselves. It was, after all, the only liturgical ceremony performed by the clergy for women only.[58] It seems that women wanted to participate in a public ritual centered on the work of their bodies. They wanted the church to officially recognize the work and agency of the female body in all of its fleshly power.[59] The same protective women who helped a mother through her pregnancy and labor

[54] See Pierce, "'Green Women' and Blood Pollution," 203.

[55] Gail McMurray Gibson, "Blessing from Sun and Moon: Churching as Women's Theater," in *Bodies and Disciplines: Intersections of Literature and History in Fifteenth-Century England*, ed. Barbara A. Hanawalt and David Wallace (Minneapolis: University of Minnesota Press, 1996), 143.

[56] Pierce, "'Green Women' and Blood Pollution," 206.

[57] See Becky R. Lee, "The Purification of Women after Childbirth: A Window onto Medieval Perceptions of Women," *Florilegium* 14 (1995–1996): 43–44.

[58] Gibson, "Blessing from Sun and Moon," 149.

[59] Gibson, "Blessing from Sun and Moon," 147.

would accompany the new mother to the door of the church on the day of her purification, signaling the public power that groups of women held in medieval society.[60] Many women showed up for the churching ritual with the female entourage that stayed with them during the forty days of their lying-in. Many women dressed up in furs or other fine clothes.[61] Even after the Reformation condemned churching, many women still demanded it and sought out churching ceremonies.[62] The churching ritual recognized the pain, fear, and labor that the new mother had endured. It was one moment when the church focused on the mother and not her baby.[63] It offered her the security of the corporate body of Christians and the warm feelings of familiar Christian ritual. It allowed women to take up space in the church for their own needs.

Women understood that their bodies had a profound agency and place in medieval society even though they were seen as intellectually and rationally inferior to males. Women also understood that their bodies cemented filial relationships through the sharing of breast milk. They understood that they were mediators and protectors of young offspring who were slated to inherit family thrones or dynasties. This all translated theologically to an awareness among women that their maternal bodies were powerful visual examples of God's power to feed the world, to forgive it, and to give it life. In that regard, the ritual of churching meant something different for women than it did for men. While churching was officially a way to cleanse the postpartum body of its shame, it seems that many medieval women manipulated this male-dominated tradition to serve their own views about the power of their maternal bodies and the protective role of the othermothers among them.

Mothering has never been for the fainthearted. Despite official scholastic teachings about the passivity of the female body, Christian mothers were anything but passive. As survival strategists, women utilized an eclectic array of tools, prayers, ritual, and magic to help them and their babies get through the dangers of childbirth and the vulnerable postpartum period. They banded together as

[60] Lee, "Purification of Women after Childbirth," 48–49.

[61] Pierce, "'Green Women' and Blood Pollution," 212.

[62] Gibson, "Blessing from Sun and Moon," 143.

[63] David Cressy, "Purification, Thanksgiving, and the Churching of Women in Post-Reformation England," *Past and Present* 141 (1993): 145.

women and as Christians to call upon strong female saints like Margaret and Anne to surround them and protect them through the trials of mothering. All of this took creativity, emotional resilience, and most of all courage. Even though doctrinal theology did not celebrate women's achievements in mothering, women found a way to incorporate the Christian faith into their lives, and they made sure that in rituals like churching the church recognized their achievements as well.

5

The Prayers and Tears of Christian Mothers

Fragments of a Hidden Christian Story: Maternal Courage

While Christian women used all sorts of tools to help themselves and each other get through the perils of pregnancy and childbirth, there was only so much a mother could do to help her child survive and thrive. Although Christian writers did not celebrate the mothers who fought, took risks, or showed courage in the face of danger, there are fragmented anecdotes in the Christian tradition that portray maternal courage and risk-taking. One famous anecdote comes from the famous early church theologian Origen. He left behind a brief but powerful anecdote of his mother's courage in the face of Roman persecution. Likewise, Saint Augustine's mother Monica is remembered for her tenacity and persistence. The medieval saint Birgitta of Sweden also portrays Mary as a strong mother, contrary to many traditions that insisted that Mary was silent and submissive. Other mothers such as the ninth-century noblewoman Dhuoda and the group of seventeenth-century mother-authors who wrote mothers' legacies took the wise steps of writing down the Christian faith for the sake of their children, especially when the mother knew she could not be there to protect and raise her child. Two mothers' legacies from the seventeenth century, *A Mother's Blessing*, written in 1616 by Dorothy Leigh, and *The Mother's Legacy to Her Unborn Child*, written in 1622 by Elizabeth Joscelin, show the concerns of Puritan mothers for the spiritual and physical well-being of their children.

It should come as no surprise to modern readers that the Christian faith included practical, strategic, and strong mothers, even though they have been basically invisible in official Christian doctrine and theology. Anthropological studies have shown how mothers from all cultures have found resourceful and creative ways to keep their children alive. In fact, strategizing for survival seems to be wired into mothers and their offspring.[1] From the ways women pick their mates[2] to how women manage households and budgets,[3] mothers very frequently consider the well-being of their offspring before they consider themselves. Christian mothers have been no different, despite the lack of Christian support for such adaptive behaviors.

The Courage and Tears of Mother Mary

In the High Middle Ages, Christian writers centered their theological attention upon the love, affection, and empathy shared between Mary and Jesus. Birgitta of Sweden (d. 1373), through her work *Meditations on the Life of Christ* (also known as *The Mirror of the Blessed Life of Christ*), was a part of this trend. She focused on Mary's care for Jesus and described their mother-child bond both in intimate ways and within domestic contexts. In her vision of the Nativity, Birgitta utilized the maternal act of dressing, in particular, to show Mary's close bond with her son. A mother of eight children herself, Birgitta was perhaps reflecting on her own maternal activities and sense of domestic order when she described in depth how Mary carefully prepared the swaddling clothes for Jesus. She envisioned Mary dressing both the baby Jesus after his birth and the

1 As Sarah Hrdy and others have shown, the maternal body mediates tradeoffs of nutrients and other life-giving chemical processes as the mother's body and the embryo compete and cooperate. Hrdy, *Mother Nature: Maternal Instincts and How They Shape the Human Species* (New York: Ballantine, 2000), 95.

2 Hrdy, *Mother Nature*, 235–65.

3 See reports such as Viviana A. Zelizer, "The Gender of Money," *Wall Street Journal*, January 27, 2011, https://www.wsj.com/articles/BL-IMB-1033; and Ana Revenga and Sudhir Shetty, "Empowering Women Is Smart Economics," *Finance & Development* 49, no. 1 (2012): 40–43, https://www.imf.org/external/pubs/ft/fandd/2012/03/revenga.htm.

adult Jesus after he died. Birgitta even depicted Mary giving birth on her own, no midwife needed. In Birgitta's vision, Mary snips the umbilical cord herself and wraps up the newborn Jesus (who was perfectly clean when he came out of his mother's uterus).[4] When Jesus cries, she joyfully picks him up to comfort him.[5] All of these visions showed that Mary was a competent and willing mother.

However, Birgitta's vision of the Nativity took the theology of Mary to a whole other level. In Birgitta's treatment of Mary, she gives *Mary* a narrative voice. In Birgitta's vision, Mary is not a quiet, ponderous mother simply observing the events of her life in silence. Rather, the vision lets Mary speak about her own experiences as a mother. Birgitta allows Mary to narrate her own suffering as she begins to understand what will happen to her child. Birgitta called Mary "the most afflicted of all mothers" because of her foreknowledge of Christ's death. In Birgitta's vision, Mary says,

> When I contemplated the places where, as I learned through the prophets, his hands and feet would be nailed at the crucifixion [Psalm 21:17], my eyes filled with tears and my heart was torn by sadness. My son looked at my crying eyes and then became deathly saddened. When I contemplated his divine power, I was consoled again, realized that this was the way he wanted it . . . So my joy was always mixed with sorrow.[6]

It is strange and surprising to hear Mary's voice in this way. Mary speaks of her sorrow and her knowledge of God. This is a complex picture of Mary as a woman who understood not only what it meant to suffer as a mother but also what it meant to live in the presence of God. In Birgitta's vision, Mary portrays *herself* as a realistic and wise mother, one who knew how to care for children, and one who showed great attention to her divine son. She acknowledged his power, but as a mother, finally, she felt the pain of her son's pain.

4 Birgitta of Sweden, *Revelations* 7.21, in *Birgitta of Sweden: Life and Selected Revelations*, ed. Marguerite Tjader Harris, trans. Albert R. Kezel, Classics of Western Spirituality (Mahwah, N.J.: Paulist Press, 1990), 188. See also Mary Dzon, "Birgitta of Sweden and Christ's Clothing," in *The Christ Child in Medieval Culture: Alpha Es Et O!*, ed. Mary Dzon and Theresa M. Kenney (Toronto: University of Toronto Press, 2012), 117–44.

5 Birgitta of Sweden, *Revelations* 7.21, pp. 189 and 203.

6 Birgitta of Sweden, *Revelations* 1.10, p. 266.

The Mothers of Origen and Augustine

The strangeness of hearing Mary's voice only deepens the silence of other famous mothers in the Christian tradition. In particular, one of the most famous early church theologians, Origen of Alexandria, had a mother who saved his life, yet we do not even know her name, much less hear her voice in the tradition. As the story goes, Origen's mother successfully navigated her son's survival through the extreme social circumstances of the persecutions of Christians in 202 by the Emperor Septimus Severus. Origen's mother was not of aristocratic lineage, nor did her family have wealth the way Paula's or Melania's did. She gave birth to nine children and lived in Alexandria as an illegal Christian with her husband, Origen's father, who was a well-known professor. He was executed in the massacre of Christians. After her husband's death, the Roman state took away the family's wealth, suggesting that Origen's mother was not even a Roman citizen.[7] She and Origen were left in poverty.

When the teenage Origen, perhaps seventeen years old, was agitated to join the ranks of martyrs like his father had, his mother stepped in. She knew he would die if he went out, so she hid Origen's clothes—such was her maternal strategy. Sure enough, Origen did not go out without his clothes. He stayed home. Origen's mother may have deprived him of the eternal crown of martyrdom, but she saved his life. While the strategy that Origen's mother utilized to save her son makes for a humorous story, it illustrates her wit, her wisdom, and her courage. Her story indicates that perhaps hundreds if not thousands of mothers in the Roman Empire had to be courageous and resourceful in order to protect their children during this frightening era. Because of the quick actions of his mother, Origen lived and went on to become the Bishop of Alexandria. Today he is seen as one of the most creative and most important early Christian theologians.

Another mother about whom Christians have heard much is Monica, the mother of Augustine of Hippo. Monica was even made a saint by the Catholic Church, and yet Augustine never thought to put her own voice or her first-person perspective into the relatively rich material about her that he left in his writings. Monica was in many ways the maternal strategist *par excellence*. While very little is known about

[7] John Anthony McGucken, ed., *The Westminster Handbook to Origen*, Westminster Handbooks to Christian Theology (Louisville: Westminster John Knox, 2004), 3.

Monica, she seems to have been a model but average Christian woman. That is, she did not relinquish her motherhood for martyrdom or the ascetic life. Most likely, she would have had no formal education, and yet, it seems that when she was in her early forties, Monica took on a professional job and became a teacher of rhetoric! Not only was she a good Christian mother, she was a *working* mother.[8] Despite this advanced career, Monica remained keenly aware of the status of wives within the ancient world: she apparently "joked" about how wives were slaves, and she gave advice to her neighbors on how to avoid the eyebrow-raising event of being beaten by their husbands.[9] Monica and her husband Patricius had worldly ambitions for their children. They insisted that Augustine get a good, classical education so that he could enjoy some rank and status in Roman society. Once her husband died, Monica continued to successfully manage the family's finances, including being able to pay the high fees for Augustine's education. She raised two other children, both of whom survived to adulthood, and she enjoyed grandchildren. All of these things show her to have been a competent and successful mother.

Although it seems that Augustine avoided Monica's prayers and tears for him when he was a young man, the mother and son stayed close their entire lives. Throughout his life, Monica made strategic decisions for the sake of Augustine's success. It was Monica who forced him to leave his long-time mistress and the mother of his only son so that he could marry a woman of proper Roman societal status. She traveled with Augustine when he moved to Milan to teach rhetoric; she even participated in his philosophical discussions.[10] On these travels, they faced dangerous skirmishes among the Roman military.[11] When she died, Augustine gave a lengthy description of her life and their lives together. He called her an "outstanding peacemaker" who put up with her husband's physical violence and infidelities with patience and strategic submission.[12] He called her a woman of "blameless conduct"[13] and noted that on their travels together

8 Gillian Clark, *Monica: An Ordinary Saint* (New York: Oxford University Press, 2015), 10.

9 Augustine, *Confessions*, trans. Sarah Ruden (New York: The Modern Library, 2018), 9.19, p. 261.

10 Clark, *Monica*, 11.

11 Clark, *Monica*, 11.

12 Augustine, *Confessions* 9.19, 21, p. 261.

13 Augustine, *Confessions* 9.21, p. 262.

with his companions, she "cared for us as if she'd given birth to us all."[14] Although in later studies of Monica, she is often portrayed as being overly attached to her son, rather than being misremembered as an over-involved, hand-wringing mother, Monica deserves to be remembered as a highly successful Christian mother.[15]

Dhuoda's *Handbook for William*

While Origen's and Augustine's mothers were both able to accompany their children into adulthood, other Christian mothers were not so lucky. They had to find ways to give their children Christian guidance and a sense of God's love from afar.

One mother's singular voice from the ninth-century Carolingian empire rings out in this regard. Her name was Dhuoda. She wrote what was called a "handbook." These little books were also known in medieval times as "mirrors," or moral-theological guides written for lay people, and were popular among the upper and educated classes.[16] She wrote her handbook in 841 and sent it to her son William in 843. He was fourteen years old. William was a "much desired son" and his mother loved him dearly.[17] Dhuoda was part of the nobility and was married to a nobleman, Bernard of Septimania. Bernard was an enemy of King Charles the Bald. Once he lost a battle with Charles' allies in the Frankish nobility, Bernard had to submit to the king. Because the relationship between the two men was so distrustful, Bernard was forced to bring his two sons with him into the company of King Charles, and William was taken as a hostage. In the highly masculinized, unstable culture of the Frankish kingdoms, Dhuoda was forced to give up William and his baby brother into the company of Charles the Bald because of her husband's politics.[18]

14 Augustine, *Confessions* 9.22, p. 263.

15 See in particular Peter Walcot, "Plato's Mother and Other Terrible Women," in *Women in Antiquity*, ed. Ian McAuslan and Peter Walcot, Greece and Rome Studies 3 (Oxford: Oxford University Press, 1996), 114–33.

16 Carol Neel, introduction to *Handbook for William: A Carolingian Woman's Counsel for Her Son*, by Dhuoda, ed. and trans. Carol Neel (Washington, D.C.: Catholic University of America Press, 1991), xxiv.

17 Dhuoda, prologue to *Handbook for William*, 6.

18 Dhuoda never learned the name of her baby son because the boys were taken with their father before they could be named and baptized. It is likely that he was named Bernard after his father. See Marie Anne Mayeski, *Dhuoda:*

Like other women of the nobility, Dhuoda was obliged to stay in the family territory and supervise their land in Frankish Septimania. She was desperate for her beloved sons because once they were taken with their father into the military company of Charles the Bald, Dhuoda never saw any of them again. Her sense of loss is palpable in her writing. She wrote, "I am well aware that most women rejoice that they are with their children in this world, but I, Dhuoda, am far away from you, my son, William."[19] It seems that she grieved the loss of her boys for the rest of her life and was plagued by isolation and depression. Her husband Bernard was eventually executed. William was killed in a skirmish after that. He may have been about seventeen or eighteen.

As for her infant son, Dhuoda never did learn the exact whereabouts of him, who, she noted poignantly, had come "forth from my body by God's mercy."[20] Historians wonder if he grew up to become the famous Bernard Plantevelue, or Bernard Hairyfeet, who is well-known for his attempt to murder king Charles the Bald in 856. If baby Bernard indeed grew up to be Hairyfeet, then Dhuoda's son would have had the amazing luck of growing up into adulthood and establishing the important medieval duchy of Aquitaine. He would have become the father of one of the most important kings, William the Pious, who endowed the important Benedictine abbey, Cluny, which became one of the most important centers of medieval Christendom.[21] She would have been the grandmother of one of the most important Christian kings. However, it is unclear if the famous Bernard Plantevelue was in fact Dhuoda's son; taken as an infant from his mother's nourishing and protective body, it is also just as likely that the baby died.

Dhuoda was a typical noble Frankish mother in the Carolingian age when the nobility took Christian piety very seriously. Her advice to William was typical of early medieval theology, which saw itself tightly woven into a moral life. Her main concern in her *Handbook for William* was for him to live a moral life before God and to be a just person within their highly masculinized, violent

---

Ninth Century Mother and Theologian (Scranton, Pa.: University of Scranton Press, 1995), 11–12.

19 Dhuoda, epigraph to *Handbook for William*, 2.

20 Dhuoda, prologue to *Handbook for William*, 6.

21 Neel, introduction to *Handbook for William*, x–xi.

culture. Dhuoda exhorted William to avoid evil and violent men and to seek out men who are moral: "good men seeking after worthy goals."[22] She assured him that God would grant God's kingdom and reward for those who "struggle for good."[23] She emphasized his moral education and his moral life. One typical Christian way to live a moral life and to find happiness was to engage in the spiritual exercises of reading Scripture and studying the mysteries of theology. She directed William to read and study Paul and the church Fathers and to probe the mysteries of the Trinity.[24] Her use of the Trinity is noteworthy because it is a diversion into a highly academic and theoretical doctrine within a very practical handbook. Perhaps she was demonstrating her knowledge of Christian theology, or perhaps she was affirming the superiority of the Christian God over other pagan gods.

Dhuoda utilized a Christian imagination to encourage William to be successful in his military duties. Her guidance indicates her belief that being an honorable man in a masculine society would please God. She wrote, "What is essential, my son William, is that you show yourself to be such a man on both levels that you are both effective in this world and pleasing to God in every way."[25] With this sentiment, Dhuoda expressed what seems to be an almost-universal sentiment among mothers: the desire that their child fit into society and be a productive citizen. She wanted William to be pleasing to God and to be "useful to man."[26] She drew upon military imagery to describe William's rise in heaven as well. He would "climb to the ranks of heaven" when he sought out good men. On a light-hearted note, Dhuoda, like any good mother of a teenager, suggested that maybe William's friends could read her *Handbook* too.[27]

It is remarkable that Dhuoda taught her child the spiritual value of a highly political life and that being a lay person in contrast to being part of the clergy class could provide a direct line to salvation. Dhuoda seems to have been pushing against the idea that being part of the clerical or praying classes was the best way to ensure eternal life. She assured William that a career in the military was not

22 Dhuoda, *Handbook for William* 3.7, p. 31.
23 Dhuoda, *Handbook for William* 1.1, pp. 8–9.
24 Dhuoda, *Handbook for William* 2.1, p. 16.
25 Dhuoda, prologue to *Handbook for William*, 5.
26 Dhuoda, *Handbook for William* 3.9, p. 33.
27 Neel, introduction to *Handbook for William*, xx.

going to jeopardize his eternal life, but she warned him that secular glory would not last. Therefore, William needed to live a secular, political life for the sake of God and not earthly glory. She taught him that earthly goods and honor were God's reward to those who obeyed the patriarchal order of family and kingdom.[28]

Another way to look at Dhuoda's *Handbook for William* is to see it as the main textbook of his faith education. She saw herself as the one best suited to give him that, noting, "you will have other teachers to present you with works of fuller and richer usefulness, but not anyone like me, your mother, whose heart burns on your behalf."[29] Dhuoda put together a variety of Christian ideas, texts, and Scripture (mostly from the Old Testament) for the growth of William's faith. She seems to have prioritized giving him a straightforward understanding of God's mercy and how the merciful divine will could be reflected on earth. She offered William a vision of a God who is able to fulfill all needs, who is great, and who is sublime.[30] In other words, along with her admonishment to William to live a moral life before God, Dhuoda presented him with a comforting and faithful God. Dhuoda seemed to want to communicate that God is on William's side. She wrote, "Beseech the Lord, cherish him and love him. If you do this, he will be your guardian, your leader, your companion, and your country—*the way the truth and the life*—endowing you most generously with prosperity in this world."[31] In these discussions, we see a mother who assured her son that the path which he was forced to take into the military would not prevent him from eternal life and that he would experience God's riches on earth—as long as he dedicated his work and his life to God.[32]

Another priority for Dhuoda was her sons' relationships: both their family ties and their ties to others who would be honorable and loving. She exhorted William to be a generous and loving person. She stressed that the fundamental tie that holds all of humanity together is love; it is the link to all military success and to political power too. She referred to the poetry of Donatus, saying that

28 Dhuoda, *Handbook for William* 3.3–4, 8, pp. 24–25, 31–32.
29 Dhuoda, *Handbook for William* 1.7, pp. 12–13.
30 Dhuoda, *Handbook for William* 1.1, p. 9.
31 Dhuoda, *Handbook for William* 1.7, p. 13.
32 Dhuoda, *Handbook for William* 3.3, pp. 23–25.

William should "love all so that you may be loved by all, and cherish them that you may be cherished."[33] It is clear that she was trying to raise a man who could have rank and stature among men but who also could exercise gentleness and compassion. She reminded him to not forget the poor and to "love justice."[34] Sticking together as family and following one another in offense and defense was the way that William and Bernard could flourish in their chaotic lives.[35] She exhorted William to find his way to those who are worthy to "love God."[36] She told William that his baby brother was "your flesh and your brother."[37] She implored them to find the good, find the helpers, and stick together as brothers. She spoke of love and compassion when she knew that they would be faced with the roughness of a military society. One can almost hear Dhuoda's grief and worry for her boys in her rhetoric.

Despite the way that the family hierarchy and patriarchal structures of Carolingian society seemed to betray her motherhood, they were still important to Dhuoda. She reminded William that God is a *Father* who controls the entire universe. She told William to fear God, love God, and believe in God.[38] Later on in the *Handbook*, she told William to "fear, love, and be faithful to your lord and father, Bernard, in all things . . . *For God hath made the father . . . He that obeyeth the father shall be a comfort to his mother*."[39] Dhuoda spent almost an entire chapter (book 3) explaining how William must revere his father, Bernard. Clearly, she was working with an image of God who is directly related to earthly fathers and patrilineal authority. Obedience to earthly fathers would bring divine reward, and "fatherly power" was the supreme power on earth.[40] She instructed William to pray for his father Bernard and for Bernard's dead relatives.[41] At the end of the *Handbook*, she even listed William's patrilineal relatives so that he would remember them and remember the family of which he is a member. Dhuoda's thoughts on God and the structure

33 Dhuoda, *Handbook for William* 3.10, p. 35.
34 Dhuoda, *Handbook for William* 4.8, p. 59.
35 Dhuoda, *Handbook for William* 3.10, p. 13.
36 Dhuoda, *Handbook for William* 1.1, p. 7.
37 Dhuoda, *Handbook for William* 1.7, p. 13.
38 Dhuoda, *Handbook for William* 3.5, pp. 27–29.
39 Dhuoda, *Handbook for William* 3.1, p. 21 (emphasis original).
40 Dhuoda, *Handbook for William* 2.2, pp. 16–17, and 3.3, pp. 23–25.
41 Dhuoda, *Handbook for William* 8.7, p. 84.

of the Trinity that placed God as the biological *father* above any other male leader reflect her typical Frankish values, which prioritized the patrilineal family lines before any kind of loyalty to a king or other male authority.[42] The Trinity in Dhuoda's eyes was about order and obedience to a clear line of masculine authority.

Dhuoda urged William to obey his father and do all good things *for her sake* as his mother.[43] But she did this even as she utilized the typical rhetoric of Christian women writers such as Hildegard of Bingen or Julian of Norwich who downplayed their intelligence and religious authority. Dhuoda minimized her authority and intelligence as a woman even though she was probably one of the very few women in her time who were highly educated. She identified herself as a "fragile" person, with a "weakness of mind," who was "unworthy,"[44] and "weak as a shadow."[45] She repeatedly noted that she is "wretched, dust and ashes."[46] Her comments to William also suggest that she knew it was not her place to talk about God. She asked William to excuse her brashness in daring to talk about God to him.[47] Yet, the educated references that she made to the Latin Vulgate translation of Scripture and to church Fathers such as Augustine and Gregory the Great belies her self-minimization. Her *Handbook* displays a highly educated, literate woman.

In other words, while Dhuoda rejected any pretense of general female intelligence, she used her privilege as the *mother* to William.[48] The *Handbook* reveals Dhuoda exercising her maternal authority by taking up the pen. In her prayer in the Prologue, she says to God about William, "he will never have another like me."[49] This suggests that she was fully aware that she was the one person in William's life who had authority over his spiritual and moral well-being.[50] Her manual is so unique because it gives us insight into the way that this ninth-century, upper-class, Frankish mother described her own profound grief at the loss of her children and how she chose to pass on

42 Neel, introduction to *Handbook for William*, xix.
43 Dhuoda, *Handbook for William* 3.1, p. 21.
44 Dhuoda, prologue to *Handbook for William*, 5.
45 Dhuoda, *Handbook for William* 1.4, p. 9.
46 Dhuoda, *Handbook for William* 1.1, p. 7.
47 Neel, introduction to *Handbook for William*, xxi.
48 Dhuoda, prologue to *Handbook for William*, 4.
49 Dhuoda, epigraph to *Handbook for William*, 4.
50 Dhuoda, *Handbook for William* 1.7, p. 13.

the Christian faith to them in her absence. Sadly, historians have no idea whether Dhuoda's sons ever saw her *Handbook* to them or if they ever used it for their own sakes. The fact that her *Handbook* even exists at all shows that she exercised her maternal agency in the best way she knew how in the violent and unpredictable circumstances of her life and the lives of her sons.

Dorothy Leigh

Around nine hundred years later, written works by mothers on the topics of Christian theology, spirituality, and morality grew into their own literary genre. The singular voice of the ninth-century Carolingian Christian mother, Dhuoda, was joined by a chorus of seventeenth-century Puritan and Protestant mothers. These maternal handbooks came to be called "mothers' legacies." They were meant to be the voice of the mother to her child on all things having to do with Christianity and the spiritual life as well as guidance on how to fit into society in her absence. But morality and practical guidance were not their main characteristics. These mothers' manuals display a sophisticated understanding of Christian theology. They also display their authors' clear sense of maternal identity. These mothers were not necessarily going to leave the spiritual lives and salvation of their children up to the clerical class or institutional church.

Dorothy Leigh was perhaps the most influential author of a mother's legacy in the seventeenth century. Leigh was born into an aristocratic and well-pedigreed English family under the reign of King James VI and I.[51] Her exact birthdate is unknown. Her mother's legacy, entitled *The Mother's Blessing. Or, The Godly Counsel of a Gentle-Woman Not Long Since Deceased, Left behind for Her Children*, was published in 1616. It seems that she died not long after its publication. It became so popular and widely read that it went through at least nineteen editions before 1640.[52]

[51] See Sylvia Brown, ed., *Women's Writing in Stuart England: The Mothers' Legacies of Dorothy Leigh, Elizabeth Joscelin, and Elizabeth Richardson* (Gloucestershire: Sutton Publishing, 1999), 6. Their popularity reached an apex in the eighteenth century and only began to wane in the nineteenth. See the list of other mother's legacies and writings by mothers in Brown, *Women's Writing in Stuart England*, vi–vii.

[52] Catharine Gray, "Feeding on the Seed of the Woman: Dorothy Leigh and the Figure of Maternal Dissent," *English Literary History* 68, no. 3 (2001): 563–92, here 564.

Historians and literary critics have interpreted Leigh's work in light of the many other "conduct manuals" that arose in the early seventeenth century.[53] They have shown how Leigh's work seems to be not just a private manual or a document for her family but a public writing that both engaged politics and critiqued church leaders. In fact, it was widely seen in its time as a companion to the widely read and respected book called *The Father's Blessing*, which was a distilled version of the political writings of King James I.[54] Because it was so publicly connected to *The Father's Blessing*, Leigh's work can be seen as the maternal version of the politics and religion of the day. It offered up something unheard of: a maternally minded public theology.

Leigh apparently had ties to a radical group of English Puritans that was part of the splintering of moderate Puritanism and Arminian Christians in the early seventeenth century. Her home county of Essex was zealously Protestant. Preachers in her day were highly respected and were paid for their sermons. In good, Puritan, "modernizing" fashion, Leigh spoke against certain Roman Catholic traditions as outdated, including the churching of postpartum women.[55] It is possible that one of her sons, William, became the Rector of Groton Suffolk, but there is very little historical documentation on what happened to her other sons.[56]

Leigh wrote her *Mother's Blessing* to her three sons: George, John, and William. It seems like they were already older teenagers or young adults at the time the manual was written. Her manual was meant to show the public that she was being a good Christian mother and that she had the spiritual authority to speak directly to her sons. Leigh began her manual by orienting the readers to herself as a wife and mother. By writing this, she claimed, she was fulfilling her wifely and maternal duties. She was raising her boys with a good religious education and instilling in them a

53 Gray, "Feeding on the Seed of the Woman," 564–65.

54 James I wrote *Basilicon Doron*, published in 1599 as a letter to his son about what a good monarch looked like. It was a way to help his subjects get more acquainted with him as king. *The Father's Blessing* was published in 1616, the same year as Dorothy Leigh's *The Mother's Blessing*. The two were even sold sometimes bound together in one volume. See Gray, "Feeding on the Seed of the Woman," 563.

55 Gray, "Feeding on the Seed of the Woman," 570.

56 Gray, "Feeding on the Seed of the Woman," 570.

Christian moral compass. With it, she wanted to ensure that her sons were brought up "godly."[57] She spent much of the manual instructing her boys on how to pray and how to have a private, pious life and household. They were to pray privately, pray often, and to not neglect prayer.[58] But Leigh's was no moralistic theology. She displayed a robust knowledge of pneumatology, making it clear to her sons that it is the Holy Spirit who teaches us and instructs us to pray, to ask God for help, and to be thankful when God helps us.[59] She directed her sons to cast their cares upon God, assuring them that God would help them and listen to them, even if their prayers were weak.[60] In this regard, Leigh taught her boys that God was a loving and attentive God who is interested in their personal and public lives.

To Leigh, acts of private prayer and devotion to God were signs of truly godly men. Leigh warned her boys that earthly fame and riches corrupt people and that they should avoid these things. If they sinned, God would forgive them, but they were not to make a habit out of sinning or seeking wealth; having wealth but shunning it were signs of godly men, as was shunning the fancy trappings of Roman Catholicism with its incense, saints, and outmoded ways of worshiping. She urged them to become preachers and to attend church regularly. In other words, Leigh was bringing up deeply Puritanical, Calvinistic, Protestant young men.

Leigh also demonstrated a sophisticated understanding of incarnational Christology with maternal dimensions, using birthing imagery to communicate Christ's presence to her sons. First, she summarized Hebrews chapter 2 saying that Christ "took our flesh" upon himself. She instructed her sons to become Christlike: "he taught us to join our flesh unto him by faith."[61] Then, she tied in the maternal functions of labor and birth to deepen her incarnational Christology. She turned to Isaiah 49:15, which asks, "Can a mother forget the child of her womb?" She extended the rhetoric of Isaiah

[57] Brown, *Women's Writing in Stuart England*, 17.

[58] Dorothy Leigh, *The Mother's Blessing. Or, The Godly Counsel of a Gentle-Woman Not Long Since Deceased, Left Behind for Her Children* (London: 1616), chs. 16, 19, 20, 32.

[59] Brown, *Women's Writing in Stuart England*, 41.

[60] Leigh, *Mother's Blessing*, chs. 16, 32.

[61] Brown, *Women's Writing in Stuart England*, 23. I have modernized some of her words, like "join" for "iyone" and "she" for "shee."

by adding, "As if he should say, is it possible, that she, which hath carried her child within her, so near her heart, and brought it forth into this world with so much bitter pain, so many groans and cries, can forget it?"[62] Leigh expounded upon Scripture on this particular point, drawing out in fully human terms what a woman goes through to bring a baby into the world. She emphasized the physical and mental challenges that it takes to bear a child. Her maternal imagery suggests that the spiritual process of having Christ become a part of our own inner lives is a birthing process—actually, a divine process of maternal labor.

Leigh's maternal imagery did not stop there. She drew upon Scripture to communicate to her sons that she would not stop laboring to help them grow into godly men. While she labored to physically bear them, she said that she was laboring to make sure that Christ was formed in them. She continued,

> Will she not labor now till Christ be formed in it? Will she not bless it every time it sucks on her breasts, when she feel the blood come from her heart to nourish it? Will she not instruct it in the youth, and admonish it in the age, and pray for it continually? Will she not be afraid that the child which she endured such pain for, should endure endless pain in hell?[63]

Leigh connected the laboring, nursing mother who will never forget her child to Paul's words in Galatians 4:19, which state, "my little children, for whom I am again in the anguish of childbirth until Christ is formed in you!"[64] She asked in light of this Scripture, "And can any man blame a mother (who indeed brought forth her child with so much pain) though she labor again will Christ be formed in them?"[65] She then connected these thoughts back to maternal love and instinct, claiming "every man knows that the love of a mother to her children is hardly contained within the bounds of reason."[66]

Leigh's use of Paul here is quite radical. For one, she used Paul to claim her authority as a mother in a time when Paul was most often

62 Brown, *Women's Writing in Stuart England*, 23.
63 Brown, *Women's Writing in Stuart England*, 23.
64 Gal 4:19 (NRSV).
65 Brown, *Women's Writing in Stuart England*, 23.
66 Brown, *Women's Writing in Stuart England*, 23.

used to *silence* women in the home and church.[67] Further, she almost likened herself to him with her claim that she labored to form her children bodily. Like Paul, she claimed that she was forming them spiritually in their young adulthood.[68] Clearly, Leigh connected the labor of a mother with the Christian's work to be a disciple of Christ, but she also drew upon the mother-child bond of attachment to claim the authority to instruct her boys and speak to them about their faith. Christ, to her, was less a savior who rescues sinners from hell (although she noted that she was concerned about that too) and more a teacher, the presence of whom would develop and grow within her boys. All this happened because of her urging, her maternal instruction, and—especially—*her maternal voice in their heads*.

Finally, Leigh was not just doing moral instruction or even giving a theology for the private, familial sphere. In her work, she branched out into a political stance that most likely grew out of her religious beliefs. Her work could be seen as something akin to a public sermon, which a woman could never actually deliver from the pulpit in the seventeenth century.[69] This makes her work interesting from a literary and historical perspective, and it deserves more attention as a political statement. Although the political dimension of her work is beyond the scope of the present work, it is worth noting that Leigh was forging a maternally informed, political theology. Her rhetoric in *The Mother's Blessing* challenges the ideas of a patriarch-king that were baked into the content of King James' 1616 *Basilicon Doron* through Leigh's themes of maternal care and motherwork.[70] She conjured a Christian imagination that replaced patriarchal notions of God with a loving and zealous mother.

Elizabeth Joscelin

Elizabeth Joscelin's legacy, entitled *The Mother's Legacy to Her Unborn Child* and published in 1622, is another example of a Puritan mother who sought to pass down the Christian faith to her child and to be a maternal presence even though she would not be physically there. It is actually based on Dorothy Leigh's earlier model.[71]

67 Gray, "Feeding on the Seed of the Woman," 571.
68 Gray, "Feeding on the Seed of the Woman," 571.
69 Gray, "Feeding on the Seed of the Woman," 575.
70 Gray, "Feeding on the Seed of the Woman," 564.
71 Brown, *Women's Writing in Stuart England*, 98.

Elizabeth Joscelin was born in Cheshire, England in 1596 to parents who seemed to be estranged from one another. At age six, her mother died. Thomas Goad, who eventually edited Joscelin's works and claimed to have known her personally, wrote that she was deeply influenced by witnessing the death of her mother. This childhood experience may have influenced her own *Mother's Legacy*.[72] She was then raised by her maternal grandfather and inherited the lands that were in her mother's family. Her grandfather likely educated Elizabeth in Latin, the humanities, and other languages. Elizabeth herself had a good marriage to her husband Taurell Joscelin, who seemed to encourage her to keep learning even after marriage. Despite her educated status, Elizabeth expressed her deep wishes to get pregnant, praying "long often and earnestly" for a child.[73] Joscelin, like many women of her day, was deeply aware of the dangers of childbirth and the high chances that she would not survive it. With these harsh realities in mind, she wrote *Mother's Legacy* several months before her due date. Unfortunately, her fears came true, and she succumbed nine days after giving birth to a daughter. She was 27 years old.

Unlike Leigh's public maternal theology, Joscelin's *Mother's Legacy* was not meant to be a public document. She made it clear that this was a private document meant for her child. She made little comment on the current state of the church or on any public or political affairs. She, like Leigh, thematized the notion of "motherly zeal" and noted that she felt compelled to write out of such strong maternal feelings.[74] Joscelin was pained to think that her child would miss out on having a mother; she hoped that as the child read the *Legacy*, she or he would hear the motherly love that Joscelin had for her child.[75] Being the good English Puritan that she was, Joscelin's main concern was that her child be instructed properly in the Christian faith. She noted that she did not care if the child was a boy or a girl; either gender was to be instructed in the Christian religion, clearly reflecting the unique opportunities that she herself had had growing up. She insisted that the baby be nursed by a woman of character despite her race ("no matter the

72 Brown, *Women's Writing in Stuart England*, 93.

73 Brown, *Women's Writing in Stuart England*, 93.

74 Brown, *Women's Writing in Stuart England*, 106.

75 Elizabeth Joscelin, *The Mother's Legacy to Her Vnborn* [Unborn] *Childe* [Child], ed. Jean D. LeDrew Metcalfe (Toronto: University of Toronto Press, 2000), 60, line 79.

complexion").[76] She wanted to make sure the child would grow up in a house that did not swear or have abusive talk and that the child would attend school. If the child were a boy, he should be encouraged to be a minister, which, in many Puritan mothers' eyes, was an honorable career. As Joscelin put it, ministers are happy and beloved by God, even if the office is not appreciated by high society. If the child were a daughter, Joscelin wanted her to be raised by her father and his wife and their daughters.[77]

One of the most prominent Christian teachings present in Joscelin's writing is her belief in the providence of God. She leaned heavily upon the providential will of God for the care of her child. In noting the possibility of her own death, she stated that "all things work for the best to those who love God."[78] Similar to Leigh's confidence in the goodness of God, Joscelin expressed her trust that God would take care of her child and that God's benevolent will would uphold and work towards human flourishing. Joscelin insisted that God has "great mercies" and "infinite mercies."[79] This is an important aspect of the maternal manuals as a genre; these Christian mother-authors clearly wanted to communicate to their children that God was working on their side and that God's will meant that *good* would come to them despite life's hardships.

Joscelin's Puritanism was also on display in the detailed instructions to her unborn child about the duties we owe God, in particular, behavioral duties. She wrote at length about the sin of slothfulness on the one side and the danger of pride on the other.[80] She warned her child of the vices of drunkenness, swearing, denying one's sinfulness, and not keeping the Sabbath.[81] She also warned that the Devil lurks in these sins.[82] She clearly believed in the rules of Puritan society, with its shunning of alcohol consumption and its strict keeping of the Sabbath. In some ways, her writing gives weight to the famous thesis by Max Weber on the

[76] In yet another angle of the complex history of wet-nursing and breastfeeding, mothers in the seventeenth century had a stereotype about women with darker complexions—that they were more robust with healthy milk.
[77] Brown, *Women's Writing in Stuart England*, 107, 111.
[78] Brown, *Women's Writing in Stuart England*, 106.
[79] Brown, *Women's Writing in Stuart England*, 111, 112.
[80] Brown, *Women's Writing in Stuart England*, 114–17.
[81] Brown, *Women's Writing in Stuart England*, 122–24.
[82] Joscelin, *Mother's Legacy*, 65, line 140 and 63, line 128f.

industriousness of the Puritans, for Joscelin was concerned that her child not be lazy or idle.[83] Joscelin expressed hopes that her child would grow into an intelligent, wise person and learn to endure life's sufferings with patience. She wanted her child to feel the closeness of Jesus, but she also made a point that we deserve to suffer because of our sins. She instructed her child to cast their cares on Jesus Christ because, she noted, Jesus suffered more than her child would ever suffer.[84]

Clearly, Joscelin saw it as her maternal duty to instruct her child in the Christian faith. It is also clear that in Joscelin's eyes, being a godly Puritan was the best way to live life, for it helped its adherents become wise, happy people. It guided Puritans to keep up with their duties to the social ordering of time by keeping the Sabbath, and it curbed vicious and destructive behavior. From the perspective of the history of ideas, Joscelin's *Legacy* is a good example of how English Puritans believed in God's providence for their personal and societal benefit. Her *Legacy* demonstrated her belief that God was on the side of English Puritan individuals and society. In other words, Joscelin's private maternal guidance to her child showed the way the modern world was taking shape in theological terms. She was concerned that the inner, *private* moral and spiritual well-being of her child should reflect commonly held beliefs in the *public* about what a good Puritan life looked like.

Faith as a Tool for Life

The theological manuals by these most unique mothers illustrate a long tradition of theologically astute and faithful mothers who passed down important pieces of the Christian faith to their children. They did not just teach their children Christian morality but also Christian theology. Their concerns were not so much salvation per se, although that was a part of their work, but rather that their children live lives that were happy, successful, and in relationship to God. For Dhuoda, that meant teaching her sons to survive in a deeply male world and to find honor, gentleness, and justice in a very rough military environment. For Dorothy Leigh, it meant

83 See Max Weber, *The Protestant Ethic and the Spirit of Capitalism*, 3rd Roxbury ed. (Los Angeles: Roxbury, 2001 [1905]).

84 Brown, *Women's Writing in Stuart England*, 119–20, 130–31.

becoming a good English Puritan, avoiding vices, and allowing Christ's form of gentleness and service to be born in one's heart. For Elizabeth Joscelin, it meant making sure her child had all the proper structures of care from those who would parent her child after her own death. This meant securing a proper family structure, a nurturing home life, a good education, and regular church attendance for her child.

The genre of mothers' legacies is a complicated one. The women who wrote these legacies wrote as *mothers*. They utilized the agency that motherhood gave them in society and used it to directly instruct their children in the Christian faith and its moral codes. By relying so heavily upon their roles as mothers, writers such as Dorothy Leigh and Elizabeth Joscelin reinforced the gender stereotypes about mothers that prevailed in their day. They upheld and affirmed the essentialist philosophical ideas that all women were meant to be maternal. And yet, precisely because they were following the cultural expectations of women in their era, they were able to write with any authority in the first place. They were able to claim authority over their subject matter and over their experiences, especially their experiences of Christian devotion and the Christian faith *as mothers*. Writers like Leigh and Joscelin leveraged their roles as mothers to permit themselves to write about theology without having to hide or apologize for their femaleness. They were mothers. In this way, these mothers' legacies uphold gender stereotypes and subvert them at the same time. They demonstrate that mothers had complex and sophisticated understandings of the Christian faith and made choices about what to prioritize when it came to handing down the faith to their children.

Similar to Dhuoda, mothers like Leigh and Joscelin prioritized many things from the Christian faith that were not emphasized by the myriad male authors, preachers, and theologians of their respective times. Like Dhuoda, Leigh and Joscelin utilized the Christian faith in the name of their children's spiritual and emotional well-being. They emphasized the love of God and God's faithfulness to their children. They also focused on aspects of the faith that taught justice and mercy so that their children could learn how to care for others and be just and merciful people in society. Finally, they all picked up the pen so that their children could sense and experience the presence and comfort of their mothers when their mothers were no longer around. In this way, the writings and voices of these women give us evidence that *they saw themselves* as a part of God's own workings in the lives of their children.

6

White Mothers' Theology, Black Mothers' Bible

White Supremacy and God's Providential Will

The Christian imagination of the fair-skinned, European, Protestant mother was imported to the New World and then forged on North American soil. In the vast hills, forests, mountains and plains of North America, there were no European-style cities, traditions, or ancient family lines to honor. There were no urban landscapes or social classes to negotiate. Instead, European Christian settlers encountered expanses of wilderness and unexpected numbers of Indigenous peoples with sophisticated cultures. They battled illness and harsh weather and had no familiar governmental or religious institutional structures upon which to lean. In the absence of these recognizable social structures, individual homes—with their nuclear family arrangements and domestic cultures—became centers for establishing the Christian piety and economic systems necessary to establish a new European-style society. The challenges of importing European culture, dress, religion, and social structures into North America demanded new emphases on the identities and work of women, especially those who were mothers. The richness and horror that constitutes the history of American settlement and colonization makes the study of motherhood in America deeply complex.

Each wave and group of settlers brought their own cultural and religious attitudes towards mothers into their new North

American communities. For instance, the Puritans who settled in New England imported conservative and "pure" views of Calvinistic Christianity to the shores of the New World. Other European settlers brought with them complex theological and secular ideas about mothering that had been shaped by sixteenth-century Reformations and Humanism, especially French Romantic ideas about maternal "affective" love. Still, other settlers quickly became involved in the slave trade, for labor was needed to build up an industrial economy like those they were accustomed to in Europe.

The European Christian theology that helped shape motherhood in the American colonies operated with two deeply held assumptions. The first assumption held that the light-skinned, "white," European race was supreme; it was superior to other peoples from across the globe with darker skin. The second assumption held that it was God's providential will for European settlers to take over the land and become economically prosperous. In the process, European Christians sought to bring non-European peoples into their cultural, religious, and linguistic orbit, regardless of the human price paid for Black and Brown people's erasure and suffering.[1] Not only did official church doctrine and clergy uphold these assumptions, European mothers themselves overwhelmingly upheld them too. The white Protestant mother figure was seen by secular and religious male leaders as the anchor of the household and as an ideal model of morality, and mothers worked hard to live up to it.

These ideas led many white Protestant mothers to internalize such idealistic messages about themselves.[2] Although white Protestant mothers formed a "maternalism" that eventually agitated for social reforms like the abolition of slavery and Indigenous rights, the tragic irony is that white Protestant mothers

1 See Louise Michele Newman, *White Women's Rights: The Racial Origins of Feminism in the United States* (New York: Oxford University Press, 1999), 116–31.

2 As with most studies of women in America, this study will also regrettably not address the rich religious lives of Catholic mothers, as many Catholic communities were marginalized in American society during the eighteenth and nineteenth centuries. See Elizabeth Kolmer, "Catholic Women Religious and Women's History: A Survey of the Literature," in *Women in American Religion*, ed. Janet Wilson James (Philadelphia: University of Pennsylvania Press, 1978), 127–40.

came to see motherhood *as it was performed in middle-class, same-race, same-sex marriages within a domestic sphere* as the great calling of God to all women. Precisely this theological belief propelled white Protestant *mothers* to participate in the destruction of mother-child relationships among Indigenous women and enslaved African women on North American soil.[3] God destined *white* women—and it seems no other kind of women—to be the "Messiahs" of humanity.

Standing in stark contrast to the white Protestant support of light-skinned, European-descended mothers was the negative understanding that Christianity had about Indigenous mothers and enslaved African mothers. These groups of women were not simply absent from or neutral figures in the Christian imagination; they were actively demonized. Indigenous mothers for instance, were seen as bad mothers by "civilized" white women. Indigenous families were destroyed by white, maternally led "missions" to Native communities.[4] Regarding women of African descent, they too, were demonized. Many women who came from Africa were enslaved and had no rights over their bodies or the lives of their children. They were often forced to become mothers through rape and sexual exploitation.

The realities of American plantation slavery and racial theories that promoted devastating prejudices against dark-skinned women require that any exploration of mothers in the Christian imagination distinguish how the Christian imagination was engaged by white Protestant mothers as a weapon against mothers of other skin colors. Much more scholarly work needs to be done on how the Christian imagination applies to Indigenous mothers; they deserve their own close study because they were already mothering within sophisticated social, spiritual, and religious networks as the original peoples of the Americas. Because

3 White Protestant mothers also worked to "Americanize" many different immigrant groups. They were both prejudiced against and helpful to unmarried mothers and other mothers outside of the heteronormative domestic sphere, offering education about breastfeeding and infant care. Amidst all this, they stripped immigrant groups of their own ethnic and cultural practices. See, for example, Regina Kunzel, *Fallen Women, Problem Girls: Unmarried Mothers and the Professionalization of Social Work, 1890–1945*, Yale Historical Publications (New Haven: Yale University Press, 1993).

4 See Newman, *White Women's Rights*, 22–55.

of the complexity of motherhood in America as a topic of study, this chapter has humble aims. It only skims the surface of these complex phenomena and the vastly different experiences of mothering and Christianity among white Protestant, Indigenous, and enslaved African mothers.

The Holy (White) Household

The Christian imagination of God's providential will and white racial superiority fell heavily upon Protestant mothers. They took it to heart and played it out within the domestic sphere—a sphere that took on a kind of cult status in early America. It was the one stable institution on a continent that had very few developed European social systems, and it became a place where women could exercise their agency. It was also a place of religious education where children learned how to be Christians and, just as importantly, *Europeans* in the New World. The domestic sphere reflected God's will for men and women. It represented a microcosm of the covenant of God with Abraham and his descendants.

Protestantism built an entire doctrine of vocation around the "holy household" as the prime location for family and social life.[5] It had its roots in the Protestant Reformations, especially the German Lutheran Reformation. Martin Luther himself taught that God calls all women to get married, bear children, and be the heart and soul of a nuclear family and household. To him, women belonged to a husband in a heterosexual marriage. Women were supposed to be like snails who carried their homes on their backs; they were like nails in a wall, never leaving the domestic sphere to pursue other ambitions.[6] Even the Virgin Mary herself was seen as nothing more and nothing less[7] than

5 I take this phrase from the title of Lyndal Roper's study, *The Holy Household: Women and Morals in Reformation Augsburg*, Oxford Studies in Social History (Oxford: Clarendon, 1989).

6 See Luther's own words in Merry Wiesner, "Luther and Women: The Death of Two Marys," in *Disciplines of Faith: Studies in Religion, Politics, and Patriarchy*, ed. Jim Obelkevich and Lyndal Roper (London: Routledge/Kegan Paul, 1987), 299. See also Martin Luther, *Luther's Works*, vol. 1, ed. Jaroslav Pelikan et al. (St. Louis: Concordia, 1955), 203.

7 Meanwhile, it must be noted that Catholic Reformation forces in the Roman Catholic Church were upholding the devotion to Mary. She was instrumental to Counter Reformation theology, not because of her maternal intercessory powers but because of all the feasts and devotion to her in popular

a deeply faithful Christian mother.[8] Luther noted in his *Commentary on the Magnificat* that after the Annunciation, Mary returned to the business of her household duties such as milking cows, washing dishes, sweeping, and cooking.[9] At the center of the new Christian domestic sphere stood one individual—the mother.

The theology of the household as a microcosm of the church increasingly became the norm in American Protestantism.[10] Puritan mothers in America were expected to read the Bible for their own edification in the privacy of their homes and to have a prayer life in their homes. The home was where children would learn Christian piety and theology. Ministers published catechetical tracts specifically for mothers to teach their children, such as the 1790 publication *Mother's Catechism*.[11] It is a dense piece of work that outlines the basics of Protestant theology in the form of a question and answer between a mother and her child. Educational manuals and educational leaders in general poured more attention and resources into educating girls how to be good domestic

---

culture. She was part of their struggle for political and economic power. See Bridget Heal, *The Cult of the Virgin Mary in Early Modern Germany: Protestant and Catholic Piety, 1500–1648* (Cambridge: Cambridge University Press, 2007), 3–22; Martin Luther, *House Postil*, in *Luthers Werke: Kritische Gesamtausgabe*, vol. 52 (Weimar: Böhlau, 1915), 689, cited in Jaroslav Pelikan, *Mary through the Centuries: Her Place in the History of Culture* (New Haven: Yale University Press, 1996), 154.

8 Reformation preachers emphasized the humanity and even fallibility of Mary, with Philip Melanchthon even speaking of Mary's "negligence" in losing the preteen Christ in the Temple (Luke 2:41–52). See Heal, *Cult of the Virgin Mary in Early Modern Germany*, 275. See also Beth Kreitzer, *Reforming Mary: Changing Images of the Virgin Mary in Lutheran Sermons of the Sixteenth Century*, Oxford Studies in Historical Theology (Oxford: Oxford University Press, 2004), 159.

9 Cited in Heal, *Cult of the Virgin Mary in Early Modern Germany*, 28.

10 See Catharine E. Beecher and Harriet Beecher Stowe, *Principles of Domestic Science as Applied to the Duties and Pleasures of Home: A Text-book for the Use of Young Ladies in Schools, Seminaries, and Colleges* (New York: J.B. Ford, 1873), 191. See also Gayle Kimball, *The Religious Ideas of Harriet Beecher Stowe: Her Gospel of Womanhood*, Studies in Women and Religion 8 (New York: Mellen, 1982).

11 John Willison, *The Mother's Catechism for the Young Child: Or, a Preparatory Help for the Young and the Ignorant, in Order to Their Easier Understanding the Assembly's Shorter Catechism: Together with Forms of Prayer, Both for Week-Days and Sabbath-Days, also, Graces, Both before and after Meat; for Children* (Glasgow: Printed by J. and M. Robertson, 1790).

workers and taught them the economy of the household so that they could both raise children in the faith and raise good white citizens of American civil society.[12] By the nineteenth century, Catharine Beecher—the well-known author and educational reformer who emphasized education for young children—wrote that the life of the nursery and kitchen would reap fruit "through eternal ages" because in them, the habits, virtues, and characters of Christians were formed—all under a mother's care.[13]

Perhaps the most famous writer in nineteenth-century America was Harriet Beecher Stowe, author of *Uncle Tom's Cabin,* which became a national bestseller. In it, the female characters who make the action happen utilize all their power *in* the home.[14] Harriet Beecher Stowe even co-authored a book with her well-known sister Catharine Beecher entitled *The American Woman's Home* (1869), which was directed at white Protestant women of the upper-middle classes. It was meant to heal divisions after the Civil War. Part of Beecher Stowe's intention was to bring Christianity and white Christian, middle-class norms to the underdeveloped South.[15] Another prolific maternalistic author of literature for women about the home was Lydia Marie Child. She wrote the widely-circulated *The Mother's Book* (1831) and *The Frugal Housewife* (1832). Child liked to see herself as a self-sacrificing Christian mother.[16] She wrote that within the home, mothers "created a 'religion of love' by securing a home 'in which love reigns.'"[17] In other words, the female American hero was a white mother.

While white Protestant mother-authors like the Beecher sisters and Lydia Maria Child promoted the archetype of the strong, solitary Christian mother in the home, their thoughts and realities were much more complex. Beecher Stowe is a case in point. For all of her idealizing of the domestic sphere as a place of strength,

12 Colleen McDannell, *The Christian Home in Victorian America, 1840–1900* (Bloomington: Indiana University Press, 1986), 132.

13 Catharine E. Beecher and Harriet Beecher Stowe, *The American Woman's Home* (New Brunswick, N.J.: Rutgers University Press, 2002 [1869]), 24.

14 Myra Jehlen, "The Family Militant: Domesticity Versus Slavery in *Uncle Tom's Cabin,*" *Criticism* 31, no. 4 (1989): 383–400, here 390.

15 Beecher and Beecher Stowe, *American Woman's Home*, xvii.

16 Helene G. Baer, *The Heart Is Like Heaven: The Life of Lydia Maria Child* (Philadelphia: University of Pennsylvania Press, 1964), 226.

17 McDannell, *Christian Home in Victorian America*, 128.

civilization, and peace, Harriet Beecher Stowe struggled with her own role as mother of six children. She described the chaos of having small children who would not even let her finish dressing properly and who were constantly getting into mischief.[18] She also described how motherhood was turning her into a dull and "uninteresting person," a "mere drudge with few ideas beyond babies and housekeeping."[19] Beecher Stowe longed for a room of her own and even set one up for herself almost a half-century before Virginia Woolf made such a longing famous.[20]

Moral Mothering and Maternal Self-Sacrifice

The evangelical moralism of the Reformation that established the domestic sphere as a place of true Christian faith under the guidance of the mother also left a legacy that claimed *white* European mothers were special. Motherhood was so important to the Protestant imagination that even the process of birthing was given positive Christian symbolism in sixteenth-century Germany. Birthing women were seen as experiencing the cross in the same way that Jesus Christ did. Like pregnant women, Jesus suffered for the sake of new life. Because of this analogous connection between birthing mothers and Jesus himself, Martin Luther and Lutheran pastors insisted that female saints favored by women such as Anne or Margaret could offer nothing of comfort or help to mothers in labor. Instead, women in childbirth were encouraged to turn directly to Christ to make meaning of their suffering.[21] Devotional literature

18 Harriet Beecher Stowe, *The Life of Harriet Beecher Stowe: Compiled from Her Letters and Journals by Her Son, Charles Edward Stowe* (New York: Houghton, Mifflin, 1890), 90–92.

19 Stowe, *Life of Harriet Beecher Stowe*, 92.

20 Stowe, *Life of Harriet Beecher Stowe*, 104.

21 See Martin Luther, "Vom ehelichen Leben (1522)," in *D. Martin Luthers Werke: Kritische Gesamtausgabe*, ed. Karl Drescher, vol. 10/2 (Weimar: Böhlau, 1907), 296. There he says, "This is also how to comfort and encourage a woman in the pangs of childbirth, not by repeating legends of Saint Margaret and other silly old wives' tales but by speaking thus: 'Dear Grete, remember that you are a woman, and that this work of God in you is pleasing to him. Trust joyfully in his will and let him have his way with you. Work with all your might to bring forth the child. Should it mean your death, then depart happily, for you will die in a noble deed and in subservience to God.'" Translation from *Luther's Works*, vol. 45, ed. and trans. Walther I. Brandt (Philadelphia: Fortress, 1962), 40.

such as Jakob Zader's *Cross-School for Pregnant and Bearing Women* (1610/1612) reflected this Lutheran theology that glorified the self-sacrificial nature of giving birth.[22]

Humanism also encouraged maternal self-sacrifice. Humanist philosophers believed that the mother-child relationship was a "medium for repairing human failures."[23] Thinkers like Erasmus of Rotterdam (1466–1536) believed that God endowed women with special capacities for morality that were absent in men. Erasmus and other male humanists argued that the mother-child bond of attachment brought out the innate morality of women and the God-given capacities for self-sacrifice that male thinkers believed were unique to females. To humanists, the mother-child bond of attachment created an energy that would transform the mother into someone who was a better, more moral person after having a child. A mother would be willing to sacrifice herself for her child, and hence, she would raise moral children who in turn would contribute to an orderly society and build up a better civilization.

These potent Reformation and humanist ideas played out in Puritan households throughout the early American colonies. The famous Puritan preacher, Cotton Mather (1663–1728), used his pulpit to instruct Puritan mothers to fast and pray for the welfare of their children. He preached that good mothers would labor twice for their children: once in birth and again for their spiritual well-being.[24] The novel *Pamela*, written by Samuel Richardson in 1744, tells the tale of a mother who gave everything for the well-being of her young son and even jeopardized her own health to make sure he was breastfed. The novel lays out the image of a moral, pious,

[22] See Kathleen M. Crowther, *Adam and Eve in the Protestant Reformation* (Cambridge: Cambridge University Press, 2010), 177–79. The German original title is *Schwangern und geberenden Weibern Creutz Schuel / darinn sie sich mit hertzlichem Trost und Gebet /sowohl als mit ihrem Wochengeräthlich / zu ihrer Kindergeburt / täglich rüsten und schicken können* (Wittenberg, 1612).

[23] Brigitte H. E. Niestroj, "Women as Mothers and the Making of the European Mind: A Contribution to the History of Developmental Psychology and Primary Socialization," *Journal for the Theory of Social Behavior* 24, no. 3 (1994): 281–303, here 284.

[24] Janet Wilson James notes that these were common themes in Cotton Mather's sermons. See Janet Wilson James, "'Vertuous Women Found': New England Ministerial Literature 1668–1735," in *Women in American Religion*, 67–87, here 70.

and Christian mother who sacrifices everything, even herself, for the good of her children. James Miller, writing in the Presbyterian paper *Weekday Religion*, gave such self-sacrificial behavior divine sanction. He wrote that women working in the home were engaging in "self-forgetful ministries."[25]

The humanist ethics of the Reformation era, which promoted maternal self-sacrifice, lifted mothers in the Protestant imagination to new heights. Mothers were seen as saviors because they had a "natural godly character" and they engaged in "conscious religious activities."[26] Lydia Sigourney (1791–1865) in her *Letters to Mothers* stated that mothers shared omnipotence with God, and she praised the "omnipotent quality of maternal influence."[27] Henry Wright, in his book *The Empire of the Mother*, stated that the mother stands between "God and her unborn babe," and with the right moral attitude, white mothers had the potential to be "the Messiah and Savior of the race."[28] A newspaper statement from the *Public Ledger and Daily Transcript* (1848) viewed mothers as being "next to God, all powerful."[29] Journalism, novels, and literature were filled with the theological idea that mothers were the mediators between the unsaved world of men and children and the love of God.

White mothers were also seen as the mediators of civilization in a land that felt profoundly uncivilized to European colonizers. Christianity, after all, was the heart of civilization in European lands. The "Republican Motherhood" of early America already promoted the centrality of the mother as European settlers pushed westward across North America.[30] Mothers became "true women"

[25] James Miller, *Weekday Religion* (Philadelphia: Presbyterian Board of Publication, 1880), quoted in McDannell, *Christian Home in Victorian America*, 128.

[26] McDannell, *Christian Home in Victorian America*, 130.

[27] Lydia Sigourney, *Letters to Mothers* (Hartford: Hudson and Skinner, 1838), quoted in Deborah C. DeRosa, "Seditious Histories: The Abolitionist Mother-Historian," in *Domestic Abolitionism and Juvenile Literature 1830–1865* (Albany: SUNY Press, 2003), 81.

[28] Henry Clark Wright, *The Empire of the Mother Over the Character and Destiny of the Race* (Boston: Bela Marsh, 1863), cited in Kimball, *Religious Ideas of Harriet Beecher Stowe*, 78–79.

[29] Nyasha Junior, *An Introduction to Womanist Biblical Interpretation* (Louisville: Westminster John Knox, 2015), 24.

[30] See Jodi Vandenberg-Daves, "Inventing a New Role for Mothers," in *Modern Motherhood: An American History* (New Brunswick, N.J.: Rutgers University Press, 2014), 11–31.

when they educated their children in virtuous living and when they taught them to read and write. Mothers "manufactured" good citizens of American society.[31]

Such soaring religious rhetoric about mothers reached an apex in the nineteenth century. Magazines and other widely circulated tracts trumpeted white women as the mothers of the entire human race. *Godey's* magazine promoted the idea that women's duties were holier than the work of men. Women's work was nothing less than civilizing men and children.[32] Tracts such as the *Presbyterian Review* promoted the Christian commitment to women becoming mothers, remaining in the home, being morally superior people, and sacrificing themselves for the good of their children, men, and households. The following quote encapsulates the white Protestant Christian imagination about mothers:

> Woman reaches her highest glory, not on the platform, nor even in the missionary field as teacher or laborer, but in the center of the home. There is the throne of her power, and above every other name that can be given her is that of mother. The world needs more teachers, and missionaries, and helpers, but not so much as it needs Christian wives and mothers . . . Unquestionably, it is in the relation of mother that the influence of woman is the most powerful in the world. Nor is there a nobler being on the earth than a self-sacrificing Christian mother, "She who rocks the cradle rules the world."[33]

Mothers embodied the virtues of industriousness, cleanliness, frugality, and—most significantly and perhaps long-lastingly—self-sacrifice.

The lofty rhetoric that scaffolded motherhood in eighteenth- and nineteenth-century Protestant thought had a polarizing effect on ideas about women and coalesced around the "Cult of True

31 Barbara Welter, "The Cult of True Womanhood: 1820–1860," *American Quarterly* 18, no. 2 (1966): 151–74. This was a part of the "Republican Motherhood" movement in the Revolutionary War and beyond.

32 Kimball, *Religious Ideas of Harriet Beecher Stowe*, 79.

33 Samuel J. Niccolls, "Woman's Position and Work in the Church," *Presbyterian Review* 10, no. 38 (1889), quoted in *Women and Religion in America*, ed. Rosemary Radford Ruether and Rosemary Skinner Keller, vol. 1, *The Nineteenth Century* (San Francisco: Harper and Row, 1981), 229.

Womanhood."[34] Either you were a mother—and hence moral and Christian—or you were a whore, a shrew, or other kind of unnatural woman.[35] When a woman did not strictly perform these Christian duties of house, husband, and children, they were often rejected and seen as not a true woman. There was little room in the Christian imagination for any other kind of female agency or way of being woman in the world. The medieval religious structures of nunneries and convents that allowed women to take on all kinds of work as alternatives to motherwork, including secular, profitable work such as that of the Beguines in France, were greatly diminished and restricted.[36] Female saints like Mary, Anne, and Margaret, who were favored by women themselves, were erased from Protestant thought. The most valuable and approved position of a woman in American Protestantism was mother.

The Cult of True Womanhood led to serious debate and splits among women in North America. Critics of Victorian norms and the Protestant cult of the mother such as Frances (Fanny) Wright argued that such norms and religious rhetoric placed a tremendous burden upon women to be consistently performing religiosity and morality in ways that did not let women be "flesh and blood."[37] She was the first woman to address a mixed-gender audience in the United States on social issues and was a dedicated abolitionist and reformer.[38] But she was also despised among white Christian mothers for how she refused to maintain the middle-class values of humility, domesticity, religiosity, and self-sacrifice for one's children. A true woman and good Christian mother remained in the home with "her Bible and a well-balanced mind."[39] True women were white Christian mothers who protected the virtue of themselves, their husbands, and their children. They were not out and about fulfilling their ambitions or lecturing to men.

[34] See Barbara Welter, *Dimity Convictions: The American Woman in the Nineteenth Century* (Athens: Ohio University Press, 1976).

[35] Naomi Miller and Naomi Yavneh, *Maternal Measures: Figuring Caregiving in the Early Modern Period* (Burlington, Vt.: Ashgate 2000), 121.

[36] Laura Swan, *The Wisdom of the Beguines: The Forgotten Story of a Medieval Women's Movement* (Katonah, N.Y.: BlueBridge, 2014), 71–84.

[37] Kimball, *Religious Ideas of Harriet Beecher Stowe*, 77.

[38] For more on the amazing Frances (Fanny) Wright, see Celia Morris, *Fanny Wright: Rebel in America* (Urbana: University of Illinois Press, 1992).

[39] Welter, "Cult of True Womanhood," 172.

White Mothers and the "Christian" Mission to Indigenous Mothers

The potent imagination about the importance of white mothers that dominated Protestant theology in America had spectacular results for the European colonizers. White European mothers actively engaged in the male violence that colonized vast stretches of North America. Rather than being a passive onlooker to destructive American policies, Protestant maternalism was inextricably tied up in the devastating theology of Manifest Destiny, which specifically identified the mission of Christianity to "civilize" the peoples who were already dwelling in North America.[40] Protestant maternalism supported the coercive schooling of Indigenous people in the virtues of Christian Europeans. These virtues, such as obedience to male figures, cleanliness, silence, and domesticity, were exemplified by white Protestant mothers. Protestant maternalism helped Christian Europeans fulfill their economic ambitions and what they thought was their destiny to settle and take the land upon which Indigenous people lived.[41]

A key piece to the theology of Protestant motherhood was the fact that white women saw their destiny tied to the destiny of white men. A pamphlet by Samuel J. Niccolls argued that white men and women were locked in a bond that could not be broken:

> Nature and experience teach that the two sexes are joined together in indissoluble wedlock, and neither socially nor morally can one prosper without the other. As in Paradise, so now, they must rise or fall together: "The woman's cause is man's; they rise or sink/Together, dwarfed or God-like, bond or free."[42]

As a part of the male ambition to rule over American lands, white mothers were expected to protect the domestic "sacred space" from the influences of cross-racial relationships. They were to make the home a space where men could find respite and familiarity. The mixing of Protestant faith in God and the agenda of white European colonial thought literally found a home in the domestic

[40] The term Manifest Destiny was first used publicly by the journalist John O'Sullivan in 1845.

[41] See John F. Berens, *Providence and Patriotism in Early America 1640–1815* (Charlottesville: University Press of Virginia, 1978), 113–170.

[42] Niccolls, "Woman's Position and Work in the Church," 267.

sphere. Protecting the household as a *religious* space also meant that white Protestant mothers had to protect it as a *culturally white European* space.

There were numerous Christian missions that involved Protestant mothers. Women who were involved in social and political reform groups such as the National Congress of Mothers sought to bring the domestic, maternal voice out from the home and apply its morality and religiosity to the endeavors of colonizing North American land. One president of the National Congress of Mothers, Hannah Schoff, wrote in 1905 that "there is the spirit of the Lord that is the mother that mothers all children, and it is because the world lacks that, that the conditions of the children of this country have not been better."[43] Amelia S. Quinton stated about white Protestant women, "Let *us* women give to the destitute tribes Christian homes and missions, for without these no race can rise."[44] Just as male colonizers saw themselves as engaging in benevolent paternalism among Indian peoples, so white women saw themselves as "maternalists."[45] Tucked into this statement is white Protestant mothers' beliefs that Indigenous women were not providing proper homes for their children and, moreover, that white mothers would be able to civilize the Indian peoples without the kind of brutality and violence that they witnessed their men doing.[46]

Despite this notion of a kinder, gentler colonizing hand popular among maternalists, the Christian imagination—with its rhetoric about white women as high priestesses of the home and moral messiahs of humanity—had devastating consequences for Indigenous mothers. Protestant positioning of white mothers as

[43] Quoted in Margaret D. Jacobs, "Maternal Colonialism: White Women and Indigenous Child Removal in the American West and Australia, 1880–1940," *Western Historical Quarterly* 36 (2005): 453–76, here 462.

[44] Amelia S. Quinton, "Annual Address," in *Indian's Friend* (1889), quoted in Newman, *White Women's Rights*, 116.

[45] Jacobs, "Maternal Colonialism," 456.

[46] On this point, see Frances Willard's address in *Transactions of the National Council in the United States* (1891), quoted in Newman, *White Women's Rights*, 116. Women such as Amelia S. Quinton and Alice Fletcher, as well as many other female participants in the Indian Reform movement, felt that the way Indian peoples were being handled both by European men and by the U.S. government was brutal and unnecessary. These women advocated for Indian rights even though Fletcher was involved in slicing up Indian land into parcels of private property, which in the end hurt Indigenous cultures.

agents of God's civilizing will in an untamed landscape gave white mothers license to view Indigenous women as uncivilized—*and as bad mothers*. White mothers such as Estelle Reel joined social reform groups in order to civilize Indigenous children because it seemed to them that the children's own Indigenous mothers were not caring for them or educating them properly.[47] White Protestant mothers believed that Indigenous mothers were slaves to their men and they seemed to believe that the word "squaw" was derogatory.[48] They believed that Indigenous women were sexually promiscuous and that they did not care about their children: the Indigenous practice of cradle boarding infants was exhibit A for child neglect.[49] Reel and many other white Christian mothers believed it was their maternalistic duty to rescue Indigenous children from the supposed savagery of their own cultures and the putatively neglectful style of their own mothers. It was mostly the women's domain in the colonial project to dispossess—or separate—children from their Indigenous, biological mothers in the name of "civilizing" the children.

Hence, many white Christian mothers harmed Indigenous people by directly targeting the most intimate of human bonds: that of mother and child. One would think that because white Protestant women were mothers who experienced the strength of the mother-child bond themselves, they would honor the mother-child bond among Indigenous people. If anyone understood in the most visceral and intimate fashion what it means to be bonded with one's child, it would have been them. But sadly, the opposite was true. White Protestant women remained firmly entrenched in their religious and cultural beliefs that *they* knew best what was right for every home and that the only form of "civilization" was the Christian form.[50] Any sense that the mother-child bond was a shared experience among Indigenous women was subjugated to white women's views of themselves as superior.

[47] Estelle Reel was the superintendent of Indian education for the Office of Indian Affairs from 1898–1910. See K. Tsianina Lomawaima and T. Tsianina Lomawaima, "Estelle Reel, Superintendent of Indian Schools, 1898–1910: Politics, Curriculum, and Land," *Journal of American Indian Education* 35, no. 3 (1996): 5–31.

[48] Newman, *White Women's Rights*, 116–17.

[49] Jacobs, "Maternal Colonialism," 463–64.

[50] Jacobs, "Maternal Colonialism," 462.

Enslaved African Mothers

No exploration of Christianity and motherhood in North America could be complete without comparing and contrasting how white Protestant mothers and Black enslaved mothers engaged the faith. Slavery is a shameful part of American history that must inform any analysis of the Protestant imagination and its relationship to motherhood in the eighteenth and nineteenth centuries in America. While white Protestant mothers were struggling for their place in the gender hierarchy of the European colonies and supporting white racial supremacy, enslaved African mothers were learning the Bible and utilizing it to help their own biological children and the children of others in the face of the desperately inhumane "Christian" policies of the transatlantic slave trade. Every aspect of Black American motherhood has been touched by the legacy of slavery and Black women's subsequent disenfranchisement in American society. In particular, they have been uniquely impacted by the traumas of sexual violence suffered by enslaved African mothers.[51] From the fact that Black women are a major part of the work force but continue to earn less than their white counterparts,[52] to their struggles with the government-sanctioned infusion of illegal drugs into Black communities,[53] to acts of police violence upon the sons of Black mothers[54] and the sexism that Black mothers face in their own church communities,[55] it is not an exaggeration to claim that enslaved women and their descendants have mothered under

[51] See for instance, Delores Williams, *Sisters in the Wilderness: The Challenge of Womanist God-Talk* (New York: Orbis, 1993), 15–19.

[52] See "Five Facts about Black Women in the Labor Force," U.S. Department of Labor, accessed November 5, 2021, https://blog.dol.gov/2021/08/03/5-facts-about-black-women-in-the-labor-force.

[53] On how President Ronald Reagan set racist policies while encouraging the drug supply within Black communities, see Ibram X. Kendi, *Stamped from the Beginning* (New York: Nation Books, 2016), 424–39.

[54] See for instance Morgan Hornsby, "'Stranger Fruit': Black Mothers and the Fear of Police Brutality," The Marshall Project, March 22, 2021, https://www.themarshallproject.org/2021/03/22/stranger-fruit-black-mothers-and-the-fear-of-police-brutality; Rita Omokha, "They Were Sons," *Vanity Fair*, May 6, 2021, https://www.vanityfair.com/news/2021/05/they-were-sons-mothers-of-black-men-killed-by-police-remember-their-losses.

[55] See for instance TeResa Green, "A Gendered Spirit: Race, Class, and Sex in the African American Church," *Race, Gender and Class* 10, no. 1 (2003): 115–28.

impossible conditions that still impact Black women and their families today.[56]

The legal, social, economic, and political cultures that grew up around the chattel slave trade of African men and women in North America deeply influenced how the Christian faith treated enslaved African mothers. Although none of these topics or numerous others on the realities of Black Christian motherhood can be explored here in appropriate detail, it is important to understand that in relation to mothering and the Christian faith, enslaved African mothers were subjected to a different set of experiences, beliefs, and challenges than white Protestant mothers. In other words, Black mothers experience an entirely different engagement with the Christian imagination. In a nutshell, it can be plausibly argued that while white Protestant mothers engaged in a theology of supremacy, enslaved African mothers were constructing their own Christian theologies of *survival.* Although Christianity was imposed upon enslaved African mothers, they were adaptable enough to engage this foreign faith as a tool for helping their destroyed families stay in touch and their oppressed children survive.[57]

At its most fundamental, the Christian imagination about enslaved African mothers was influenced by pseudoscientific theories of the different "races" of humanity. These pseudoscientific theories ranked human ethnicities and groups based on their outward appearances and cultural practices.[58] "Whiteness" was a European ideal of beauty,[59] and European cultural practices were seen as superior to all other cultures, including Islamic, African, Asian, and Indigenous North American cultures. As such, dark-skinned enslaved women were seen as inferior humans to white women. Therefore, they supposedly did not need the kinds of legal and social protections that white women deserved. One of the most destructive laws of the colonial time period was the law of "*partus*

[56] See Patricia Hill Collins, *Black Feminist Thought* (New York: Routledge, 2009), 51–215.

[57] Margaret D. Jacobs, *White Mother to a Dark Race: Settler Colonialism, Maternalism, and the Removal of Indigenous Children in the American West and Australia, 1880–1940* (Lincoln: University of Nebraska Press, 2009).

[58] See J. Kameron Carter, *Race: A Theological Account* (New York: Oxford University Press, 2008), 80–108, esp. 91.

[59] See Nell Irvin Painter, *A History of White People* (New York: W. W. Norton, 2010), 59–71.

sequitur ventrem."[60] This devastating and deeply inhumane law considered enslaved African women's children the property of their masters.[61] In other words, the children of enslaved African mothers *were not theirs*. This law also encouraged white masters to sexually assault enslaved women in order to produce more enslaved children.[62] Enslaved African mothers faced the constant threat of being separated from their children, often never to see them again.

Pseudoscientific racial theories also influenced the medical treatment of enslaved African women. Medical professionals often mistreated enslaved African mothers based on false racial biases. Black women were mistakenly believed to be tougher than white women and therefore more able to work in fields. It was even believed that they felt less pain than white women, a legacy which today still haunts Black mothers within the American medical system.[63] Such racial theories also doubted that enslaved mothers made deep and lasting bonds with their children. Both points are false. Enslaved mothers suffered the same kinds of pregnancy ailments and birth pains as any woman of lighter-colored skin; their bodies worked in the same ways as those of white women in labor and in nursing; and the bonds between mother and child were as strong as any mother-child bond in the white population.

Black feminists were already writing about these issues in the nineteenth century. They showed the traumatic, tragic realities of splitting up enslaved children and babies from their mothers. Sojourner Truth wrote about this issue as did Frances Watkins

[60] In English: "That which is brought forth follows the womb."

[61] Junior, *Introduction to Womanist Biblical Interpretation*, 43, citing the law: *partus sequitur ventrem*. See also Katherine Clay Bassard, *Transforming Scriptures: African American Women Writers and the Bible* (Athens: University of Georgia Press, 2011), 3.

[62] See Karen Cook Bell, *Running from Bondage: Enslaved Women and Their Remarkable Fight for Freedom in Revolutionary America* (Cambridge: Cambridge University Press, 2021), 23.

[63] Modern practices of gynecology and the C-section were developed using enslaved mothers' bodies, usually without any kind of pain relief. See Brynn Holland, "The 'Father of Modern Gynecology' Performed Shocking Experiments on Enslaved Women," History.com, December 4, 2018, https://www.history.com/news/the-father-of-modern-gynecology-performed-shocking-experiments-on-slaves; "Medical Exploitation of Black Women," Equal Justice Initiative, August 29, 2019, https://eji.org/news/history-racial-injustice-medical-exploitation-of-black-women/.

Harper in her well-known poem from 1854, "The Slave Mother."[64] Harper's poem depicts in heart-wrenching imagery the sheer, unbearable anguish that slave mothers experienced as they were forced to give up their children:

> Saw you the sad, imploring eye?
> Its every glance was pain,
> As if a storm of agony
> Were sweeping through the brain.
>
> She is a mother pale with fear,
> Her boy clings to her side,
> And in her kyrtle vainly tries
> His trembling form to hide.
>
> He is not hers, although she bore
> For him a mother's pains;
> He is not hers, although her blood
> Is coursing through his veins!
>
> He is not hers, for cruel hands
> May rudely tear apart
> The only wreath of household love
> That binds her breaking heart . . .
>
> They tear him from her circling arms,
> Her last and fond embrace.
> Oh! never more may her sad eyes
> Gaze on his mournful face.
>
> No marvel, then, these bitter shrieks
> Disturb the listening air:
> She is a mother, and her heart
> Is breaking in despair.[65]

[64] See Nell Irvin Painter, *Sojourner Truth: A Life, A Symbol* (New York: W. W. Norton, 1996), 11–12.

[65] Just a few lines of the 1854 poem will have to suffice here to illustrate this reality for slave mothers. Frances Watkins Harper, *The Slave-Mother*, in *American Poetry: The Nineteenth Century* (New York: Library of America, 1993), available online at https://www.poetryfoundation.org/poems/51977/the-slave-mother-56d23017ceaad.

Such traumatic scenes of children being sold away from their mothers were common; they were witnessed live in slave auctions and depicted in art of the period as well. The practice of selling babies and children from their enslaved mothers is a clear and indisputable example of how Christian ideals did not resist the greater forces of racism, white supremacy, economic exploitation, and abuse that enslaved African mothers experienced.

Unfortunately, despite Christianity's universal message of God's love for the world and the promise of Jesus Christ as the salvation for all humanity, white Christians did not apply these humanizing aspects to dark-skinned, enslaved women. In fact, Protestant theology actively promoted the so-called "Curse of Ham" from Genesis chapter 9.[66] The white Protestant interpretation of this biblical story, where Noah actually curses Ham's son Canaan (and not Ham, in fact), was used to support the white supremacist belief that dark-skinned peoples were inferior. It pointed to the Bible to show that it was God's will that people with dark skin were to be subject to white European rule. Sermons and teachings about obedience to one's master abounded. Biblical passages like Ephesians 6:5 (NRSV), "slaves obey your earthly masters with fear and trembling, in singleness of heart, as you obey Christ," were fixtures in preaching and teaching to enslaved people.

Because Christians believed people with dark skin were descendants of Ham and therefore cursed, they debated whether they ought to try to convert slaves from their pagan ways. Throughout the American colonies and well into the nineteenth century, Christian leaders argued about converting and baptizing enslaved people to Christianity. If enslaved peoples became believers, they would then have the right to take Sundays off from work, for example, and they would be able to challenge the harsh treatment visited upon them by white masters: they would have the rights of other Christians.[67] Christianity, it seems, was not ready for that.

Enslaved African mothers fought the system of slavery at every turn. Numerous accounts of enslaved women running away—with their children, ahead of their children, or following

[66] Stephen R. Haynes, *Noah's Curse: The Biblical Justification of American Slavery*, Religion in America (Oxford: Oxford University Press, 2002).

[67] Marcus W. Jernegan, "Slavery and Conversion in the American Colonies," *American Historical Review* 21, no. 3 (1916): 504–27.

their children—can be found throughout scholarly treatments of the era of slavery in North America.[68] Frequently, slave mothers would risk the lives of their family members to reach northern states, taking young children along with them. Their plight was dangerous and lonely.[69] Even when an enslaved woman escaped to freedom, if she could not produce papers of her identity or emancipation, she could go to prison, and her children would be taken from her.[70] Enslaved mothers were constantly rebelling against their masters and constantly bearing the brunt of punishment. They were also constantly protective of the well-being and fate of their own children and the children of other enslaved mothers around them.[71] Enslaved African women mothered as fugitives. They mothered as rebels against the slave system. They mothered without any legal or social power.

For enslaved African mothers, the Bible was the most reliable source for understanding the white, European Christian faith. Many of the stories from the Bible were able to be handed down orally. Further, the Biblical stories depicted a God who was vastly different from the God that enslaved people heard preached. White preachers utilized their pulpits to uphold the slave system and validate white supremacy; they constantly referred to Jesus' sayings about the blessedness of the "meek" and obedience to one's master.[72] Even slaves who became preachers were not as trusted

[68] See for example the Cairns Collection of American Women Writers at the University of Wisconsin-Madison, https://www.library.wisc.edu/specialcollections/collections/the-william-b-cairns-collection-of-american-women-writers-1650-1940/; William L. Andrews, ed., *Six Women's Slave Narratives*, Schomburg Library of Nineteenth-Century Black Women Writers (New York: Oxford University Press, 1988); S. Charles Bolton, *Fugitivism: Escaping Slavery in the Lower Mississippi Valley 1820–1860* (Fayetteville: University of Arkansas Press, 2019); Sydney Nathans, *To Free a Family: The Journey of Mary Walker* (Cambridge, Mass.: Harvard University Press, 2013); and Ronnie W. Clayton, ed., *Mother Whit: The Ex-Slave Narratives of the Louisiana Writers' Project* (New York: Peter Lang, 1990), among others.

[69] Annie Burton's and Kate Drumgoold's narratives in *Six Women's Slave Narratives*, 11ff., 6ff.

[70] Bell, *Running from Bondage*, 133.

[71] Linda Brent, *Incidents in the Life of a Slave Girl* (Boston: Linda Brent, Boston Stereotype Foundry, 1861), 36. Brent depicts her grandmother's constant efforts to secure the freedom of her children with reliance on God's help.

[72] Frequently used Bible passages were Col 3:22–25; Eph 6:5–8; and 1 Pet 2:18–20.

as the Bible itself.[73] White supremacist uses of Christianity aimed for docility among rebellious and restless slaves, leading enslaved peoples to turn to the Bible to hear and understand a very different message about themselves and about God.

Shaped by their harrowing experiences of mothering and the moral dissonance between what they heard preached compared to what they heard from the Bible, enslaved African mothers developed a unique hermeneutic of reading Scripture that focused on survival, connection, and internal dignity, including loving one's self.[74] Black slave mothers viewed the Bible through the lenses of survival and self-love, and they did everything they could to convey those messages to their children. Many enslaved African mothers looked for messages of endurance and justice from the Bible. They sought out passages that gave them strength and courage to go on. One popular passage was that of Philippians 4:13: "I can do all things in him who strengthens me." Other passages spoke to how enslaved mothers had to do so much undercover, in the dark, and in constant anxiety and fear. Proverbs 30:5b spoke to those realities: "Weeping may remain for a night, but rejoicing comes in the morning."

As free and enslaved African people began adopting Christianity, Black spirituality grew into a rich mixture of Christian beliefs and traditional African religious practices.[75] Enslaved African mothers drew upon both Christian ideas and African supernaturalism in their struggles to keep themselves and their children alive. Much of this "slave religion" took place in secret places such as "hush harbors" or in other extra-ecclesial ways.[76] Much more scholarly attention needs to be paid to how enslaved mothers engaged in the ritual of "conjuring" to protect themselves and

[73] Albert J. Raboteau, *Slave Religion: The "Invisible Institution" in the Antebellum South* (New York: Oxford University Press, 1978), 290–318.

[74] Williams, *Sisters in the Wilderness*, 19–20.

[75] Yvonne Chireau, "The Uses of the Supernatural: Toward a History of Black Women's Magical Practices," in *A Mighty Baptism: Race, Gender, and the Creation of American Protestantism*, ed. Susan Juster and Lisa MacFarlane (Ithaca, N.Y.: Cornell University Press, 1996), 174–75.

[76] Raboteau, *Slave Religion*, 211–88. "Hush Harbors" have been a recent topic of interest. See Jessica Brodie, "The Message of the Hush Harbor: History and Theology of African Descent Traditions," *South Carolina United Methodist Advocate*, March 1, 2019, https://advocatesc.org/2019/03/the-message-of-the-hush-harbor-history-and-theology-of-african-descent-traditions/.

to thwart the domination of their owners.[77] While white Protestant preachers debated whether to even convert their slaves to Christianity, Black mothers and their children were constructing a new form of Reformation Christianity: one that would help them in their impossible situations.

Along with survival, enslaved Black mothers fought to keep connections to their children and extended families. They did not have the luxury of an exalted domestic sphere or the freedom to move about in order to maintain familial connections. Because slave mothers had no control of the destiny or safety of their children, they often relied on othermothers to help raise them. These were aunts, neighbors, grandmothers, helpers—anyone who cared. For Black mothers, this othermothering was a part of their sense of the connection of all Black people. The story of Hagar became paradigmatic of God's promises to enslaved African mothers. Hagar was a mother who could do nothing but rely on the promise of God to save her and her child. Her story shows that God did indeed save Hagar and her child, suggesting that God would do the same for enslaved women in America. The saying that "we are all Aunt Haggie's Children" encapsulates the Black mother's hermeneutic of connection—and the connection to God's promises for those who suffer.[78] Thanks to the tenacity of enslaved African mothers, the collective Black religious consciousness today has a robust sense of spiritual fortitude.

A further priority for enslaved African mothers' use of the Bible was the commitment to self-love and teaching their children to love themselves. Enslaved African mothers often drew upon the Song of Solomon and the Shulamite woman to claim their own agency and desire: "I am black but beautiful."[79] Black mothers did what they could to pass this self-love down to their children, teaching them on the one hand to act with care towards others because the Bible commands it but, on the other hand, also teaching them to discard those parts of the Bible that don't affirm love of self, cultural pride, and connection to community. One famous example of this is the

77 Chireau, "Uses of the Supernatural," 176–77, 187. As Chireau points out, academic scholarship still lacks a robust paradigm into which enslaved African women's spirituality fits.

78 Teresa L. Fry Brown, *God Don't Like Ugly: African American Women Handing on Spiritual Values* (Nashville: Abingdon, 2000), 83–84.

79 Bassard, *Transforming Scriptures*, 19–21.

grandmother of the well-known theologian Howard Thurman, who had been born into slavery. As the story goes, Howard Thurman's grandmother told of how white ministers often abused the Pauline passages on slavery. She claimed that if she ever learned to read the Bible, she would never again read those parts of Paul.[80]

It was these "higher goods" that constituted what Womanist theologians have called a "Mother Whit."[81] This was the instinct that enslaved African mothers developed for danger, for abusive people, as well as for chances to assert one's dignity, or even to rebel and escape. Biblical passages and stories that supported the knowledge to survive, to hold on, to connect, and to love oneself were the passages that held meaning for enslaved African Christian mothers.

Frances Harper Watkins' 1869 poem "Moses: A Story of the Nile"[82] illustrates the complexity of enslaved African mothers' positions in the survival and faith of their children. By the 1860s, there was a nascent Black theology movement, especially among freed slaves and free Black people. They were becoming ministers and forming Christian communities that became places for education, housing, and other forms of care for Black people. Early Black theologians saw themselves as the Ethiopian and Egyptian princes that are mentioned in the Exodus and Psalm 68:31. Such princes were taken out of their countries and sent to the promised land—America—to build up a new society. In other words, Black people were beginning to see how Christianity could be used for their *own* empowerment. Although much of Harper's epic poem focuses on Moses' fate among the Egyptians, his decision to return to his Hebrew family, and the grief of Pharoah's daughter at his departure, the depiction of Jochebed, Moses' Hebrew biological mother, gives insight into the figure of the enslaved African mother.

[80] From Howard Thurman, *Jesus and the Disinherited* (New York: Abingdon-Cokesbury Press, 1949), 30–31.

[81] Brown, *God Don't Like Ugly*, 83–84.

[82] Barbara Johnson makes the argument that Moses' life and his decision to return to his people rather than living a privileged life is a reflection of Harper's own decisions. She was born a free Black woman who could have lived a nice life, but instead, she chose to return to her people, so to speak, and use her work and her platform to fight for the rights of those enslaved. See Barbara Johnson, *Moses and Multiculturalism* (Berkeley: University of California Press, 2010), 42–43.

Harper depicts Moses' return to his biological family from the house of the Pharoah as bittersweet. She describes how he finds them toiling and aged under their labor, poor, and in rough physical shape. Once she has her own son back in her presence, Moses' mother recounts how she strategized for his survival when he was an infant, how she decided to save him from Pharaoh's murderous plan, how she wove the grass for Moses' "ark," and how she laid him among the grasses and lilies of the Nile.[83] She tells him that she never lost faith in him, even when news came to the family that he might take an oath to become a permanent member of the Pharoah's family.[84] Harper then has Moses answer his mother in a very moving monologue that credits her—and it seems her alone—with making him the person he is. He tells her that when he was about to take an oath to the Pharaoh, Moses remembered his biological mother. It was this memory of his time with his mother that gave him the strength and resolve to refuse the oath.[85]

Harper illustrates the nature of the Christian faith among enslaved mothers. The faith of Moses' mother was a hushed, silent faith in the face of overwhelming powers and prejudices. But it was an effective faith nonetheless. The words of Moses' mother show that mothers facing poverty and oppression indeed found ways to save their children and help them survive. The fact that Moses' mother had heard news of the oath ceremony also shows that disenfranchised mothers who were separated from their children still tried to keep track of them and find out how they were doing. Although Moses' biological mother had no power in the system, as long as she had him in her presence, she could—and did—help him. When he was not in her presence, she believed in God and in her son.

Sojourner Truth, earlier known as Isabella when she was an enslaved mother, tells of the terrors and violence of being an enslaved mother. As a young woman, she was ignorantly proud that she had borne five children for her master—they were, after all, new laborers and economic wealth. From her own brutalized childhood, it was so ingrained in her to never steal or bother her

83 Frances Watkins Harper, "Moses: A Story of the Nile," in *Complete Poems of Frances E.W. Harper*, ed. Maryemma Graham, Schomburg Library of Nineteenth-Century Black Women Writers (New York: Oxford University Press, 1988), 44.

84 Harper, "Moses," 44.

85 Harper, "Moses," 40, 46.

masters that she let her children go hungry just to uphold her moral standards. However, she also took tremendous risks on behalf of her children. In 1872, when her master John Dumont reneged on his promise to free her and her enslaved husband Tom, as was their right under New York State law, Isabella took her little baby Sophia and simply left. She carried her baby, walking several miles to a safe house, where she then went on to freedom. She also took a huge risk in pursuing her son Peter when he had been illegally sold into slavery, and she attributed her courage to the power of God in her.[86] Sojourner Truth in many ways is an example of the "outraged mother" who was forced to raise children in a system that brutalized both Black mothers and their families but who still depended upon maternal instincts and felt maternal anguish when their children suffered the injustices that were a part of the American plantation slavery complex.[87] They depended upon friends, themselves, and God to get them through the severity of their life circumstances.

Other free Black women such as Jarena Lee and Zilpha Elaw engaged their Christian faith by becoming preachers along with being mothers.[88] They joined the ranks of hundreds of female itinerant preachers in the eighteenth and nineteenth centuries and engaged in benevolent work such as opening schools for Black children. These Black women who found their voices in the fledgling Black church viewed preaching and speaking publicly as their rights as Christians. This right was based in their *biblical* mandate rather than in some kind of *natural* right requiring secular feminists to fight for themselves.[89] Many felt that they were divinely sanctioned by God to travel freely and preach. Although their authority was often questioned, these Black mothers saw themselves as both nurturers of the Black community and as authorities on the Word.

[86] Rosetta R. Haynes, *Radical Spiritual Motherhood: Autobiography and Empowerment in Nineteenth-Century African American Women* (Baton Rouge: Louisiana State University Press, 2011), 148.

[87] Haynes, *Radical Spiritual Motherhood*, 154–55.

[88] Haynes argues that preachers like Jarena Lee, Zilpha Elaw, and Sojourner Truth (aka Isabella) had complex relationships to their children and to themselves as biological mothers, perhaps due to their difficulties within the racist chattel-slavery system in America. See Haynes, *Radical Spiritual Motherhood*, 81–84 and 153–55.

[89] Haynes, *Radical Spiritual Motherhood*, 29.

These radical, spiritual mothers often chose to remain unmarried after their husbands died in order to focus on their benevolent work and preaching. This gave them a spiritual power not unlike the Roman matrons in the early church who insisted on remaining celibate in order to fulfill an ideal of virginity. For many Black mothers who became spiritual mothers, celibacy was a form of sexual empowerment, allowing them to avoid the sexual exploitation that was such a devastating part of their motherhoods.[90]

Many of them cared for their own children while preaching or relied on extended family to help raise their children. Although they had paying jobs and traveled far and wide to preach, they also took on the cult of domesticity, both in order to fight negative stereotypes that they were ungovernable and unable to settle into society as well as to make themselves appear as respectable citizens next to their white counterparts. They enjoyed an "elasticity of the domestic sphere" that allowed them to have voice in the public sphere.[91]

The Complexities of White Protestant Maternalism

Protestant motherhood is a deeply complex issue, especially in American history and theology, where white supremacist notions have deeply impacted the Christian imagination, causing the realities of mothering and Christianity to be vastly different for free white women, enslaved women, and Indigenous women. Many white Protestant mothers found themselves both benefiting from white European supremacy and critiquing it for its inhuman treatment of non-European peoples.

Well-known Protestant mother-authors such as Lydia Maria Child and Harriet Beecher Stowe simultaneously promoted the evangelical conservativism of mothers in the home on the one hand *and* used their platforms as mothers on the other hand to call for social change, not just for themselves but also for enslaved African peoples and Indigenous peoples. Beecher Stowe connected the domesticity of the mother character Rachel Halliday to Christianity and anti-slavery politics. Lydia Marie Child gained widespread fame with her domestic manuals directed towards white Protestant mothers. However, she also wrote novels and pamphlets that

90 Haynes, *Radical Spiritual Motherhood*, 50.
91 Haynes, *Radical Spiritual Motherhood*, 62.

advocated for the rights of Indigenous people and enslaved Africans such as *An Appeal in Favor of that Class of Americans Called Africans* (1833). It is considered one of the first book-length treatments of abolition. She also wrote a book entitled *An Appeal for the Indians* (1868).

Other first-wave feminists utilized their roles as mothers to fight for white women's rights. Leaders such as Elizabeth Cady Stanton, Lucretia Mott, and Julia Ward Howe used the notion of maternal power to argue for more involvement by white women in the male-dominated public sphere. They were seen as "maternal feminists" for the ways they honored the religious agency and moral authority of mothers. Some maternal feminists such as Stanton blamed the Protestant clergy and the institutional church for confining women to the domestic sphere, essentially roping them off from public power, foreshadowing the modern feminist movement for women's ordination. Most confounding about the first-wave maternal feminists is their racism. Leaders of the women's suffrage movement, Elizabeth Cady Stanton and Susan B. Anthony, received support for their cause regarding the white women's vote from none other than ex-slave and abolitionist Frederick Douglass himself. But when it came time to fight to extend the vote to Black men, Stanton and Anthony refused.[92] What is worse, Black women were not even up for consideration.

First-wave feminists seemed to embrace the Christian and humanist ideas that the mother-child bond encouraged women to become moral agents, not just in their households but also in the public sphere. And yet they harbored a heinous blind spot to the struggles of enslaved, Indigenous, and African women who were also *mothers with bonds to their children.* Indigenous and enslaved African mothers also had moral compasses. They fought for their freedoms and the good of their children too. They loved their families and worked for their well-being just as white women who were struggling in the wildernesses of the New World did. But nineteenth-century, white, maternal feminists' call for an empathetic, moral, and Christian response to the suffering of

[92] For a brief but informative treatment of this issue, see Becky Little, "How Early Suffragists Left Black Women out of Their Fight," History.com, November 8, 2017, https://www.history.com/news/suffragists-vote-black-women.

other people was no match against powerful economic forces, political interests, and racial theories that kept dark-skinned mothers enslaved and wiped Indigenous populations off of North American lands.

Conclusion

Mothers and the Christian Imagination

This study has been an exercise in the old adage, "Change the way you look at things and the things you look at change." Only, it has flipped the script; in this book, I have changed the *things* we look at in the Christian tradition in the hopes that the *way* we look at the tradition can also change. By focusing on the numerous examples and stories of Christian women who were mothers and by paying special attention to how they utilized the faith for the benefit of themselves and their children, this study has sought to open new horizons for understanding Christianity and its theological narrative.

Despite patriarchy, official church doctrine, and a male-defined faith, it is fair to say that mothers have made the Christian tradition their own throughout history, and they continue to do so today. While the early church taught that women needed to leave behind their maternal bodies in order to participate in the resurrection, likening them to earthly attachments, powerful Roman mothers such as Melania and Paula utilized the new freedoms provided by ascetic Christian lifestyles to pursue their own spiritual ambitions. In another example, Christian ambivalence about the maternal body turned it into the most appropriate location for explaining God's deep love for humanity. Although thinkers like Tertullian used the limiting rhetoric of uterine shame, what they really pointed to was the way God relied on the uterine generosity of the maternal body for the greatest display of divine love: the Incarnation. Indeed, the church has celebrated Mary as a virgin, but thinkers from Anselm to Bernard of Clairvaux called upon her as a protective mother. While the medieval church was trying to clamp down on superstitions and the use of magic in the name of the all-powerful God, women banded together in their use of all kinds of material aids, spells, and prayers in a sisterhood that included midwives and female saints such as Margaret, Mary, and Anne in order to survive the perils of pregnancy, birth, and the postpartum period. Although the rite of churching was meant to purify the woman from the shame of birth, such groups of women turned it into a celebration of their hard motherwork and the generativity of the maternal body.

Mary's dominance faded after the Reformation, but the centrality of the mother in the Christian imagination did not. It was imported to the New World, where Christian motherhood took on new forms of power and empathy that were lived out by countless white Protestant mothers who saw themselves as the bearers of civilization and European values in a land of abundant nature. However, their heroism was an unmitigated disaster for innumerable enslaved African women and Indigenous mothers. The singular narrative of Christianity's colonial destiny in the New World that white Protestant mothers participated in bulldozed its way through Indigenous lands and resulted in the enslavement of African families. In order to survive, Black mothers did as so many centuries of women did before them: they adapted the aspects and promises of Christianity for a faith that would help them and their children. By directing their children to the faithfulness and goodness of God, enslaved mothers leveraged the best parts of the Christian tradition to help their children survive a brutally inhumane system of slavery. As Frances Watkins Harper showed in her poetry on Moses, the Christian faith—with its commitment to the justice of God and its biblical stories of strong people overcoming impossible situations—helped enslaved African women mother through suffering, uncertainty, inhumanity, and separation. Outraged mothers such as Sojourner Truth depended on God as she fought for freedom for her children.

Twenty-one centuries of Christian thought have shown that women who are mothers will continue to utilize the best parts of Christian teaching to help their offspring grow into adulthood. They will utilize the offerings of the institutional church for the well-being of themselves and their children. They will seek out Christian rituals and practices that help them cope with mothering as well as ones that help them celebrate the power of their bodies. If modern scientific theories are correct, babies will continue to attach to their mothers, just as mothers will attach to their children. The evolutionary and biological processes that have driven successful mothers to be strategists of survival and givers of nourishment and comfort will continue in modern motherhood. As their Christian sisters did in the past, successful mothers will continue to find the aspects of the Christian faith that offer the most protective, merciful, comforting, and educational advantages to their children.

Christian mothers throughout history have revealed those elements of the Christian religion that have been the most important to them. Eternal life was one of those concerns. Monica was desperate that her son Augustine become a Christian to avoid hell. Dhuoda insisted that her words to her son William were because she was concerned for his salvation. It could be argued that Roman mothers like Monica and Paula, and even Perpetua, believed that their spiritual glory would translate into eternal security for their children. But the eternal well-being of their offspring did not come at the expense of the well-being of their children here on earth. Monica did everything she could to give Augustine the best secular education. Dhuoda insisted that God would protect her sons in their servitude to the king, and Elizabeth Joscelin insisted that her children be well taken care of.

Another aspect of the Christian faith that was a priority for mothers was believing in a loving, comforting God. The maternal concept of God belied the view of a God who was out to war. In Julian of Norwich's maternal theology, God was a forgiving, gentle, nurturing being who cared for wayward humans. Tertullian depicted a loving, caring God who was willing to enter humanity through the vulnerable space of a woman's uterus. When fear pervaded Christian culture around the turn of the first millennium, it was Mary to whom Christians turned for comfort and for the promise of eternal life. Despite male control of Christian theology, lay people time and time again turned to maternal images and figures such as Margaret, Mary, and Anne, among many other female saints, in their times of need. It seems that those things that young children need—protection, comfort, and warmth—are also things that adults need. They have found them in the maternal aspects of the Christian faith.

Today, Christian mothers are joining the complex conversations around motherhood that are taking place in all corners of public discourse, from blogs, to conferences, to books. There is a thriving cottage industry of literature and self-help guidance aimed at white Christian mothers today. Bookstore shelves are stuffed with materials directed towards mothers on how to raise Christian children, create a Christian home, and find God's purpose in the everyday practices of motherwork. Conversations among Christians about mothering, especially within American Evangelical and Roman Catholic circles, are popular. What needs to be analyzed more closely is whether the broad field of contemporary Christian parenting (which is mostly directed towards mothers) is a continuation of the institution of white Protestant motherhood that suffocated the voices and creativity of non-white mothers or whether it represents a new chapter in how mothers are adapting the Christian faith to their modern needs.

In contrast to the lively conversations about motherhood among white Evangelical and Roman Catholic women, there seems to be a more muted conversation about Black motherhood and Christianity going on today. While Black women have been the backbone of the Black church in America, it seems that Black Christian mothers are charting their own path regarding how they mother their children and raise them up in the faith. Black Christian motherhood does not have the same overtones of raising up citizens who would be obedient to a white patriarchy, or dominating cultural themes in the way that white Christian mothers have done and still do.[1] Perhaps this is because Black mothers were not allowed to build up their own ideologies of motherhood *or* Christianity. White people defined both of these institutions for and *upon* Black mothers. In any case, more analysis is needed on how Black mothers have adapted the Christian faith for the sake of themselves and their children in a white-dominated society.

1 See for example, a Black mother's struggle with Christianity: Rita B. Dandridge, "The Motherhood Myth: Black Women and Christianity in *The Deity Nodded*," *MELUS* 12, no. 3 (1985): 13–22.

As this study has made clear, mothers have utilized the wealth of Christian teachings and practices in ways that have celebrated their strength and helped their children. But despite their adaptability and creative uses of the faith, Christian theology has not necessarily been empowering to women. Its ambivalence towards the female body, its biases against motherwork as a purely earthly and undignified endeavor, and its misgivings about female agency have been barriers to its own enrichment. For too long, Christian theology has placed the destiny of women solely in the identity of motherhood, and it has placed its understanding of motherhood solely in its negative paradigm of the female. The question today is whether modern Protestant theology will break its centuries-long theological notion of "motherhood" to instead see and respect mothers themselves. If there is one task before the Christian imagination today, it is learning to talk about God in ways that allow women who are mothers to recognize themselves in Christian rhetoric. This requires taking into account all the profound changes that happen to women and their bodies in becoming mothers. How can Christian theology talk about God in ways that recognize the imperative biological work of the maternal body in bringing forth new life? Is there room in preaching and the church community to recognize the unspoken dimensions of a mother's life such as maternal grief? Do Christian churches care that twenty-first-century mothers are torn between raising their children and trying to survive in relentlessly capitalistic societies?

Although Christianity has maintained a metaphysic of shame and inferiority regarding the female body, women throughout the long centuries of the Christian faith have complicated that notion and have proven that there is no one single narrative about women in the Christian tradition. Even though they were prevented from writing scholastic treatises, mothers did not hesitate to take up the pen to write about God for the sake of their faith and the faiths of their children. Dhuoda wrote a Christian *Handbook* to her two young sons in an era when women were not taught to read or write. Julian of Norwich wrote radical visions of the motherhood of God during a time when the Catholic church may have burned her at the stake for her ideas. Since women began publishing in the seventeenth century, they have not stopped writing about their faiths or passing their faiths down to their children. Dorothy Leigh and

Elizabeth Joscelin began an entirely new genre of women's writing about the Christian faith for the sake of their children. Such women, and surely innumerably more, complexified the singular narrative Christian theology told about women. Their legacies show that mothers have had a profound understanding of God's work—and they continue to do so. Mothers were theologians of the highest kind, even if their ideas were neglected. They balanced a vision of heaven for their children while insisting on God's care for humanity here on earth.

Bibliography

Aasgaard, Reidar, Cornelia B. Horn, and Oana Maria Cojocaru, eds. *Childhood in History: Perceptions of Children in the Ancient and Medieval Worlds*. Abingdon: Routledge, 2018.

Ainsworth, Mary D. Salter, Mary C. Blehar, Everett Waters, and Sally N. Wall. *Patterns of Attachment: A Psychological Study of the Strange Situation*. New York: Routledge, 2015.

Althaus-Reid, Marcella, and Lisa Isherwood. *Controversies in Feminist Theology*. Controversies in Contextual Theology. London: SCM Press, 2007.

Ambrose. *On Virginity*. In vol. 10 of *Nicene and Post-Nicene Fathers*, Second Series. Edited by Philip Schaff and Henry Wace. Translated by H. de Romestin, E. de Romestin, and H. T. F. Duckworth. Buffalo, N.Y.: Christian Literature Publishing Co., 1896. Revised and edited for New Advent by Kevin Knight.

Andrews, William L., ed. *Six Women's Slave Narratives*. The Schomburg Library of Nineteenth-Century Black Women Writers. New York: Oxford University Press, 1988.

Angier, Natalie. *Woman: An Intimate Geography*. Rev. ed. Boston: Mariner Books/Houghton Mifflin Harcourt, 2014.

Anselm. *The Prayers and Meditations of Saint Anselm with the Proslogion*. Edited and translated by Sister Benedicta Ward. New York: Penguin Books, 1973.

Anselm of Canterbury. *The Virgin Conception and Original Sin*. In *Anselm of Canterbury: Complete Philosophical and Theological Treatises*, trans. Jasper Hopkins and Herbert Richardson, chap. 18. Jackson, Mich.: Ex Fontibus Company, 2016.

Arx, Walter von. "The Churching of Women after Childbirth: History and Significance." In *Liturgy and Human Passage*, edited by David Power and Luis Maldonado, 63–71. New York: Seabury Press, 1979.

Atkinson, Clarissa. *The Oldest Vocation: Christian Motherhood in the Middle Ages*. Ithaca, N.Y.: Cornell University Press, 1991.

Aubert, Jean-Jacques. "Threatened Wombs: Aspects of Ancient Uterine Magic." *Greek, Roman, and Byzantine Studies* 30, no. 3 (2005): 421–49.

Augustine. *Confessions*. 2 vols. Translated by Carolyn J. B. Hammond. Loeb Classical Library. Cambridge, Mass.: Harvard University Press, 2014.

———. *Confessions*. Translated by Sarah Ruden. New York: The Modern Library, 2018.

Ayşe, Saktanber. *Living Islam: Women, Religion and the Politicization of Culture in Turkey*. London: I.B. Tauris, 2002.

Baake, Odd Magne. *When Children Became People: The Birth of Childhood in Early Christianity*. Minneapolis: Fortress, 2005.

Badinter, Elizabeth. *The Conflict: How Modern Motherhood Undermines the Status of Women*. New York: Metropolitan Books, 2012.

Baer, Helene G. *The Heart Is Like Heaven: The Life of Lydia Maria Child*. Philadelphia: University of Pennsylvania Press, 1964.

Baraitser, Lisa. *Maternal Encounters: The Ethics of Interruption*. Hove, East Sussex: Routledge, 2008.

Bassard, Katherine Clay. *Transforming Scriptures: African American Women Writers and the Bible*. Athens: University of Georgia Press, 2011.

Beecher, Catharine E., and Harriet Beecher Stowe. *The American Woman's Home*. New Brunswick, N.J.: Rutgers University Press, 2002 [1869].

———. *Principles of Domestic Science as Applied to the Duties and Pleasures of Home: A Text-book for the Use of Young Ladies in Schools, Seminaries, and Colleges*. New York: J.B. Ford, 1873.

Bell, Karen Cook. *Running from Bondage: Enslaved Women and Their Remarkable Fight for Freedom in Revolutionary America*. Cambridge: Cambridge University Press, 2021.

Benjamin, Mara H. *The Obligated Self: Maternal Subjectivity and Jewish Thought*. New Jewish Philosophy and Thought. Bloomington: Indiana University Press, 2018.

Berens, John F. *Providence and Patriotism in Early America 1640–1815*. Charlottesville: University Press of Virginia, 1978.

Bettini, Maurizio. *Women and Weasels: Mythologies of Birth in Ancient Greece and Rome*. Chicago: University of Chicago, 2013.

Bolton, Brenda. "*Vitae Matrum*: A Further Aspect of the *Frauenfrage*." In *Medieval Women: Studies in Church History*, edited by Derek Baker, 253–74. Subsidia I. Oxford: Basil Blackwell, 1978.

Bolton, S. Charles. *Fugitivism: Escaping Slavery in the Lower Mississippi Valley 1820–1860*. Fayetteville: University of Arkansas Press, 2019.

Boss, Sarah Jane. "Francisco Suarez and Modern Mariology." In *Mary: The Complete Resource*, edited by Sarah Jane Boss, 256–78. Oxford: Oxford University Press, 2007.

Boss, Sarah Jane. *Mary*. New Century Theology. London: Continuum, 2004.

Boswell, John. *The Kindness of Strangers: The Abandonment of Children in Western Europe from Late Antiquity to the Renaissance*. New York: Vintage Books, 1990.

Bowlby, John. *Attachment*. Vol. 1. 2nd ed. New York: Basic Books, 1982.

Bowler, Peter J. "Preformation and Pre-Existence in the Seventeenth Century: A Brief Analysis." *Journal of the History of Biology* 4 (1971): 221–44.

Boyd, Susan C. *Mothers and Illicit Drugs: Transcending the Myths*. Toronto: University of Toronto Press, 1999.

Brent, Linda. *Incidents in the Life of a Slave Girl*. Boston: Linda Brent, Boston Stereotype Foundry, 1861.

Brinton, Valerie Rose. "Capitalism and Performance Parenting." *Journal of Psychohistory* 42, no. 2 (2014): 161–69.

Brodie, Jessica. "The Message of the Hush Harbor: History and Theology of African Descent Traditions." *South Carolina United Methodist Advocate*. March 1, 2019. https://advocatesc.org/2019/03/the-message-of-the-hush-harbor-history-and-theology-of-african-descent-traditions/.

Brown, Peter. *Body and Society: Men, Women, and Sexual Renunciation in Early Christianity*. New York: Columbia University Press, 1988.

———. *The Cult of the Saints: Its Rise and Function in Latin Christianity*. Chicago: University of Chicago Press, 2009.

Brown, Rachel Fulton. *Mary and the Art of Prayer: The Hours of the Virgin in Medieval Christian Life and Thought*. New York: Columbia University Press, 2018.

Brown, Sylvia, ed. *Women's Writing in Stuart England: The Mothers' Legacies of Dorothy Leigh, Elizabeth Joscelin, and Elizabeth Richardson*. Gloucestershire: Sutton Publishing, 1999.

Burnett, Carol Monica C. "Mother-Child Bonding in the Fathers of the Church." In *Children in Late Ancient Christianity*, edited by Corneila B. Horn and Robert R. Phenix, 75–102. Tübingen: Mohr Siebeck, 2009.

Burrus, Virginia. *Saving Shame: Martyrs, Saints, and Other Abject Subjects*. Philadelphia: University of Pennsylvania Press, 2008.

Bynum, Caroline Walker. *Holy Feast and Holy Fast: The Religious Significance of Food to Medieval Women*. Berkeley: University of California Press, 1987.

———. *Jesus as Mother: Studies in the Spirituality of the High Middle Ages*. Publications of the Center for Medieval and Renaissance Studies 16. Berkeley: University of California Press, 1982.

———. *Wonderful Blood: Theology and Practice in Late Medieval Northern Germany and Beyond*. The Middle Ages. Philadelphia: University of Pennsylvania Press, 2007.

Calvin, John. *Institutes of the Christian Religion*. Vol. 1. Edited by John T. McNeill. Translated by Ford Lewis Battles. Philadelphia: Westminster, 1960.

Carnes, Natalie. *Motherhood: A Confession*. Redwood City, Calif.: Stanford University Press, 2020.

Carter, J. Kameron. *Race: A Theological Account*. New York: Oxford University Press, 2008.

Cavadini, John, and Danielle M. Peters, eds. *Mary on the Eve of the Second Vatican Council*. Notre Dame, Ind.: University of Notre Dame Press, 2017.

Chamberlain, Ava. "The Immaculate Ovum: Jonathan Edwards and the Construction of the Female Body." *William and Mary Quarterly*, 3rd ser., 57, no. 2 (2000): 289–322.

Chazelle, Celia. "Figure, Character, and the Glorified Body in the Carolingian Eucharistic Controversy." *Traditio* 47 (1992): 1–36.

Chesler, Phyllis. *With Child: A Diary of Motherhood*. New York: Penguin, 1981.

Chireau, Yvonne. "The Uses of the Supernatural: Toward a History of Black Women's Magical Practices." In *A Mighty Baptism: Race, Gender, and the Creation of American Protestantism*, edited by Susan Juster and Lisa MacFarlane, 171–88. Ithaca, N.Y.: Cornell University Press, 1996.

Clark, Elizabeth A. *The Origenist Controversy: The Cultural Construction of an Early Christian Debate*. Princeton: Princeton University Press, 1992.

Clark, Gillian. *Monica: An Ordinary Saint*. New York: Oxford University Press, 2015.

Clayton, Ronnie W., ed. *Mother Whit: The Ex-Slave Narratives of the Louisiana Writers' Project*. New York: Peter Lang, 1990.

Cloke, Gillian. "*Mater* or Martyr: Christianity and the Alienation of Women within the Family in the Later Roman Empire." *Theology and Sexuality* 5 (1996): 37–57.

———. *This Female Man of God: Women and Spiritual Power in the Patristic Age, AD 350–450*. New York: Routledge, 1995.

Clooney, Francis X. "Melania the Elder: A Biographical Note." *Traditio* 5 (1947): 59–77.

Cohick, Lynn H., and Amy Brown Hughes. *Christian Women in the Patristic World: Their Influence, Authority, and Legacy in the Second through Fifth Centuries*. Grand Rapids: Baker Academic, 2017.

Collins, Patricia Hill. *Black Feminist Thought*. New York: Routledge, 2009.

Colonna, Vittoria, Chiara Matraini, and Lucrezia Marinella. *Who Is Mary? Three Early Modern Women on the Idea of the Virgin Mary*. Edited and translated by Susan Haskins. Chicago: University of Chicago Press, 2008.

Corretti, Carolyn, and Sukumar P. Desai. "The Legacy of Eve's Curse: Religion, Childbirth Pain, and the Rise of Anesthesia in Europe: c. 1200–1800s." *Journal of Anesthesia History* 4 (2018): 182–90.

Cressy, David. "Purification, Thanksgiving, and the Churching of Women in Post-Reformation England." *Past and Present* 141 (1993): 106–46.

Crowther, Kathleen M. *Adam and Eve in the Protestant Reformation*. Cambridge: Cambridge University Press, 2010.

Cusk, Rachel. *A Life's Work: On Becoming a Mother*. New York: Picador, 2003.

Dandridge, Rita B. "The Motherhood Myth: Black Women and Christianity in *The Deity Nodded*." *MELUS* 12, no. 3 (1985): 13–22.

Daniel-Hughes, Carly. *The Salvation of the Flesh in Tertullian of Carthage: Dressing for the Resurrection*. New York: Palgrave Macmillan, 2011.

Davidson, Basil. *Black Mother: The Years of the African Slave Trade*. Boston: Little, Brown, and Company, 1961.

Demand, Nancy. *Birth, Death, and Motherhood in Classical Greece*. Baltimore: Johns Hopkins University Press, 1994.

———. "Monuments, Midwives, and Gynecology." In *Ancient Medicine in Its Socio-Cultural Context*, vol. 1, edited by H. F. J. Horstmanshoff, Philip J. van der Eijk, and P. H. Schrijvers, 275–90. Amsterdam: Brill, 1995.

DeRosa, Deborah C. "Seditious Histories. The Abolitionist Mother-Historian." In *Domestic Abolitionism and Juvenile Literature 1830–1865*, 79–106. Albany: SUNY Press, 2003.

Dey, Claudia. "Mothers as Makers of Death." *Paris Review*. August 14, 2018. https://www.theparisreview.org/blog/2018/08/14/mothers-as-makers-of-death/.

Dhuoda. *Handbook for William: A Carolingian Woman's Counsel for Her Son*. Edited and translated by Carol Neel. Medieval Texts in Translation. Washington, D.C.: Catholic University of America Press, 1991.

Dixon, Suzanne. *The Roman Mother*. Routledge Revivals. Hoboken, N.J.: Taylor and Francis, 2014.

Duffy, Eamon. *Royal Books and Holy Bones: Essays in Medieval Christianity*. New York: Bloomsbury Continuum, 2018.

Dunn, Mary. *The Cruelest of All Mothers: Marie de L'Incarnation, Motherhood, and Christian Tradition*. New York: Fordham University Press, 2016.

Dzon, Mary. "Birgitta of Sweden and Christ's Clothing." In *The Christ Child in Medieval Culture: Alpha Es Et O!*, edited by Mary Dzon and Theresa M. Kenney, 117–44. Toronto: University of Toronto Press, 2012.

"Early Penitentials: The Canons of Theodore." Added September 8, 2015. Internet Archive. Cambridge, Corpus Christi College. MS 190. https://archive.org/details/EarlyPenitentialsTheCanonsOfTheodore.

Edin, Kathryn, and Maria Kefalas. *Promises I Can Keep: Why Poor Women Put Motherhood before Marriage*. Berkeley: University of California Press, 2005.

Ellington, Donna Spivey. *From Sacred Body to Angelic Soul: Understanding Mary in Late Medieval and Early Modern Europe*. Washington, D.C.: Catholic University of America Press, 2001.

Equal Justice Initiative. "Medical Exploitation of Black Women." Equal Justice Initiative. August 29, 2019. https://eji.org/news/history-racial-injustice-medical-exploitation-of-black-women/.

Faust, Drew Gilpin. *Mothers of Invention: Women of the Slaveholding South in the American Civil War*. Fred W. Morrison Series in Southern Studies. Chapel Hill: University of North Carolina Press, 1996.

Filippini, Nadia Maria. *Pregnancy, Delivery, Childbirth: A Gender and Cultural History from Antiquity to the Test Tube in Europe*. New York: Routledge, 2021.

Finucane, Ronald C. *The Rescue of the Innocents: Endangered Children in Medieval Miracles*. New York: St. Martin's Press, 2000.

France, James. *Medieval Images of Saint Bernard of Clairvaux*. Kalamazoo, Mich.: Cistercian Publications, 2007.

Fry Brown, Teresa L. *God Don't Like Ugly: African American Women Handing on Spiritual Values*. Nashville: Abingdon, 2000.

Fuchs, Rachel G. *Poor and Pregnant in Paris: Strategies for Survival in the Nineteenth Century*. New Brunswick, N.J.: Rutgers University Press, 1992.

Fulton, Rachel. *From Judgment to Passion: Devotion to Christ and the Virgin Mary, 800–1200*. New York: Columbia University Press, 2002.

Furman, Gloria. *Missional Motherhood: The Everyday Ministry of Motherhood in the Grand Plan of God*. Wheaton, Ill.: Crossway, 2016.

Galen. *On the Usefulness of the Parts of the Body*. Vol. 1. Translated and edited by Margaret Tallmadge May. Cornell Publications in the History of Science. Ithaca, N.Y.: Cornell University Press, 1968.

Garden, George. "A Discourse Concerning the Modern Theory of Generation." *Philosophical Transactions of the Royal Society of London* 16, no. 192 (1691): 474–83.

Garver, Valerie L. "Childbearing and Infancy in the Carolingian World." *Journal of the History of Sexuality* 21, no. 2 (2012): 208–44.

Gerontius. *The Life of Melania the Younger*. Translated by Elizabeth A. Clark. Lewiston, N.Y.: Edwin Mellen, 1984.

Gibson, Gail McMurray. "Blessing from Sun and Moon: Churching as Women's Theater." In *Bodies and Disciplines: Intersections of Literature and History in Fifteenth-Century England*, edited by Barbara A. Hanawalt and David Wallace, 139–54. Minneapolis: University of Minnesota Press, 1996.

Giles, Melinda. *Mothering in the Age of Neoliberalism*. Bradford, Ont.: Demeter Press, 2014.

Glancy, Jennifer. "The Law of the Opened Body: Tertullian on the Nativity." *Henoch* 30, no. 2 (2008): 267–88.

Gopnik, Alison, Andrew Meltzoff, and Patricia Kuhl. *How Babies Think: The Science of Childhood*. London: Phoenix, 2001.

Gössmann, Elisabeth, and Dieter R. Bauer, eds. *Maria, für alle Frauen oder über allen Frauen?* Reihe Frauenforum. Freiburg im Breisgau: Herder, 1989.

Göttner-Abendroth, Heide. *Die Göttin und ihr Heros: Die Matriarchalen Religionen in Mythos, Märchen und Dichtung*. Munich: Frauenoffensive, 1980.

Graef, Hilda. *Mary: A History of Doctrine and Devotion*. 2 vols. New York: Sheed and Ward, 1964.

Gray, Catharine. "Feeding on the Seed of the Woman: Dorothy Leigh and the Figure of Maternal Dissent." *English Literary History* 68, no.3 (2001): 563–92.

Green, TeResa. "A Gendered Spirit: Race, Class, and Sex in the African American Church." *Race, Gender and Class* 10, no. 1 (2003): 115–28.

Gregory of Nyssa. *Against Eunominus. Great Catechetical Oration. On the Soul and Resurrection. On Virginity. On the Holy Trinity. Letters*. Vol. 5 of *A Select Library of Nicene and Post-Nicene Fathers of the Christian Church*, edited by Philip Schaff and Henry Wace. Grand Rapids: Eerdmans, 1986.

———. *On Virginity*. In *St. Gregory: Ascetical Works*, translated by Virginia Wood Callahan. Washington, D.C.: Catholic University Press, 1967.

Haarer, Johanna. *Die Deutsche Mutter und Ihr Erstes Kind* [The German Mother and Her First Child]. Munich: F.J. Lehmanns, 1934.

Hallstein, D. Lynn O'Brien. "The Intriguing History and Silences of *Of Woman Born*: Rereading Adrienne Rich Rhetorically to Better Understand the Contemporary Context." *Feminist Formations* 22, no. 2 (2010): 18–41.

Harper, Frances Watkins. "Moses: A Story of the Nile." In *Complete Poems of Frances E.W. Harper*, edited by Maryemma Graham. The Schomburg Library of Nineteenth-Century Black Women Writers. New York: Oxford University Press, 1988.

———. "The Slave-Mother." In *American Poetry: The Nineteenth Century*. New York: Library of America, 1993. https://www.poetryfoundation.org/poems/51977/the-slave-mother-56d23017ceaad.

Harris, Marguerite Tjader, and Albert R. Kezel, eds. *Birgitta of Sweden: Life and Selected Revelations*. Translated by Albert R. Kezel. Classics of Western Spirituality. Mahwah, N.J.: Paulist Press, 1990.

Hart, Susan. *The Impact of Attachment: Developmental Neuroaffective Psychology*. New York: W. W. Norton, 2011.

Haynes, Rosetta R. *Radical Spiritual Motherhood: Autobiography and Empowerment in Nineteenth-Century African American Women*. Baton Rouge: Louisiana State University Press, 2011.

Haynes, Stephen R. *Noah's Curse: The Biblical Justification of American Slavery*. Oxford: Oxford University Press, 2002.

Heal, Bridget. *The Cult of the Virgin Mary in Early Modern Germany: Protestant and Catholic Piety, 1500–1648*. Cambridge: Cambridge University Press, 2007.

Heene, Katrien. *The Legacy of Paradise: Marriage, Motherhood, and Woman in Carolingian Edifying Literature*. New York: Peter Lang, 1997.

Heming, Carol Piper. *Protestants and the Cult of the Saints in German Speaking Europe, 1517–1531*. Kirksville, Mo.: Truman State University Press, 2003.

Henry, Jon. "'Stranger Fruit': Black Mothers and the Fear of Police Brutality." March 22, 2021. https://www.jonhenryphotography.com/strangerfruit.

Hesiod. *Works and Days: A Translation and Commentary for the Social Sciences*. Edited and translated by Walter C. Neale and David W. Tandy. Berkeley: University of California Press, 1996.

Heyes, Michael E. *Margaret's Monsters: Women, Identity, and the Life of St. Margaret in Medieval England*. New York: Routledge, 2020.

Ho, Sin-pan Daniel. *Paul and the Creation of a Counter-Cultural Community: A Rhetorical Analysis of 1 Cor. 5.1–11.1 in Light of the Social Lives of the Corinthians*. Library of New Testament Studies 509. London: Bloomsbury T&T Clark, 2015.

Holland, Brynn. "The 'Father of Modern Gynecology' Performed Shocking Experiments on Enslaved Women." *History*. August 29, 2017. Updated December 4, 2018. https://www.history.com/news/the-father-of-modern-gynecology-performed-shocking-experiments-on-slaves.

Horowitz, Maryanne Cline. "Aristotle and Women." *Journal of the History of Biology* 9, no. 2 (1976): 183–213.

Hrdy, Sarah Blaffer. *Mother Nature: Maternal Instincts and How They Shape the Human Species*. New York: Ballantine, 2000.

———. *Mothers and Others: The Evolutionary Origins of Mutual Understanding*. Cambridge, Mass.: Belknap Press, 2009.

Ihnat, Kati. *Mother of Mercy, Bane of the Jews: Devotion to the Virgin Mary in Anglo-Norman England*. Princeton: Princeton University Press, 2016.

Jacobs, Margaret D. "Maternal Colonialism: White Women and Indigenous Child Removal in the American West and Australia, 1880–1940." *Western Historical Quarterly* 36 (2005): 453–76.

Jacobs, Margaret D. *White Mother to a Dark Race: Settler Colonialism, Maternalism, and the Removal of Indigenous Children in the American West and Australia, 1880–1940*. Lincoln: University of Nebraska Press, 2009.

Jacquart, Danielle, and Claude Thomasset. *Sexuality and Medicine in the Middle Ages*. Princeton: Princeton University Press, 1988.

James, Janet Wilson. "'Vertuous Women Found': New England Ministerial Literature 1668–1735." In *Women in American Religion*, edited by Janet Wilson James, 67–87. Pennsylvania: University of Pennsylvania Press, 1978.

Jantzen, Grace. "Flourishing: Towards an Ethic of Natality." *Feminist Theory* 2, no. 2 (2001): 219–32.

Jeansonne, Glen. *Women of the Far Right: The Mother's Movement and World War II*. Chicago: Chicago University Press, 1997.

Jehlen, Myra. "The Family Militant: Domesticity Versus Slavery in *Uncle Tom's Cabin*." *Criticism* 31, no. 4 (1989): 383–400.

Jernegan, Marcus W. "Slavery and Conversion in the American Colonies." *American Historical Review* 21, no. 3 (1916): 504–27.

John Chrysostom. *On Virginity. Against Remarriage*. Edited by Elizabeth A. Clark. Translated by Sally Rieger Shore. Studies in Women and Religion 9. Lewiston, N.Y.: Edwin Mellen, 1983.

Johnson, Barbara. *Moses and Multiculturalism*. Berkeley: University of California Press, 2010.

Johnson, Elizabeth. "The Marian Tradition and the Reality of Women." *Horizons* 12, no. 1 (1985): 116–35.

Johnston, Eric. "The Biology of Woman in Thomas Aquinas." *The Thomist: A Speculative Quarterly Review* 77, no. 4 (2013): 577–616.

Jonas, Hans. *The Gnostic Religion: The Message of the Alien God and the Beginnings of Christianity*. 3rd ed. Boston: Beacon, 2001.

Jones, Peter Murray, and Lea T. Olsan. "Performative Rituals for Conception and Childbirth in England, 900–1500." *Bulletin of the History of Medicine* 89, no. 3 (2015): 406–33.

Joscelin, Elizabeth. *The Mothers Legacy to Her Vnborn* [Unborn] *Childe* [Child]. Edited by Jean D. LeDrew Metcalfe. Toronto: University of Toronto Press, 2000.

Julian of Norwich. *Showings*. Translated by Edmund Colledge. Classics of Western Spirituality. Mahwah, N.J.: Paulist Press, 1978.

Junior, Nyasha. *An Introduction to Womanist Biblical Interpretation*. Louisville: Westminster John Knox, 2015.

Kampen, Natalie Boymel. "Material Girl: Feminist Confrontations with Roman Art." *Arethusa* 27, no. 1 (1994): 111–37.

Karant-Nunn, Susan C. *The Reformation of Ritual: An Interpretation of Early Modern Germany*. New York: Routledge, 1997.

Kendi, Ibram X. *Stamped from the Beginning*. New York: Nation Books, 2016.

Kimball, Gayle. *The Religious Ideas of Harriet Beecher Stowe: Her Gospel of Womanhood*. Studies in Women and Religion 8. New York: Mellen, 1982.

King, Helen. *Hippocrates' Woman: Reading the Female Body in Ancient Greece*. London: Routledge, 1998.

King James. *The Fathers Blessing: Or Second Councell to His Sonne*. London: B. Alsop for Leonard Becket, 1616.

Kirkpatrick, Lee A. *Attachment, Evolution, and the Psychology of Religion*. New York: Guilford, 2005.

Kok, Jacobus, Martin I. Webber, and Jermo Van Nes, eds. *Drawing and Transcending Boundaries in the New Testament and Early Christianity*. Beiträge Zum Verstehen der Bibel 38. Zürich: Lit, 2019.

Kolmer, Elizabeth. "Catholic Women Religious and Women's History: A Survey of the Literature." In *Women in American Religion*, edited by Janet Wilson James, 127–40. Philadelphia: University of Pennsylvania Press, 1978.

Koonz, Claudia. *Mothers in the Fatherland: Women, the Family and Nazi Politics*. New York: St. Martin's Press, 1987.

Kors, Alan Charles, and Edward Peters, eds. *Witchcraft in Europe, 400–1700: A Documentary History*. Philadelphia: University of Pennsylvania Press, 2001.

Kramer, Heinrich, and Jacob Sprenger. *The Hammer of Witches: A Complete Translation of the Malleus Maleficarum*. Translated by Christopher S. Mackay. Cambridge: Cambridge University Press, 2009.

Kreitzer, Beth. *Reforming Mary: Changing Images of the Virgin Mary in Lutheran Sermons of the Sixteenth Century*. Oxford Studies in Historical Theology. Oxford: Oxford University Press, 2004.

Kristeva, Julia. "Stabat Mater." In *The Kristeva Reader*, edited by Toril Moi, translated by León S. Roudiez, 160–86. New York: Columbia University Press, 1986.

———. "Stabat Mater." In *The Portable Kristeva*, edited by Kelly Oliver, 310–32. European Perspectives. New York: Columbia University Press, 1997.

Kunzel, Regina G. *Fallen Women, Problem Girls: Unmarried Mothers and the Professionalization of Social Work, 1890–1945*. Yale Historical Publications. New Haven: Yale University Press, 1993.

Labouvie, Eva. *Andere Umstände*. Cologne: Böhlau Verlag, 1998.

Lamott, Anne. *Operating Instructions*. New York: Anchor Books, 2005.

Landau, Elizabeth. "How Much Did Grandmothers Influence Human Evolution?" *Smithsonian Magazine*. January 4, 2021. smithsonianmag.com.

Larson, Wendy. "Who is the Master of This Narrative? Maternal Patronage of the Cult of St. Margaret." In *Gendering the Master Narrative*, edited by Mary C. Erler and Maryanne Kowaleski, 94–104. Ithaca, N.Y.: Cornell University Press, 1990.

Lee, Becky R. "The Purification of Women after Childbirth: A Window onto Medieval Perceptions of Women." *Florilegium* 14 (1995–1996): 43–55.

Lefkowitz, M. R. "The Motivations for St. Perpetua's Martyrdom." *Journal of the American Academy of Religion* 44, no. 3 (1976): 417–21.

Leigh, Dorothy. *The Mother's Blessing. Or, The Godly Counsel of a Gentle-Woman Not Long Since Deceased, Left Behind for Her Children*. London: 1616.

Lester, Anne E. "Lost but Not Yet Found: Medieval Foundlings and Their Care in Northern France, 1200–1500." *Journal of the Western Society for French History* 35 (2007). https://quod.lib.umich.edu/w/wsfh/0642292.0035.001/-lost-but-not-yet-found-medieval-foundlings-and-their-care?rgn=main;view=fulltext.

Levine, Amy-Jill, and Maria Mayo Robbins, eds. *A Feminist Companion to Patristic Literature*. Feminist Companion to the New Testament and Early Christian Writings 12. London: T & T Clark, 2008.

Lewis, A. S., John Smith, and F. Crawford Burkitt, eds. *Select Narratives of Holy Women: From the Syro-Antiochene or Sinai Palimpsest as Written above the Old Syriac Gospels*. Studia Sinaitica 9–10. London: C.J. Clay and Sons, 1900.

Lewis, Nicola Denzey. *The Bone Gatherers: The Lost Worlds of Early Christian Women*. Boston: Beacon, 2007.

Leyser, Conrad, and Lesley Smith, eds. *Motherhood, Religion, and Society in Medieval Europe 400–1000: Essays Presented to Henrietta Leyser*. Farnham: Ashgate, 2011.

Lieu, Judith. *Marcion and the Making of a Heretic: God and Scripture in the Second Century*. New York: Cambridge University Press, 2015.

Linke, Uli. "Manhood, Femaleness, and Power: A Cultural Analysis of Prehistoric Images of Reproduction." *Comparative Studies in Society and History* 34, no. 4 (1992): 579–620.

Little, Becky. "How Early Suffragists Left Black Women out of Their Fight." History.com. November 8, 2017. https://www.history.com/news/suffragists-vote-black-women.

Lo Presti, Roberto. "Informing Matter and Enmattered Forms: Aristotle and Galen on the 'Power' of the Seed." *British Journal for the History of Philosophy* 22, no. 5 (2014): 929–50.

Lomawaima, K. Tsianina, and T. Tsianina Lomawaima. "Estelle Reel, Superintendent of Indian Schools, 1898–1910: Politics, Curriculum, and Land." *Journal of American Indian Education* 35, no. 3 (1996): 5–31.

Luther, Martin. *D. Martin Luthers Werke: Weimarer Ausgabe. Abteilung 1. Tischreden. Sonderedition Der Kritischen Gesamtausgabe, Gesamtwerk in 4 Abteilungen.* Edited by Ulrich Köpf. Weimar: Böhlau Nachfolger, 2000.

———. *Luther's Works.* Vol. 1, edited by Jaroslav Pelikan, Hilton C. Oswald, Helmut T. Lehmann, Christopher Boyd Brown, and Benjamin T. G. Mayes. Saint Louis: Concordia, 1955.

———. *Luther's Works.* Vol. 45, edited and translated by Walther I. Brandt. Philadelphia: Fortress, 1962.

———. "Vom ehelichen Leben (1522)." In *D. Martin Luthers Werke: Kritische Gesamtausgabe*, edited by Karl Drescher. Vol. 10/2. Weimar: Böhlau, 1907.

Lyons, Izzy, and Charles Hymas, "Mother Is No Longer Gender-Specific Term, Government Lawyers Say." *The Telegraph.* February 14, 2019, https://www.telegraph.co.uk/news/2019/02/14/mother-no-longer-gender-specific-term-government-lawyers-say/.

MacMillan, Margaret. *The Road to 1914: The War That Ended Peace.* New York: Random House, 2013.

Malone, Mary T. *Women and Christianity.* Vol. 1, *The First Thousand Years.* Maryknoll, N.Y.: Orbis, 2001.

Marlow, Lana. *Mothers in Prison: Women's Autobiography and Activism.* Riga, Latvia: VDM Verlag, 2009.

Mather, Cotton. *Elizabeth in Her Holy Retirement: An Essay to Prepare a Pious Woman for Her Lying In. Or, Maxims and Methods of Piety, to Direct and Support a Handmaid of the Lord, Who Expects a Time of Travail.* Boston: B. Green, 1710.

Mayeski, Marie Anne. *Dhuoda: Ninth Century Mother and Theologian.* Scranton: University of Scranton Press, 1995.

McCabe, Jane. Review of *Of Woman Born: Motherhood as Experience and Institution*, by Adrienne Rich. *Frontiers: A Journal of Women's Studies* (1977): 77–78.

McClain, Dani. *We Live for the We: The Political Power of Black Motherhood.* New York: Bold Type Books, 2019.

McDannell, Colleen. *The Christian Home in Victorian America, 1840–1900.* Bloomington: Indiana University Press, 1986.

McGucken, John Anthony, ed. *The Westminster Handbook to Origen*. Westminster Handbooks to Christian Theology. Louisville: Westminster John Knox, 2004.

McRae, Elizabeth Gillespie. *Mothers of Massive Resistance: White Women and the Politics of White Supremacy*. New York: Oxford University Press, 2020.

Mellon, Joelle. *The Virgin Mary in the Perceptions of Women*. Jefferson, N.C.: McFarland & Company, 2008.

Meyer, R., and S. P. Desai. "Accepting Pain Over Comfort: Resistance to the Use of Anesthesia in the Mid-Nineteenth Century." *Journal of Anesthesia History* 1 (2015): 115–21.

Migne, J. P., John Batteridge Pearson, and J. B. Pearson. *Index Alphabeticus Omnium Doctorum, Patrum, Scriptorumque Ecclesiasticorum Quorum Opera Scriptaque Vel Minima in Patrologia Latina Reperiuntur*. Ridgewood, N.J.: Gregg Press, 1965.

Miles, Margaret. *Image as Insight: Visual Understanding in Western Christianity and Secular Culture*. Boston: Beacon, 1985.

Miller, James. *Weekday Religion*. Philadelphia: Presbyterian Board of Publication, 1880.

Miller, Naomi, and Naomi Yavneh. *Maternal Measures: Figuring Caregiving in the Early Modern Period*. Burlington, Vt.: Ashgate, 2000.

Moll, Sebastian. *The Arch-Heretic Marcion*. Wissenschaftliche Untersuchungen Zum Neuen Testament 250. Tübingen: Mohr Siebeck, 2010.

Morgan, Brandon. "'We Will All Be Changed': Materiality, Resurrection, and Reaping Spiritual Bodies in Origen's *Peri Archon*." *American Theological Inquiry* 7, no. 2 (2014): 13–16.

Morillo, Susana Reboreda. "Childhood and Motherhood in Ancient Greece: An Iconographic Look." In *Motherhood and Infancies in the Mediterranean in Antiquity*, edited by Margarita Sánchez Romero and Rosa Mª Cid López, 135–50. Oxford: Oxbow Books, 2018.

Morris, Celia. *Fanny Wright: Rebel in America*. Urbana: University of Illinois Press, 1992.

Murphy, Francis X. "Melania the Elder: A Biographical Note." *Traditio* 5 (1947): 59–77.

Musurillo, Herbert, ed. *The Acts of the Christian Martyrs*. Oxford: Clarendon, 1972.

Myers, Alicia. *Blessed among Women? Mothers and Motherhood in the New Testament*. New York: Oxford University Press, 2017.

Nathans, Sydney. *To Free a Family: The Journey of Mary Walker*. Cambridge, Mass.: Harvard University Press, 2013.

Newman, Barbara. *From Virile Woman to WomanChrist: Studies in Medieval Religion and Literature*. Philadelphia: University of Pennsylvania Press, 1995.

———. *God and the Goddesses: Vision, Poetry, and Belief in the Middle Ages*. Philadelphia: University of Pennsylvania Press, 2003.

———. *Sister of Wisdom: St. Hildegard's Theology of the Feminine*. Berkeley: University of California Press, 1987.

Newman, Louise Michele. *White Women's Rights: The Racial Origins of Feminism in the United States*. New York: Oxford University Press, 1999.

Niccolls, Samuel J. "Woman's Position and Work in the Church." *The Presbyterian Review* 10, no. 38 (1889): 267–79.

Niestroj, Brigitte H. E. "Women as Mothers and the Making of the European Mind: A Contribution to the History of Developmental Psychology and Primary Socialization." *Journal for the Theory of Social Behavior* 24, no. 3 (1994): 281–303.

Nixon, Virginia. *Mary's Mother: Saint Anne in Late Medieval Europe*. University Park: Pennsylvania State University Press, 2004.

Notker. "In natale sanctarum feminarum" [The Festival of Holy Women]. In *Poetry of the Carolingian Renaissance*, edited by Peter Godman, 318–20. Norman: University of Oklahoma Press, 1985.

Oberman, Michelle, and Cheryl L. Meyer. *When Mothers Kill: Interviews from Prison*. New York: New York University Press, 2008.

Olson, Tillie. "I Stand Here Ironing." In *Tell Me a Riddle: A Collection*. Philadelphia: J. B. Lippincott, 1960.

Omokha, Rita. "They Were Sons." *Vanity Fair*. May 6, 2021.

Painter, Nell Irvin. *A History of White People*. New York: W. W. Norton, 2010.

———. *Sojourner Truth: A Life, A Symbol*. New York: W. W. Norton, 1996.

Palladius. *The Lausiac History of Palladius*. Translated by W. K. L. Clarke. Translations of Christian Literature. London: SPCK, 1918.

Pappano, M. Aziza, and Dana M. Olwan, eds. *Muslim Mothering: Global Histories, Theories, and Practices*. Bradford, Ont.: Demeter Press, 2016.

Patrologia Latina. Edited by J.-P. Migne. 217 vols. Paris, 1844–1864.

Pelikan, Jaroslav. *Mary through the Centuries: Her Place in the History of Culture*. New Haven: Yale University Press, 1996.

Philips, J. A. *Eve: The History of an Idea*. New York: Harper and Row, 1984.

Pierce, Joanne M. "'Green Women' and Blood Pollution: Some Medieval Rituals for the Churching of Women after Childbirth." *Studia Liturgica* 29, no. 2 (1999): 191–215.

Polikoff, Nancy. "Lesbians Choosing Children: The Personal Is Political Revisited." In *Maternal Theory: Essential Readings*, edited by Andrea O'Reilly. Bradford, Ont.: Demeter Press, 2007.

Raboteau, Albert J. *Slave Religion: The "Invisible Institution" in the Antebellum South*. New York: Oxford University Press, 1978.

Radice, Betty, ed. *Letters of Abelard and Heloise*. Penguin Classics. Harmondsworth: Penguin, 1974.

Radler, Charlotte. "The Dirty Physician: Necessary Dishonor and Fleshly Solidarity in Tertullian's Writings." *Vigiliae Christianae* 63 (2009): 345–68.

Raphael, Melissa. *The Female Face of God in Auschwitz*. London: Routledge, 2003.

Rebillard, Eric, ed. *Greek and Latin Narratives about the Ancient Martyrs*. Oxford Early Christian Texts. Oxford: Oxford University Press, 2017.

Revenga, Ana, and Sudhir Shetty. "Empowering Women Is Smart Economics." *Finance & Development* 49, no. 1 (2012): 40–43. https://www.imf.org/external/pubs/ft/fandd/2012/03/revenga.htm.

Reynolds, Gretchen. "Mother's Exercise May Boost Baby's Brain." *New York Times*. November 20, 2013. https://well.blogs.nytimes.com/2013/11/20/mothers-exercise-may-boost-babys-brain.

Ricci, Gabriel, ed. *Mothers in Prison*. 2nd ed. New York: Routledge, 2018.

Rich, Adrienne. *Of Woman Born: Motherhood as Experience and Institution*. New York: W. W. Norton, 1976.

Rifkin, Jeremy. *The Empathic Civilization: The Race to Global Consciousness in a World in Crisis*. New York: J. P. Tarcher/Penguin, 2009.

Robbins, Sarah. "'The Future Good and Great of Our Land': Republican Mothers, Female Authors, and Domesticated Literacy in Antebellum New England." *New England Quarterly* 75, no. 4 (2002): 562–91.

Roberts, Alexander, James Donaldson, and Arthur Cleveland Coxe, eds. *Ante-Nicene Fathers: The Writings of the Fathers Down to A.D. 325*. Peabody, Mass.: Hendrickson, 1994.

Röckelein, Hedwig, Claudia Opitz, and Dieter R. Bauer, eds. *Maria: Abbild oder Vorbild: Zur Sozialgeschichte Mittelalterlicher Marienverehrung*. Tübingen: Edition Diskord, 1990.

Roper, Lyndal. *The Holy Household: Women and Morals in Reformation Augsburg*. Oxford Studies in Social History. Oxford: Clarendon, 1989.

———. *The Witch in the Western Imagination*. Richard Lectures 1998. Charlottesville: University of Virginia Press, 2012.

Roux, Mathilde. "Five Facts About Black Women in the Labor Force." *U.S. Department of Labor Blog*. August 3, 2021. blog.dol.gov.

Rowland, Beryl, trans. *Medieval Woman's Guide to Health: The First English Gynecological Handbook*. Kent, Ohio: Kent State University Press, 1981.

Ruddick, Sara. *Maternal Thinking: Towards a Politics of Peace*. Boston: Beacon, 1995.

Ruether, Rosemary Radford, and Rosemary Skinner Keller, eds. *The Nineteenth Century*. Vol. 1 of *Women and Religion in America*. San Francisco: Harper and Row, 1981.

Schearing, Linda S. "Parturition (Childbirth), Pain, and Piety: Physicians and Genesis 3:16a." In *Mother Goose, Mother Jones, Mommie Dearest: Biblical Mothers and Their Children*, edited by Cheryl Kirk-Duggan and Tina Pippin, 85–96. Atlanta: SBL Press, 2009.

Schorr, Dorothy C. *The Christ Child in Devotional Images in Italy during the XIV Century*. New York: G. Wittenborn, 1954.

Schroeder, Caroline T. *Melania: Early Christianity through the Life of One Family*. Berkeley: University of California Press, 2018.

Schulenberg, Jane Tibbetts. *Forgetful of Their Sex: Female Sanctity and Society, ca. 500–1100*. Chicago: University of Chicago Press, 1998.

Seim, Turid Kralsen. "Motherhood and the Making of Fathers in Antiquity." In *Women and Gender in Ancient Religions*, edited by Stephen P. Ahearne-Kroll, Paul A. Holloway, and James A. Kelhoffer, 99–124. Tübingen: Mohr Siebeck, 2010.

Sellers, Tina Schermer, and Kris Thomas. "Women Called: A Qualitative Study of Christian Women Dually Called to Motherhood and Career." *Journal of Psychology and Theology* 33, no. 3 (2005): 198–209.

Shahar, Shulamith. *The Fourth Estate: A History of Women in the Middle Ages*. New York: Methuen & Co., 1983.

Sheingorn, Pamela. "'The Wise Mother': The Image of St. Anne Teaching the Virgin Mary." In *Gendering the Master Narrative: Women and Power in the Middle Ages*, edited by Mary C. Erler and Maryanne Kowaleski, 105–34. New York: Cornell University Press, 2003.

Sheridan, Susan. "Adrienne Rich and the Women's Liberation Movement: A Politics of Reception." *Women's Studies* 35 (2006): 17–45.

Sidel, Ruth. *Unsung Heroines: Single Mothers and the American Dream*. Berkeley: University of California Press, 2006.

Sigourney, Lydia. *Letters to Mothers*. Hartford: Hudson and Skinner, 1838.

Silva, Dorsía S., Laila Malik, and Abigail L. Palko, eds. *Mothers, Mothering, and Globalization*. Bradford, Ont.: Demeter Press, 2017.

Sperling, Jutta. "Squeezing, Squirting, Spilling Milk: The Lactation of Saint Bernard and the Flemish *Madonna Lactans* (ca. 1430–1530)," *Renaissance Quarterly* 71, no. 3 (2018): 868–918.

Stafford, Pauline, and Anneke B. Mulder-Bakker, eds. *Gendering the Middle Ages*. Oxford: Blackwell, 2001.

Stanton, Elizabeth Cady. *The Woman's Bible*. Boston: Northeastern University Press, 1993 [1895].

Stitt, Jocelyn Fenton, and Pegeen Reichert Powell, eds. *Mothers Who Deliver*. Albany: SUNY Press, 2010.

Stortz, Martha Ellen. "'Where or When Was Your Servant Innocent?': Augustine on Childhood." In *The Child in Christian Thought*, edited by Marcia J. Bunge, 78–102. Grand Rapids: Eerdmans, 2001.

Stowe, Harriet Beecher. *The Life of Harriet Beecher Stowe: Compiled from Her Letters and Journals by Her Son, Charles Edward Stowe*. New York: Houghton, Mifflin, 1890.

Stromberg, Joseph. "New Evidence That Grandmothers Were Crucial for Human Evolution." *Smithsonian Magazine*. October 23, 2012. smithsonianmag.com.

Swan, Laura. *The Wisdom of the Beguines: The Forgotten Story of a Medieval Women's Movement*. Katonah, N.Y.: BlueBridge, 2014.

Tacitus. *The Germany and the Agricola of Tacitus: The Oxford Translation Revised, with Notes*. Produced by Anne Soulard, Charles Aldarondo, Tiffany Vergon, Eric Casteleijn, and the Online Distributed Proofreading Team. Project Gutenberg. May 17, 2013. https://www.gutenberg.org/files/7524/7524-h/7524-h.htm.

Tertullian. *Ad Uxorem*. In volume 4 of *The Ante-Nicene Fathers: The Writings of the Fathers Down to A.D. 325*, ed. Alexander Roberts, James Donaldson, and Arthur Cleveland Coxe. Peabody, Mass.: Hendrickson, 1994.

———. "A Treatise on the Soul." Translated by Peter Holmes. In volume 3 of *The Ante-Nicene Fathers: The Writings of the Fathers Down to A.D. 325*. Edited by Alexander Roberts and James Donaldson. Peabody, Mass.: Hendrickson, 1994.

———. *On the Flesh of Christ*. In vol. 3 of *The Ante-Nicene Fathers: The Writings of the Fathers Down to A.D. 325*, edited by Alexander Roberts, James Donaldson, A. Cleveland Coxe, and Allan Menzies. Edinburgh: T & T Clark, 1989. Available online at https://www.tertullian.org/articles/evans_carn/evans_carn_04eng.htm.

Thurman, Howard. *Jesus and the Disinherited*. New York: Abingdon-Cokesbury Press, 1949.

Vandenberg-Daves, Jodi. "Inventing a New Role for Mothers." In *Modern Motherhood: An American History*, 11–31. New Brunswick, N.J.: Rutgers University Press, 2014.

Vaughn, Sally N. *St. Anselm and the Handmaidens of God: A Study of Anselm's Correspondence with Women*. Turnhout, Belgium: Brepols, 2002.

Vogt, Kari. "'Becoming Male': A Gnostic and Early Christian Metaphor." In *The Image of God: Gender Models in Judaeo-Christian Tradition*, edited by Kari Elisabeth Bøerresen, 170–86. Minneapolis: Fortress, 1995.

de Voragine, Jacobus. *The Golden Legend: Readings on the Saints*. Translated by William Granger Ryan. Princeton: Princeton University Press, 2012.

Walcot, Peter. "Plato's Mother and Other Terrible Women." In *Women in Antiquity*, edited by Ian McAuslan and Peter Walcot, 114–33. Greece and Rome Studies 3. Oxford: Oxford University Press, 1996.

Warner, Judith. *Perfect Madness: Motherhood in the Age of Anxiety*. New York: Riverhead Books, 2006.

Warner, Marina. *Alone of All Her Sex: The Myth and the Cult of the Virgin Mary*. New York: Knopf, 1976.

Weber, Ines. "The Reception of Biblical Texts and Their Normative Effect Upon Marriage, Adultery, and Divorce from the Seventh to the Eleventh Century." In *The Early Middle Ages*, edited by Franca Ela Consolino and Judith Herrin, 321–44. The Bible and Women. Atlanta: SBL Press, 2020.

Weber, Max. *The Protestant Ethic and the Spirit of Capitalism*. 3rd Roxbury ed. Los Angeles: Roxbury, 2001.

Welter, Barbara. "The Cult of True Womanhood: 1820–1860." *American Quarterly* 18, no. 2 (1966): 151–74.

Welter, Barbara. *Dimity Convictions: The American Woman in the Nineteenth Century*. Athens: Ohio University Press, 1976.

Wemple, Suzanne Fonay. *Women in Frankish Society: Marriage and the Cloister, 500 to 900*. Middle Ages. Philadelphia: University of Pennsylvania Press, 1981.

Wiegand, Sister M. Gonsalva, trans. *The Nondramatic Works of Hrosvitha*. Saint Meinrad, Ind.: Abbey Press, 1936.

Wiesner, Merry E. "Luther and Women: The Death of Two Marys." In *Disciplines of Faith: Studies in Religion, Politics, and Patriarchy*, edited by Jim Obelkevich and Lyndal Roper, 295–308. London: Routledge/Kegan Paul, 1987.

———. "Studies of Women, the Family, and Gender." In *Reformation Europe: A Guide to Research II*, edited by William S. Maltby, 159–88. St. Louis: Center for Reformation Research, 1992.

William of Malmesbury. *Miracles of the Blessed Virgin Mary*. Edited and translated by R. M. Thomson and M. Winterbottom. Rochester, N.Y.: Boydell Press, 2015.

William of St. Thierry. "Sur le Cantique." In *The Works of William of St. Thierry 2: Exposition on the Song of Songs*, translated by Mother Columba Hart. Cistercian Fathers Series 6. Spencer, Mass.: Cistercian Publications, 1970.

Williams, Delores. *Sisters in the Wilderness: The Challenge of Womanist God-Talk*. New York: Orbis, 1993.

Williams, Gerhild Scholz, ed. and trans. *Mothering Baby: On Being a Woman in Early Modern Germany. Johannes Praetorius' Apocalypsis Mysterorum Cybeles. Das ist Eine Schnakische Wochen-Comedie (1662)*. Tempe: Arizona Center for Medieval and Renaissance Studies, 2010.

Williamson, Beth. "The *Virgin Lactans* as Second Eve: Image of the Salvatrix." *Studies in Iconography* 19 (1998): 105–38.

Willison, John. *The Mother's Catechism for the Young Child: Or, a Preparatory Help for the Young and the Ignorant, in Order to Their Easier Understanding the Assembly's Shorter Catechism: Together with Forms of Prayer, Both for Week-Days and Sabbath-Days, also, Graces, Both before and after Meat; for Children*. Glasgow: J. and M. Robertson, 1788.

Wilson-Kastner, Patricia. *A Lost Tradition: Women Writers of the Early Church*. Washington, D.C.: University Press of America, 1981.

Wilson, Stephen. *The Magical Universe: Everyday Ritual and Magic in Pre-Modern Europe*. London: Hambledon and London, 2000.

Wright, Henry Clark. *The Empire of the Mother Over the Character and Destiny of the Race*. Boston: Bela Marsh, 1863.

Zelizer, Viviana A. "The Gender of Money." *Wall Street Journal*. January 27, 2011.

Zimmer, Henrich. "Das Mutterrecht der Pikten." *Zeitschrift der Savigny-Stiftung für Rechtsgeschichte, Romanische Abteilung* 15 (1894): 219–40.

Zytaruk, Maria. "Artifacts of Elegy: The Foundling Hospital Tokens." *Journal of British Studies* 54, no. 2 (2015): 320–48.

Index